"Rick Richter's book is a landmark work providing excellent tools for understanding the differences and comparisons of the two religious books and also for Christian evangelism. The common misunderstandings of the Bible exhibited in the Qur'an are clearly delineated, and the many misunderstandings of what Muslims truly believe are clearly outlined as well. I can recommend this text to both teacher and student."

—Rev. Peter Conwell Richards, missionary to Africa

"The scholarship and research as well as the approachable style go hand-in-hand with an unambiguous witness to Christ. This will be both a great help to those seeking spiritual truth and also a deep comfort to those who believe that Jesus is the Son of God and the Savior of the Nations."

—Rev. Dan P. Gilbert, president of the Northern Illinois District of the Lutheran Church–Missouri Synod

"This book's layout—a side-by-side comparison of what the Qur'an and the Bible have to say on a wide range of specific subjects—is extremely enlightening. Even without Rev. Richter's very helpful comments, this comparison design lets these two very different religions speak for themselves. The Christian Gospel simply glows from the pages of the study."

—Rev. Ronald Weidler, Batavia, IL

"It is rare that I would have a guest on my radio program more than twice. However, I have had Rick Richter on three times because his book is filled with interesting information that cannot be exhausted in a one-hour interview."

—Tom Baker, host of "Law and Gospel" radio broadcast

Comparing the Qur'an and the Bible

What They Really Say about Jesus, Jihad, and More

RICK RICHTER

BakerBooks

a division of Baker Publishing Group
Grand Rapids, Michigan

Published by Baker Books
a division of Baker Publishing Group
P.O. Box 6287, Grand Rapids, MI 49516-6287
www.bakerbooks.com

Printed in the United States of America

Library of Congress Cataloging-in-Publication Data
Richter, Rick (Eldor William).
    Comparing the Qur'an and the Bible : what they really say about Jesus, Jihad, and more / Rick Richter.
        p.   cm.
    Includes bibliographical references and indexes.
    ISBN 978-0-8010-1402-4 (pbk.)
    1. Koran—Relation to the Bible. 2. Islam—Relations—Christianity. 3. Christianity and other religions—Islam. I. Title.
BP134.B4R53 2011
220.6—dc23   2011022378

11   12   13   14   15   16   17   7   6   5   4   3   2   1

In gratitude to the Lord God,
the God of Abraham, the Father
of our Lord Jesus Christ

Contents

Preface

Comparing the Qur'an and the Bible will be beneficial to the person for whom the terrorist events of and following 9/11 have raised questions, and who has heard conflicting views regarding Islam.

What does Islam teach? Is Islam a religion of peace? How do the teachings of the Qur'an compare with the teachings of the Bible? To answer these and other questions, *Comparing the Qur'an and the Bible* goes to the primary source of Islam, the Qur'an, and the primary source of Christianity, the Bible. This guide will assist the inquiring person who wishes to discern for himself or herself what the Qur'an actually teaches and how it compares with the Bible.

Islam has increased dramatically, from approximately 460,000,000 adherents in 1973 throughout the world to 1.6 billion people in 2009. (As of 2009, Christians numbered 2.2 billion worldwide.) Islam is a significant religious and political force in the world that cannot be ignored. It is important that we become knowledgeable about a religion that affects all our lives. And Christians need to be informed and fortified in their faith if they are to share the love of Christ in a compassionate and informed way.

Highlights of This Book

Comparing the Qur'an and the Bible presents quotes from the Qur'an and the Bible, side by side, on topics such as Abraham, Allah/God, Jesus, the nature of humankind, sin, judgment, paradise, suicide, and so forth. You will have the satisfaction of personally comparing and learning what the teachings of the Qur'an and the Bible are from the primary texts themselves.

Each section begins with a table comparing Qur'an and Bible passages in parallel columns. The commentary that follows the table reflects first on the Qur'an and then on the Bible. Qur'an and Bible texts from the table that are

referenced in the commentary are indicated by boldfaced type. A summary
of each subject concludes the section.

It is recommended that chapter 14, "The Ultimate Questions of Life,"
which contrasts the questions of life and death in the Qur'an and the Bible,
be read before and after the study.

The reader will also benefit from reading chapter 15, "Sharing the Good
News with Muslims." This chapter presents a practical approach to share the
good news of Jesus Christ, based on my research and personal experience.

Since present-day Muslims pattern themselves after the life of Muhammad,
and present-day radical fundamentalists use the methodology of Muhammad, "Background Information on the Life of Muhammad" is invaluable.
Also, to understand the present tension between Shi'ites and Sunnis you need
knowledge of their historic development, which is presented in "Background
Information on Shi'ites and Sunnis."

My personal appreciation to Rev. Hicham Chehab, a former Muslim, for
his counsel with regard to the Muslim content. His personal testimony may
be found in "Testimony of a Former Muslim."

If you are a leader of a Bible study or small group, you may further discussion by utilizing the study guides at the back of the book.

May you have the joy of discovery and the satisfaction of seeing the facts
for yourself.

A Word about Primary Sources

The text used as the primary source of the Qur'an in *Comparing the Qur'an
and the Bible* is *The Glorious Qur'an: Arabic Text and English Rendering*,
translated by Mohammad M. Pickthall (10th rev. ed.; Des Plaines, IL: Library
of Islam, 1994). This explanatory translation by Pickthall was "the first English
translation of the Koran by an Englishman who is a Muslim." His "rendering" seeks to avoid "a style of language which Muslims at once recognise as
unworthy." Pickthall states, "The Koran cannot be translated. . . . The Book
is here rendered almost literally and every effort has been made to choose
befitting language."[1]

Two additional sources are used for supplementary translations. One is
The Koran, translated by N. J. Dawood (New York: Penguin, 1999). "Dawood
came to England as an Iraq State Scholar in 1945 and graduated from London
University. . . . He is best known for his translation of the Koran, the first in
contemporary English, which was published as a Penguin Classic in 1956. . . .
In the present edition the translation has been completely revised, an index has
been added and the arrangement of the *surahs* follows the traditional sequence."[2]

The second additional source is *The Koran*, translated by J. M. Rodwell
(Everyman's Library; London: J. M. Dent, 1994). In his introduction, Alan

Jones, a noted Arabic scholar from Oxford University, points out the strength of Rodwell's translation: "Where he [Rodwell] is much better than others is in his cross-referencing to biblical material, information that is crucial to one's understanding of the Qur'an." Jones numbers Rodwell among the non-Muslim translators but states clearly, *"The best and most influential translation by a Muslim is undoubtedly that of a British convert, Muhammad Marmaduke Pickthall."*[3]

The text used as a primary source for the Bible is the New International Version (NIV), 1984 edition.

Part I

1

Abraham

A. The Significance of Abraham

Muslims, Christians, and Jews all claim Abraham as their "father." Why is Abraham so important to Muslims and Christians? Why, according to the Qur'an, does Islam trace its roots back to Abraham? How is the Christian view of Abraham similar to yet different from that of Islam?

The Qur'an	The Bible

1. Abraham as spiritual father
    Surah 2:135. And they say: Be Jews or Christians, then ye will be rightly guided. Say (unto them, O Muhammad): Nay, but (we follow) the religion of Abraham, the upright, and he was not of the idolaters.
    136. Say (O Muslims): We believe in Allah and that which is revealed unto us and that which was revealed unto Abraham and Ishmael, and Isaac, and Jacob, and the tribes, and that which Moses and Jesus received, and that which the Prophets received from their Lord. We make no distinction between any of them, and unto Him we have surrendered.
	2. Abraham as means of blessing to the nations
	    Genesis 12:1–3. The LORD [Heb. YAHWEH] had said to Abram, "Leave your country, your people and your father's household and go to the land I will show you. I will make you into a great nation and I will bless you; I will make your name great, and you will be a blessing. I will bless those who bless you, and whoever curses you I will curse; and all peoples on earth will be blessed through you [Abraham]."
	    Genesis 22:18. And through your offspring [seed] all nations on earth will be blessed.
	    Matthew 1:1. Jesus Christ the son of David, the son of Abraham.

1. The Qur'an: Abraham as spiritual father

■ **According to the Qur'an, what is the significance of Abraham?**

Abraham is the spiritual father of Muslims as he is the spiritual father of Jews and Christians.

In **Surah 2:135** of the Qur'an, the call of Allah and the call through Muhammad is to return to "the religion of Abraham." Abraham "was not of the idolaters." He did not worship idols. (Idol worship was common in Muhammad's day in the city of Mecca and among the desert tribes of Arabia.) Each of the five daily prayers in Islam ends with a reference to Abraham. The Qur'an depicts Abraham as a child chiding his father for believing in idols (Surah 6:74).

■ **What is the origin of Islam?**

Islam, according to the Qur'an (**Surah 2:136**), is the religion "which is revealed unto us," that is, to Muslims through the revelation given to Muhammad, and it is the religion "which was revealed unto Abraham." Its origin is the belief of Abraham in the unity and oneness of the one God. This belief in the God of Abraham was handed down from Abraham through Ishmael, Isaac, Jacob, and the tribes. It is also the religion that Moses and all the prophets "received from their Lord" (**Surah 2:136**). Islam is a call to monotheism, the worship of one God, and the return to belief in Allah. Muslims have "surrendered" "unto Him" (**Surah 2:136**).

■ **Is Islam a form of Judaism or Christianity?**

Since, according to the Qur'an, Islam is a return to the religion of Abraham, Islam has its own origin and is not an offshoot of Judaism or Christianity. According to **Surah 2:135**, when Muslims are urged by Jews or Christians to "be Jews or Christians" so that they might be "rightly guided," Muslims are to say, "Nay, but (we follow) the religion of Abraham" (**Surah 2:135**), and "we believe in Allah," and "unto Him we have surrendered" (**Surah 2:136**). Allah is "Lord of the Worlds: The Beneficent, the Merciful" (Surah 1:2–3). Since Abraham "surrendered" to Allah, it is unequivocally stated in Surah 3:67, "Abraham was not a Jew, nor yet a Christian." In the Qur'an, Islam is not dependent on any other religion but on the revelation given to Muhammad.

2. The Bible: Abraham as means of blessing to the nations

■ **How does the Bible view Abraham?**

The Lord God makes himself known to Abram (later renamed Abraham; see Gen. 17:5). He calls him out of idolatry, the worship of the moon-god, to a new beginning, to a new land (Acts 7:2–3; Heb. 11:8). The Lord (Hebrew: Yahweh) calls Abram to "leave your country . . . and go to the land I will show you. . . . I will make you into a great nation. . . . All peoples on earth will be

In Islamic and Arabic-speaking countries, Christians use "Allah" in their Bible to denote the person of God. For this study, I use "Allah" for the Qur'an section since that name is revered by Muslims. For the Bible section I use "Lord God"—"Lord" (Yahweh, the covenant God who is the great I AM), the name revealed to Abraham (Gen. 15:1–6) and Moses (Exod. 3:14), and "God," referring to the God of creation (Gen. 2:4).

blessed through you" (**Gen. 12:1–3**). Later, to reassure Abram that he has not forgotten his promise, the Lord (Yahweh) speaks to Abram in a vision and assures Abram that his descendants will be as numerous as the stars (Gen. 15:5).

The true and living God later reveals himself to Moses as "I AM" (Exod. 3:14). This name is significant. The Lord (I AM) is the fountain and foundation of all being and of all reality. He is the Lord (I AM) who makes himself known to Abram in an act of unexpected love, while Abram's family is still in idolatry. The covenant God, Yahweh, is the great I AM. He is the Lord of Noah (Gen. 6:7–8), of Abel (Gen. 4:4), and of Adam and Eve (Gen. 2:7).

The promise to Abram is a gracious and generous promise that "all peoples on earth will be blessed through you" (**Gen. 12:3**) and that he will have "a son coming from your own body" (Gen. 15:4). This blessing is repeated in **Genesis 22:18** by the Lord: "and through your offspring [seed] all nations on earth will be blessed." The Lord (Yahweh / I AM) is the God of promise to Abraham, Isaac, Jacob, and all people of "all nations."

In keeping with the promise made to Abram, the Bible affirms that this promise was fulfilled in the offspring (or seed) of Abraham, the Messiah: "'and to your seed,' meaning one person, who is Christ" (Gal. 3:16). The Bible holds that Jesus, the Messiah, is by lineage and fulfillment the personification and embodiment of the promise to Abraham. The Bible states that the blessing to all nations (**Gen. 22:18**) is transmitted through the person of Jesus, who is "the son of Abraham" (**Matt. 1:1**).

3. Summary

The Qur'an teaches that Islam is a return to the belief of Abraham. Muslims trace their religion back to Abraham as the supreme example of belief in one God, Allah. Allah is the Lord of the worlds, the God of Abraham, Ishmael, Isaac, Jacob, the tribes, and the Prophets.

According to the Bible, the true and living Lord God is Yahweh, the great "I AM." The Lord graciously makes himself known to Abram, calls him out of idolatry, and promises that "all peoples on earth will be blessed through you" (Gen. 12:3). Christians believe in this one God, the God of Abraham, who is the Lord, the great I AM. They cherish the promise of the Lord God given to Abraham that "through your offspring [seed] all nations on earth will be blessed" (Gen. 22:18). This promise is contained, centered, and culminated in Jesus, the "offspring" of Abraham. Jesus the Messiah, in the fullest sense, is the "son of Abraham."

Since both Muslims and Christians believe they worship the God of Abraham, is this God of Abraham the same for Muslims and for Christians, or does each offer a different character and description of God? Do Muslims and Christians worship the same God? These questions will be addressed in the course of this study.

For discussion questions, see study guide 1.

B. Abraham and Righteousness

What makes a person "righteous" before God? This question is basic to any religion.

The Qur'an	The Bible

1. Abraham the upright
    Surah 3:67. Abraham was not a Jew, nor yet a Christian; but he was an upright man who had surrendered (to Allah), and he was not of the idolaters.
    Surah 2:124. And (remember) when his Lord tried Abraham with (His) commands, and he fulfilled them, He said: Lo! I have appointed thee a leader for mankind.
	2a. Abraham the righteous
	    Genesis 15:1, 5–6. After this, the word of the LORD came to Abram in a vision: "Do not be afraid, Abram. I am your shield, your very great reward." . . . He took him outside and said, "Look up at the heavens and count the stars—if indeed you can count them." Then he said to him, "So shall your offspring be." Abram believed the LORD, and he credited it to him as righteousness.
	2b. Abraham's children "credited" as righteous
	    Matthew 3:9. [John the Baptizer's words:] "And do not think you can say to yourselves, 'We have Abraham as our father.' I tell you that out of these stones God can raise up children for Abraham."
	    Galatians 3:28–29. There is neither Jew nor Greek, slave nor free, male nor female, for you are all one in Christ Jesus. If you belong to Christ, then you are Abraham's seed, and heirs according to the promise.
	    John 8:56–59. [Jesus's words:] "Your father Abraham rejoiced at the thought of seeing my day; he saw it and was glad." "You are not yet fifty years old," the Jews said to him, "and you have seen Abraham!" "I tell you the truth," Jesus answered, "before Abraham was born, I am!" At this, they picked up stones to stone him; but Jesus hid himself, slipping away from the temple grounds.

1. The Qur'an: Abraham the upright

▪ **According to the Qur'an, how did Abraham become righteous?**

The Qur'an states in **Surah 3:67**, "Abraham was not a Jew, nor yet a Christian." He was "an upright man who had surrendered (to Allah)." Abraham was "upright." Having "surrendered to Allah," he rejected idolatry and thus became the first Muslim.

The statement is made again and again in the Qur'an that unto Allah "we have surrendered." *Surrender* conveys the basic meaning of the word *Islam*, "submission" (to Allah), and of the name Muslim, "one who surrenders."

Abraham "fulfilled" Allah's commands when he was tested. Because of this, Allah appointed him "leader for mankind" (**Surah 2:124**). Abraham's obedience made him worthy of being the leader for all people.

In the Qur'an, what makes Abraham and others righteous and able to enter Paradise is their belief in Allah and their obedience in fulfilling Allah's commands (Surah 2:25; 4:57).

2. The Bible

a. Abraham the righteous

▪ **According to the Bible, how did Abraham become righteous?**

Abraham was told in **Genesis 15:5**, "Look up at the heavens and count the stars." The Lord God promised, "So shall your offspring be." And "Abram believed the LORD, and he [God] credited it to him as righteousness" (**Gen. 15:6**). Abraham was upright and righteous before God because he believed the promise of the Lord. The Lord God's promise was one of grace (undeserved love) and elicited Abraham's response of faith, whereby he was "credited" as righteous before the Lord God. Abraham's faith was great because the promise was great. He was declared righteous because of his faith in God's promise: "The promise comes by faith, so that it may be by grace" (Rom. 4:16)—that is, by the Lord God's undeserved, free favor.

b. Abraham's children "credited" as righteous

▪ **How do Abraham's offspring become righteous, according to the Bible?**

In Jesus's day the Pharisees took great pride in the fact that they were of "Abraham's seed," or natural descendants of Abraham. John the Baptizer reminded them that "out of these stones God can raise up children for Abraham" (**Matt. 3:9**). Their physical DNA did not make them spiritual children of Abraham.

Galatians 3:29 promises, "If you belong to Christ, then are you Abraham's seed, and heirs according to the promise." You become a spiritual child of Abraham only through the Christ, the Messiah. In him the promise to Abraham is fulfilled. With Abraham, Abraham's children have their faith "credited [to them] as righteousness" (Rom. 4:5).

In **John 8:56–59**, Jesus dramatically states that Abraham "rejoiced at the thought of seeing my day; he saw it and was glad." Even more strikingly, Jesus says, "Before Abraham was born, I am!" Jesus clearly identifies himself as the great "I AM."

Jesus's listeners know that it was the Lord named I AM who had revealed himself to Abram. He is the Lord who made himself known to Moses in the burning bush: "God said to Moses: 'I AM WHO I AM. This is what you are to say to the Israelites: "I AM has sent me to you"'" (Exod. 3:14).

Jesus, by stating, "Before Abraham was born, I am," presents himself as the God of Abraham. Thus those who see as Abraham "saw" by faith and are "glad" in Jesus as their God and Messiah are truly the children of Abraham and are righteous.

3. Summary

According to the Qur'an, Abraham was "upright," one who had surrendered to Allah, rejecting idolatry. He was obedient in fulfilling the commands of Allah in the time of testing. Because of his obedience, he is a leader for humankind. By belief in Allah and obedience, he would enter Paradise.

The Bible states that "Abram believed the LORD, and he [the Lord] credited it to him as righteousness" (Gen. 15:6). The Lord's gracious promise to Abraham called forth a response of faith. Abraham was declared righteous by faith in the promise. The children of Abraham are not those of natural descent, then, but those who have faith in the fulfillment of the promise embodied in the Messiah: "If you belong to Christ, then you are Abraham's seed, and heirs according to the promise" (Gal. 3:29). The gracious promise is for all people to be received by faith in Christ and for their faith to be "credited" with Abraham as "righteousness" (Rom. 4:3–5).

Jesus, the Messiah, testified, "Before Abraham was born, I am" (John 8:58). He is the great "I AM" whom Abraham "saw," in whom Abraham "believed," and in whom Abraham "rejoiced."

For discussion questions, see study guide 2.

C. Abraham and Resurrection

Did Abraham believe in the resurrection of the dead?

The Qur'an	The Bible
1. Abraham shown proof of resurrection Surah 2:260. And when Abraham said (unto his Lord): My Lord! Show me how Thou givest life to the dead, He said: Dost thou not believe? Abraham said: Yea, but (I ask) in order that my heart may be at ease. (His Lord) said: Take four of the birds and cause them to incline unto thee, then place a part of them on each hill, then call them, they will come to thee in haste. And know that Allah is Mighty, Wise.	**2. Abraham lives** Matthew 22:31–32. [Jesus's words:] "But about the resurrection of the dead—have you not read what God said to you, 'I am the God of Abraham, the God of Isaac, and the God of Jacob'? He is not the God of the dead but of the living."

1. The Qur'an: Abraham shown proof of resurrection

■ **What is the story of resurrection that the Qur'an relates?**

Surah 2:260 states that Abraham desired a sign of the resurrection, not because he doubted but so that "my heart may be at ease." Allah told him to divide four birds and place a part of them on four hills, then call them, and they would come to him. The Qur'an does not tell us that Abraham actually did this; however, the strong implication is that he believed and passed the test. Abraham received proof of the resurrection in that Allah was able to restore the divided birds back to life.

2. The Bible: Abraham lives

■ **What did Jesus say to the Sadducees who did not believe in the resurrection?**

In Matthew 22:31–32 Jesus quotes the Lord God as saying, "I am the God of Abraham." It is obvious, Jesus notes, that God was saying that Abraham, Isaac, and Jacob were not dead but living in fellowship with him, the living God (something the Sadducees denied). Once this truth was established, the veracity of the resurrection would follow.

Likewise, the Bible states that Abraham's belief in the resurrection was evidenced in his willingness to sacrifice Isaac, "even though God had said to him, 'It is through Isaac that your offspring will be reckoned.' Abraham reasoned that God could raise the dead, and figuratively speaking, he did receive Isaac back from death" (Heb. 11:18–19).

3. Summary

The Qur'an and the Bible both affirm Abraham's belief in the bodily resurrection. The Qur'an presents the example of the four birds cut into pieces and by implication called back to life.

The Bible cites Abraham's belief that the Lord God could raise Isaac from the dead if necessary. Jesus reminds skeptics that the Lord God is the great "I AM"; no one can have fellowship with him and not be alive. He is the God not of the dead but of the living.

For discussion questions, see study guide 3.

D. Abraham and the Ka'aba

Why are the Ka'aba and the annual hajj pilgrimage to the Ka'aba so important? Did Abraham actually build the Ka'aba?

The Ka'aba

"The Ka'aba, the focal point of Mecca, is an ancient stone building some thirty-three feet wide, forty feet long, and fifty feet high. A black stone (thought to be a meteorite) is set in a corner of the building. . . . As Islamic tradition records, Abraham was commanded to sacrifice Ishmael, but God offered a ram in his stead. Abraham, in gratitude to Allah, built a place of worship, called it Ka'aba, and requested that people make an annual pilgrimage to it. In years to come, local Arabs corrupted the ritual, set up idols in the structure, and began a tradition of polytheism. Muhammad finally restored monotheism and the pilgrimage."

Ergun Mehmet Caner and Fetthi Emir Caner, *Unveiling Islam* (Grand Rapids: Kregel, 2002), 128–29.

The Qur'an	The Bible
1. Abraham builds the Ka'aba in Mecca	**2. Abraham and Arabia**
Surah 2:125. And when We made the House (at Mecca) a resort for mankind and a sanctuary, (saying): Take as your place of worship the place where Abraham stood (to pray). And We imposed a duty upon Abraham and Ishmael, (saying): Purify My House for those who go around and those who meditate therein and those who bow down and prostrate themselves (in worship).	Acts 7:2–3. To this he [Stephen] replied: "Brothers and fathers, listen to me! The God of glory appeared to our father Abraham while he was still in Mesopotamia, before he lived in Haran. 'Leave your country and your people,' God said, 'and go to the land I will show you.'"

1. The Qur'an: Abraham builds the Ka'aba in Mecca

■ **Why was the Ka'aba built?**

The Qur'an in **Surah 2:125** states that Allah "made the House (at Mecca)" a "resort for mankind and a sanctuary." "The place where Abraham stood (to pray)" at Mecca was to be the "place of worship." According to the Qur'an, Abraham and Ishmael built the Ka'aba here and dedicated it (Surah 2:127).

According to Islamic tradition, Abraham built the Ka'aba in gratitude after Allah offered a ram as a ransom in the place of Ishmael (Surah 37:107). Even before Muhammad's time, the people of Mecca held the belief that Abraham had built the Ka'aba.

In the Qur'an, Allah speaks of himself as "We" (see, for example, **Surah 2:125**). In the Hebrew Bible, one of the names of God is *Elohim*, which is also plural. The full meaning of "We" and *Elohim* is realized in Jesus's revelation of one God in three divine persons: Father, Son, and Holy Spirit.

Ka'aba means "cube" in Arabic. The structure has the form of a "cube" thirty-three feet wide, forty feet long, and fifty feet high.

All Muslims have the "duty" once in their lifetime to take the hajj, the holy pilgrimage to Mecca.

There may be exceptions: "And pilgrimage to the House is a duty unto Allah for mankind, for him who can find a way thither" (Surah 3:97). The exception may be physical or financial inability.

The hajj is observed on the eighth day of the twelfth month of the Islamic lunar calendar. All Muslims are dressed in unsewn garments like those they will be buried in, signifying their being of equal status and dead to the world. The observance is as follows:

1. The Ka'aba is circled seven times while reciting prayers and verses from the Qur'an.
2. The pilgrims run seven times between two hills of Mecca to depict Hagar frantically searching for water for her son Ishmael. They finally drink from the well of Zamzam to signify the quest of Hagar fulfilled.
3. They travel thirteen miles to the plain of Arafat, where Muhammad preached his last sermon. There they stand all day in honor of Muhammad, to purify themselves in submission and repentance.
4. They go to Mina, the site of Abraham's willingness to sacrifice Ishmael. There they cast seven stones at a pillar to recall Abraham and Ishmael resisting the temptation of the devil.
5. Pilgrims offer a sacrifice in remembrance of the ram offered in place of Ishmael. Steps 1 and 2 are repeated.[1]

The pilgrimage concludes with the Eid ul Adha, or Feast of the Sacrifice, commemorating Abraham's willingness to sacrifice his son. "The Feast of Sacrifice is a worldwide Muslim celebration that lasts for three days, a time for rejoicing, prayer, and visiting with family and friends."[2]

The hajj is an example of the ritual, prayer, devotion, and self-discipline that are necessary, along with the mercy of Allah, to enter Paradise. The prophet Muhammad said that a person who performs the hajj properly "will return as a newly born baby [free of all sins]."[3]

2. The Bible: Abraham and Arabia

■ Did Abraham go to Arabia?

According to the Bible, the sacrifice of Isaac (not Ishmael) was not at Mina but in the "region of Moriah" (Gen. 22:2), thought to be what is now the Temple Mount in Jerusalem (2 Chron. 3:1).[4]

Rather than going to Arabia and building the Ka'aba in what is now Mecca, according to the Bible Abraham traveled from Ur of the Chaldeans to Haran

(**Acts** 7:2–3; cf. Gen. 11:31), to Shechem (Gen. 12:6), to Bethel (Gen. 12:8), to Egypt (Gen. 12:10), to the Negev (Gen. 13:1), to Bethel (Gen. 13:3), "in the land of Canaan" (Gen. 13:12), to "the oaks of Mamre" near Hebron (Gen. 13:18 RSV), to the Negev and Gerar (Gen. 20:1), and to Beersheba (Gen. 21:32). He finally was buried by his sons, Isaac and Ishmael, in the cave of Machpelah (Gen. 25:9). Nowhere in the Bible is it suggested that Abraham went into what today is Saudi Arabia, although this is not impossible. Clearly, according to the Bible, the site of the sacrifice was not Mina but in the "region of Moriah."

3. Summary

For Muslims there is no doubt that Abraham built the Ka'aba as a place of worship. It is a central place of worship that unites all Muslims in the worship of Allah. Abraham built it out of gratitude that he was spared offering his son in sacrifice. The Ka'aba and Islamic tradition propound that the son to be sacrificed was Ishmael.

In the Bible there is no mention of Abraham's going to Arabia. The Bible precisely states that the place of the sacrifice was not Mina but the "region of Moriah" and, as we shall see, that the son to be sacrificed was Isaac. (See "D. Ishmael or Isaac Offered as a Sacrifice" in chapter 2.)

For discussion questions, see study guide 3.

2

Ishmael and Isaac

A. Ishmael

What significance does Ishmael have in the Qur'an and in the identity of the Arabs? What prominence is Ishmael given in the Bible?

The Qur'an	The Bible
1a. The birth of Ishmael	**2a. The birth of Ishmael**
Surah 37:101. So We gave him tidings of a gentle son.	**Genesis 16:1–2.** Now Sarai, Abram's wife, had borne him no children. But she had an Egyptian maidservant named Hagar; so she said to Abram, "The LORD has kept me from having children. Go, sleep with my maidservant; perhaps I can build a family through her." Abram agreed to what Sarai said.
1b. The standing of Ishmael	**2b. The standing of Ishmael**
Surah 4:163. Lo! We inspire thee as We inspired Noah and the prophets after him, as We inspired Abraham and Ishmael and Isaac and Jacob and the tribes, and Jesus and Job and Jonah and Aaron and Solomon, and as we imparted unto David the Psalms.	**Genesis 25:13, 16, 18.** These are the sons of Ishmael. . . . These are the names of the twelve tribal rulers. . . . And they lived in hostility toward all their brothers.
Surah 14:39. Praise be to Allah Who hath given me, in my old age, Ishmael and Isaac! Lo! my Lord is indeed the Hearer of Prayer.	**Genesis 37:28.** [Joseph's brothers] sold him [Joseph] for twenty shekels of silver to the Ishmaelites, who took him to Egypt.
Surah 19:54. And make mention in the Scripture of Ishmael. Lo! he was a keeper of his promise, and he was a messenger (of Allah), a Prophet.	
55. He enjoined upon his people worship and almsgiving, and was acceptable in the sight of his Lord.	

1. The Qur'an

a. The birth of Ishmael

■ **What does the Qur'an say about Ishmael's birth?**

Allah gave to Abraham the "tidings of a gentle son" (**Surah 37:101**). According to Islamic interpretation, the son was Ishmael, since the birth of Isaac follows in verse 112 of Surah 37.

b. The standing of Ishmael

■ **What status is Ishmael given in the Qur'an?**

In **Surah 4:163**, Ishmael is given the highest status, being listed alongside Noah, Abraham, the prophets, Isaac and Jacob, the tribes, Jesus, Job, Jonah, Aaron, Solomon, and David.

In **Surah 14:39**, both Ishmael and Isaac are sons to Abraham "in my old age" in answer to prayer, for which Abraham praises Allah.

Surah 19:54–55 presents Ishmael as "keeper of his promise, . . . a messenger (of Allah), [and] a Prophet." He was a man of piety who "enjoined upon his people worship and almsgiving, and was acceptable in the sight of his Lord." According to Surah 19, he was acceptable because he worshiped Allah and did acts of piety and charity.

2. The Bible

a. The birth of Ishmael

■ **How is it that Ishmael is born?**

In **Genesis 16:1–2**, Sarai tells Abraham to "sleep with my maidservant" (Hagar) with the hope that "perhaps I can build a family through her." Abraham "agreed" with Sarai. The Lord God had promised that "a son coming from your own body will be your heir" (Gen. 15:4). The plan of the Lord God, however, is that this would be through Sarai (Gen. 17:15–16).

b. The standing of Ishmael

■ **What status is Ishmael given in the Bible?**

The Bible does not give any prominence to Ishmael. He is clearly the son of the maidservant (Gen. 16:1–2). However, the Lord God has loving concern for the maidservant, Hagar, and for Ishmael, her son. When the two are banished, the Lord God hears Ishmael's crying and provides a well of water for him and Hagar (Gen. 21:15–19). The Lord God promises to make Ishmael "into a great nation" (Gen. 21:18). Ishmael is then richly blessed with twelve sons who become the heads of twelve tribes (**Gen. 25:13, 16**), but "they lived in hostility toward all their brothers" (**Gen. 25:18b**). The strife felt in the household of Abraham continues to this day. While the Bible often speaks of the "God of Abraham, Isaac, and Jacob," Ishmael is never listed among the patriarchs.

The Arabs receive their ancestry and identity from Ishmael and are called Ishmaelites in the Bible (**Gen. 37:28**).

3. Summary

The Qur'an designates Ishmael as the "keeper of the promise," "a messenger," and "a Prophet." The Qur'an lists in order Abraham, Ishmael, Isaac, and Jacob.

The Bible lists the patriarchs as "Abraham, Isaac, and Jacob," with no mention of Ishmael. This is, no doubt, because the promise of the everlasting covenant to all people was given through Isaac, the son of the inheritance. The Arabs today receive their identity through Ishmael and strongly believe they are descendants of Abraham through Ishmael.

For discussion questions, see study guide 4.

B. Conflict in the Household of Abraham

If we are to understand the conflict between Jews and Arabs in the world today, we must visit the historical background and discover the root of the conflict in the household of Abraham between Hagar and Sarah.

The Qur'an	The Bible
1. Hagar and Sarah No specific account of conflict between Hagar and Sarah.	**2. Hagar and Sarah** **Genesis 16:4.** She [Hagar] began to despise her mistress [Sarai]. **Genesis 16:6.** Sarai mistreated Hagar; so she fled from her. **Genesis 16:9.** [The angel told Hagar,] "Go back to your mistress and submit to her." **Genesis 21:9–10.** [Ishmael] was mocking, and she [Sarah] said to Abraham, "Get rid of that slave woman and her son, for that slave woman's son will never share in the inheritance with my son Isaac."

1. The Qur'an: Hagar and Sarah

▪ Does the Qur'an illuminate the roots of the conflict?

The Qur'an does not mention the origin of the conflict.

2. The Bible: Hagar and Sarah

▪ What do we learn about Hagar?

Genesis 16:4: After Hagar gave birth to Ishmael, she "began to despise her mistress." Hagar seems to become filled with pride and lords her pregnancy over her mistress, Sarai.

■ **How does Sarai in turn treat Hagar?**

Genesis 16:6: Sarai in turn "mistreated" Hagar so badly that Hagar "fled from her" into the wilderness. Sarai, filled with jealousy and hostility toward Hagar, becomes abusive. The situation becomes intolerable for Hagar and she flees into the wilderness with her son.

■ **What does the angel of the Lord tell Hagar?**

See **Genesis 16:7–12:** She is to return to Sarai and submit to her. God will increase her descendants so that "they will be too numerous to count." She is to name her son Ishmael, which means "God hears." Ishmael will be "a wild donkey of a man" who will "live in hostility toward all his brothers."

■ **What happens at the festival when Isaac is weaned?**

Genesis 21:9: Ishmael "was mocking," perhaps poking fun at Isaac. With this, Sarah (as Sarai has now been renamed by God; see Genesis 17) reaches the limit of her endurance.

■ **What is Sarah's reaction?**

In **Genesis 21:10,** Sarah demands that Abraham "get rid of that slave woman and her son," for Ishmael "will never share in the inheritance with my son Isaac." This is as the Lord God had stated clearly to Abraham: "Your wife Sarah will bear you a son, and you will call him Isaac. I will establish my covenant with him as an everlasting covenant" (Gen. 17:19).

3. Summary

The conflict in Abraham's household is basically between Hagar and Sarah. The conflict begins with the contempt of Hagar toward Sarah and escalates with Sarah's harsh treatment of Hagar. Ishmael's "mocking" of Isaac is the "last straw," and Sarah insists that Hagar and Ishmael leave. There is to be no question as to which son receives the inheritance: Ishmael "will never share in the inheritance with my son Isaac." Sarah states emphatically what the Lord God had already explicitly set forth to Abraham: it is Isaac who is the son of the covenant.

For discussion questions, see study guide 4.

C. Abraham's Concern for Ishmael and the Covenant Promise to Isaac

How is Abraham affected by the conflict in his household between Hagar and Ishmael and Sarah and Isaac? What is the solution?

The Qur'an	The Bible
1. Abraham's concern for Ishmael The Qur'an is silent on this.	2. Abraham's concern for Ishmael **Genesis 21:11–13.** The matter distressed Abraham greatly because it concerned his son. But God said to him, "Do not be so distressed about the boy and your maidservant. Listen to whatever Sarah tells you, because it is through Isaac that your offspring will be reckoned. I will make the son of the maidservant into a nation also, because he is your offspring."

1. The Qur'an: Abraham's concern for Ishmael

■ **How did Abraham react to the dismissal of Ishmael?**

The Qur'an is silent on this.

2. The Bible: Abraham's concern for Ishmael

■ **What was Abraham's reaction to the dismissal of Ishmael?**

Genesis 21:11–13 states that "the matter distressed Abraham greatly because it concerned his son" (Ishmael). Abraham was upset over the situation.

■ **What is God's clear message to Abraham concerning the covenant promise?**

In **Genesis 21:11–13**, the Lord God reaffirms: "It is through Isaac that your offspring will be reckoned." The Lord God holds to his word: "Your wife Sarah will bear you a son, and you will call him Isaac. I will establish my covenant with him as an everlasting covenant" (Gen. 17:19).

With regard to Ishmael, the Lord God assures Abraham, "I will make the son of the maidservant into a nation also, because he is your offspring" (**Gen. 21:13**). Ishmael will also be greatly blessed with sons who would be "twelve tribal rulers" (Gen. 25:16). (Islamic tradition also holds that the twelve sons became twelve Arab tribes.)

> In the ancient Near East, the son of a maidservant could have equal rights with a son of a wife. See Genesis 46, where Jacob has twelve sons. Four of them are by bondwomen, yet they are numbered among Jacob's twelve sons and are given an inheritance.

The Lord God's covenant promise of a blessing to all nations will flow through Abraham's offspring (seed; Gen. 22:18).

According to Genesis 25:9, when Abraham died "his sons Isaac and Ishmael buried him in the cave of Machpelah."

3. Summary

Abraham is greatly distressed and torn over the conflict in his household. He loves both of his sons. He recognizes that Isaac is the son of the promise and the "everlasting covenant," but his heart goes out to Ishmael. The Lord God confirms that Isaac will receive the promise and through him Abraham's "offspring will be reckoned." God also reassures Abraham that Ishmael will not be forgotten; he too will be richly blessed.

It is well to remember that the Lord God promised Abraham and Sarah a son in their old age. The Lord God had in mind Isaac, the son of promise, all along. It was because Abraham and Sarah began to doubt that Ishmael was conceived and complications ensued.

Might not Abraham's deep love for his two sons and his concern for Ishmael as well as for Isaac, and the fact that Isaac and Ishmael came together to bury their father (see Gen. 25:9), be an inspiration for understanding between Jews and Arabs today?

For discussion questions, see study guide 5.

D. Ishmael or Isaac Offered as a Sacrifice

The Qur'an and the Bible both agree that Abraham was willing to sacrifice his son, but which of the two sons was Abraham willing to sacrifice? Both the Qur'an and the Bible attach great significance to this test of Abraham.

The Qur'an	The Bible

1. Ishmael offered as sacrifice
    Surah 37:102. And when (his son) was old enough to walk with him, (Abraham) said: O my dear son, I have seen in a dream that I must sacrifice thee. So look, what thinkest thou? He said: O my father! Do that which thou art commanded. Allah willing, thou shalt find me of the steadfast.
    103. Then, when they had both surrendered (to Allah), and he had flung him down upon his face,
    104. We called unto him: O Abraham!
    105. Thou hast already fulfilled the vision. Lo! thus do We reward the good.
    107. Then We ransomed him with a tremendous victim.
	2. Isaac offered as sacrifice
	    Genesis 22:2. Then God said, "Take your son, your only son, Isaac, whom you love, and go to the region of Moriah. Sacrifice him there as a burnt offering on one of the mountains I will tell you about."

1. The Qur'an: Ishmael offered as sacrifice

■ **Who is the son Abraham was to sacrifice? Does the Qur'an name him specifically?**

While **Surah 37:102** does not mention Ishmael by name, specifying only "when (his son) was old enough to walk," Islam holds that the son to be sacrificed was Ishmael. (The context does imply that the son was Ishmael. The account of Isaac follows with v. 112.) "Muslim interpreters a generation after Muhammad concluded that the prophet was descended from the slave woman Hagar's boy, Ishmael. Later scholarly opinion determined that Ishmael was also the son who went under the knife."[1] The commitment of Abraham and Ishmael to Allah is reenacted in the hajj (annual pilgrimage) when pilgrims throw stones at a stone pillar signifying Abraham and Ishmael's resistance to the devil and their resolve to carry out the sacrifice. It should be noted that Allah "ransomed" Abraham's son.

2. The Bible: Isaac offered as sacrifice

■ According to the Bible, which son is offered as sacrifice?

According to the Bible, the son offered as sacrifice is specifically Isaac: in Genesis 22:2 God instructs Abraham, "Take your son, your only son, Isaac, whom you love, and go to the region of Moriah. Sacrifice him there as a burnt offering."

3. Summary

Both the Qur'an and the Bible say that Abraham was tested by the command of God to sacrifice his son. There is an irreconcilable difference, though, for the tradition of Islam, which comes over two thousand years later than the biblical account, holds it was Ishmael, while the biblical account, from the days of Moses, states clearly that the son to be sacrificed was Isaac. In both sources Abraham passes the test and the Lord God mercifully spares the son.

For discussion questions, see study guide 5.

E. Isaac

1. Prophet/Patriarch

What standing and what role does Isaac have according to the Qur'an and the Bible?

The Qur'an	The Bible
1a. Isaac among the prophets	**1b. Isaac the patriarch**
Surah 3:84. Say (O Muhammad): We believe in Allah and that which is revealed unto us and that which was revealed unto Abraham and Ishmael and Isaac and Jacob and the tribes, and that which was vouchsafed unto Moses and Jesus and the Prophets from their Lord. We make no distinction between any of them, and unto Him we have surrendered.	**Exodus 3:6.** "I am the God of your father, the God of Abraham, the God of Isaac and the God of Jacob."

a. The Qur'an: Isaac among the prophets

■ How is Isaac described in the Qur'an?

Isaac is given the high status of being listed with Abraham, Ishmael, Jacob and the tribes, Moses, Jesus and the Prophets (**Surah 3:84**). Note that Ishmael is listed before Isaac in "Abraham and Ishmael and Isaac."

b. The Bible: Isaac the patriarch

■ **How is Isaac described in the Bible?**

In the Bible, Isaac is often listed among the patriarchs and prophets: "the God of Abraham, the God of Isaac and the God of Jacob" (**Exod. 3:6**). Ishmael is never so listed. The Bible states that "Abraham gave the name Isaac to the son Sarah bore him" (Gen. 21:3). Isaac means "laughter." Both Abraham and Sarah laughed upon being told that they would have a son (Gen. 17:17; 18:12). After all, Abraham would be one hundred years old and Sarah ninety years old when Isaac was born. Sarah laughed in unbelief and, it seems, Abraham perhaps in disbelief and delight.

2. Isaac and Righteousness

How are Isaac and Jacob "righteous" in the Qur'an and the Bible?

The Qur'an	The Bible
2a. Righteous by good deeds and worship of Allah **Surah 21:72.** And We bestowed upon him Isaac, and Jacob as a grandson. Each of them We made righteous. 73. And We made them chiefs who guide by Our command, and We inspired in them the doing of good deeds and the right establishment of worship and the giving of alms, and they were worshippers of Us (alone).	**2b. Righteous by faith** **Galatians 3:6–8.** Consider Abraham: "He believed God, and it was credited to him as righteousness." Understand, then, that those who believe are children of Abraham. The Scripture foresaw that God would justify the Gentiles by faith, and announced the gospel in advance to Abraham: "All nations will be blessed through you." **Romans 9:6–8.** It is not as though God's word had failed. For not all who are descended from Israel are Israel. Nor because they are his descendants are they all Abraham's children. On the contrary, "It is through Isaac that your offspring will be reckoned." In other words, it is not the natural children who are God's children, but it is the children of the promise who are regarded as Abraham's offspring.

a. The Qur'an: Righteous by good deeds and worship of Allah

■ **How are Isaac and Jacob righteous before Allah?**

In the Qur'an, both Isaac and Jacob "We made righteous" (**Surah 21:72**). Allah is the one who made them righteous. Isaac and Jacob were "inspired" by Allah in "the doing of good deeds and the right establishment of worship and the giving of alms," and the worship of Allah alone (**Surah 21:73**). It is by their "doing . . . good deeds" and being "worshippers of Us [Allah] (alone)" that they are righteous. (See also Surah 2:177.)

b. The Bible: Righteous by faith

■ **How are Isaac and Jacob righteous before God?**

The promise given to Abraham is reaffirmed to Isaac (Gen. 26:2–4) and to Jacob (Gen. 28:13–15). Isaac and Jacob are righteous before God, as was their father/grandfather Abraham, by faith in the promise: "Abram believed the LORD, and he credited it to him as righteousness" (Gen. 15:6). As noted above, this verse from Genesis is quoted by Paul in **Galatians 3:6–8**.

David pleads, "Do not bring your servant into judgment, for no one living is righteous before you [God]" (Ps. 143:2). Righteousness is "from God . . . through faith in Jesus Christ" (Rom. 3:22). Since "Abraham's faith was credited to him as righteousness" (Rom. 4:9), "the promise comes by faith, so that it may be by grace," and Abraham "is the father of us all"(Rom. 4:16).

■ **Who are the recipients of the promise made to Abraham?**

As **Romans 9:6–8** says, not "natural children" but "children of the promise" are called "Abraham's offspring." This promise of righteousness by faith is available to the natural descendants of Isaac and Ishmael and for *all* peoples. The promise to Abraham is that "all nations will be blessed through you" (**Gal. 3:8**; Gen. 12:3).

3. Summary

In the Qur'an, Isaac is listed after Abraham and Ishmael, whereas in biblical lists Isaac is included as the son of Abraham and no mention is made of Ishmael. In Surah 21:72, Isaac and Jacob are "made righteous" and "inspired" in the "doing of good deeds." Throughout the Qur'an "righteousness" is always by belief in Allah and the doing of good deeds (see Surah 2:177). In the Qur'an it is not by faith in the promise of the "offspring [seed]" to Abraham that one is righteous before God (Gen. 15:6).

In the Bible, Isaac and Jacob are "righteous" because, like their forefather Abraham, they receive the gracious promise given to Abraham and believe in the promise, to be fulfilled in the Messiah, the "offspring" of Abraham. It is by faith in the promised Messiah that one is declared righteous before God. Such faith is demonstrated in the fruit of righteousness (Matt. 7:17; Phil. 1:11).

For discussion questions, see study guide 5.

3

Jews, Christians, Muslims

A. Jews and Christians in the Qur'an and the Bible

In view of the present tensions between peoples in the Middle East, what does the Qur'an say about Christians and Jews? In comparison, what does the Bible say about non-Christians?

The Qur'an	The Bible

1a. Approach to Christians and Jews
    Surah 2:109. Many of the People of the Scripture long to make you disbelievers after your belief, through envy on their own account, after the truth hath become manifest unto them. Forgive and be indulgent (toward them) until Allah give command. Lo! Allah is Able to do all things.
    Surah 2:113. And the Jews say the Christians follow nothing (true), and the Christians say the Jews follow nothing (true); yet both are readers of the Scripture. Even thus speak those who know not. Allah will judge between them on the Day of Resurrection concerning that wherein they differ.
1b. Sabbath breakers become apes
    Surah 2:65. And ye know of those of you [Jews] who broke the Sabbath, how We said unto them: Be ye apes, despised and hated!
	2a. Jews and non-Jews one in Christ
	    Ephesians 2:13, 14, 16. But now in Christ Jesus you who once were far away have been brought near through the blood of Christ. For he himself is our peace, who has made the two one and has destroyed the barrier, the dividing wall of hostility. . . . And in this one body to reconcile both of them to God through the cross, by which he put to death their hostility.
	2b. God's love in Christ is for all
	    Romans 5:6, 8, 10. When we were still powerless, Christ died for the ungodly. . . . While we were still sinners, Christ died for us. . . . For if, when we were God's enemies, we were reconciled to him through the death of his Son, how much more, having been reconciled, shall we be saved through his life!

The Qur'an

66. And We made it an example to their own and to succeeding generations, and an admonition to the Godfearing.

1c. Friendship with Jews and Christians to be avoided

Surah 5:51. O ye who believe! Take not the Jews and Christians for friends. They are friends one to another. He among you who taketh them for friends is (one) of them. Lo! Allah guideth not wrongdoing folk.

1d. Hell for Christians

Surah 5:72. They surely disbelieve who say: Lo! Allah is the Messiah, son of Mary. The Messiah (himself) said: O Children of Israel, worship Allah, my Lord and your Lord. Lo! whoso ascribeth partners unto Allah, for him Allah hath forbidden Paradise. His abode is the Fire. For evil-doers there will be no helpers.

73. They surely disbelieve who say: Lo! Allah is the third of three; when there is no God save the One God. If they desist not from so saying a painful doom will fall on those of them who disbelieve.

1e. Reward for those who believe in Allah and do right

Surah 2:62. Those who are Jews, and Christians, and Sabaeans—whoever believeth in Allah and the Last Day and doth right—surely their reward is with their Lord, and there shall no fear come upon them neither shall they grieve.

1f. The Jews most hostile

Surah 5:82. Thou wilt find the most vehement of mankind in hostility to those who believe (to be) the Jews, and the idolaters. And thou wilt find the nearest of them in affection to those who believe (to be) those who say: Lo! We are Christians. That is because there are among them priests and monks, and because they are not proud.

1g. Jews lost, except for a few

Surah 4:155. Then because of their breaking of their covenant, and their disbelieving in the revelations of Allah, and their slaying of the Prophets wrongfully, and their saying: Our hearts are hardened—Nay, but Allah hath set a seal upon them for their disbelief, so that they believe not save a few—

The Bible

2 Corinthians 5:19–21. God was reconciling the world to himself in Christ, not counting men's sins against them. And he has committed to us the message of reconciliation. We are therefore Christ's ambassadors, as though God were making his appeal through us. We implore you on Christ's behalf: Be reconciled to God. God made him who had no sin to be sin for us, so that in him we might become the righteousness of God.

John 3:16–18. For God so loved the world that he gave his one and only Son, that whoever believes in him shall not perish but have eternal life. For God did not send his Son into the world to condemn the world, but to save the world through him. Whoever believes in him is not condemned, but whoever does not believe stands condemned already because he has not believed in the name of God's one and only Son.

The Qur'an	The Bible
156. And because of their disbelief and of their speaking against Mary a tremendous calumny. **Surah 98:6.** Lo! those who disbelieve, among the People of the Scripture and the idolaters, will abide in fire of hell. They are the worst of created beings. **Surah 5:86.** But those who disbelieve and deny Our revelations, they are owners of hell-fire.	

1. The Qur'an

a. Approach to Christians and Jews

■ **What is the approach of the Qur'an toward Christians and Jews?**

Surah 2:109: Christians and Jews are "People of the Scripture" (or of "the Book"). Muslims are to "forgive and be indulgent" toward them until Allah commands otherwise.

Surah 2:113: Jews and Christians accuse one another of following "nothing (true)," and both will be judged by Allah on the day of resurrection.

b. Sabbath breakers become apes

■ **How are unobservant Jews characterized?**

Surah 2:65 describes an unusual situation where Jews who "broke the Sabbath" were turned into apes. Surah 5:60 has those "who serveth idols" also being turned into apes and swine.

c. Friendship with Jews and Christians to be avoided

■ **How are Muslims to relate to Christians and Jews?**

Surah 5:51 forbids Muslims to take "Jews and Christians for friends."

d. Hell for Christians

■ **What destiny awaits Christians, according to the Qur'an?**

Surah 5:72: Those who say "Allah is the Messiah, son of Mary" (such as Christians), who "ascribeth partners unto Allah" (that is, those who believe in the Trinity or are idolaters), to that person "Allah hath forbidden Paradise. His abode is the Fire."

According to the following verse (**Surah 5:73**), doom awaits those who believe that "Allah is the third of three." This refers to Christians who believe in three divine persons in the Godhead. It is based on a false understanding, for Christians do not believe that each person of the Godhead is "the third of three."

e. Reward for those who believe in Allah and do right
■ **What reward awaits the Muslim?**

Surah 2:62 states that only those who believe in Allah and the Last Day and do right will have their reward "with their Lord." In other words, belief in Allah and right living gain one eternal life.

f. The Jews most hostile
■ **Does the Qur'an rank Jews and Christians as better or worse than each other?**

Surah 5:82: The "most vehement of mankind in hostility" to Islam are the Jews and idolaters. Christians, especially monks, because of their humility, are the most near "in affection to those who believe" (Muslims). However, they must say, "Our Lord [Allah] we believe" (Surah 5:83).

g. Jews lost, except for a few
■ **What destiny awaits Jews and other unbelievers, according to the Qur'an?**

Surah 4:155–56: The Jews in general are lost and sealed in their disbelief, "save a few," because of "their breaking of their covenant, and their disbelieving in the revelations of Allah, and their slaying of the Prophets," and because of their saying, "Our hearts are hardened" and their "speaking against Mary," the mother of Jesus.

Surah 98:6 and Surah 5:86 leave no doubt that disbelievers among the Christians and Jews and idolaters, those who "deny Our revelations," "will abide in fire of hell."

2. The Bible

a. Jews and non-Jews one in Christ
■ **What is the biblical view of people of differing ethnic and cultural groups?**

The scriptures in Ephesians 2:13–16 state that all people (Jews, Gentiles, Arabs, and all "who once were far away") "have been brought near through the blood of Christ." Christ has broken down barriers and removed walls of hostility by uniting all people in "one body" on the cross. All people have been reconciled to God "through the cross."

b. God's love in Christ is for all
■ **How did God's love reach out to all?**

In Romans 5:6–10 we learn that when we were still "powerless," "ungodly," "sinners," and "enemies," "we were reconciled to him through the death of his Son." We did not first have to prove ourselves by believing in God and doing

Some object that the Christian faith is intolerant and narrow, since it requires faith in God's one and only Son. However, if a cure for cancer were developed and made available as a gift to all people, we would herald it as a gift beyond compare. We would not blame the giver of the cure if people refused the cure, or were uninformed of it, and as a result died of cancer. So we should not blame God when the Bible states that "whoever believes in him is not condemned, but whoever does not believe stands condemned already" (**John 3:18**). Rather, let all people give thanks to God that he offered his Son "to be sin for us" that we might "become the righteousness of God" in him, and let all those who believe "appeal" to and "implore" everyone in the name of Christ to "be reconciled to God" (**2 Cor. 5:19–21**).

what is right, before God loved us in Christ. God's love was proffered, and was unmerited, undeserved, and unconditional in his Son, Jesus the Messiah.

God's grace in Christ is extended to all. (In contrast, in the Qur'an, "Allah loveth not the disbelievers" [Surah 3:32].)

■ **What was God accomplishing in Christ?**

"God was reconciling the world to himself in Christ" (**2 Cor. 5:19–21**). God's love and reconciliation in Christ are for all sinful human beings, regardless of status or race.

■ **According to John 3:16–18, what was God doing in providing the great gift of his Son?**

The original Greek of **John 3:16** can be translated literally thus: "So loved God the world that he gave his one and only Son." To such a degree God loved all the people of the world, without distinction, that he gave his beloved Son as the Lamb of God for the sins of the world (John 1:29). It is through faith in God's Son, just as Abraham had faith, that one has eternal life. God has provided a cure for the sin-sickness in the heart of humankind. Through the giving of his Son, God restores the fellowship with him broken by Adam and Eve and gives the gift of eternal life to all who believe in his Son.

B. Christianity and Arabs: A Historical Note

■ **Was Christianity known among the Arab tribes?**

The accusation has been leveled that Christians did not spread the gospel in the Arabian Peninsula and hence Islam had fertile ground in which to take root. But the book *Christianity among the Arabs in Pre-Islamic Times*, by J. Spencer Trimingham, "details the extent of Christianity throughout the

Saudi peninsula prior to Muhammad's rise. Basically, the entire Saudi peninsula was ringed with Jewish or Christian tribes."[1]

C. Summary

The present hostility of some Muslims toward Jews and Christians becomes easier to understand when one reads in the Qur'an material ranging from expressions of indulgence toward Jews and Christian to a curse upon Jewish sabbath breakers, turning them to apes, commands to avoid friendship with Jews and Christians, and statements that Jews are most hostile to Muslims, that only "a few" (Surah 4:155) Christian priests and monks will be saved (those who believe in Allah [Surah 5:83]), that most Jews will be lost, and that Jews and Christians along with idolaters who disbelieve in Allah will be "owners of hell-fire."

In the New Testament, by contrast, God loves all the people of the world so much that he sends his one and only Son, Jesus the Messiah, to be the Savior of all people from sin. God freely gives forgiveness of sins and the gift of eternal life through faith in Jesus. His love in Christ is extended to all, breaking down barriers between people by reconciling them to God and to one another through the blood of Jesus shed on the cross. This proffered love of the Lord God in Christ toward all people is in sharp contrast with the words of the Qur'an toward Christians, Jews, and idolaters.

For discussion questions, see study guide 6.

4

Allah / Lord God

Central to any faith is the concept of God. Who is God and what is the character of God in his very essence? The Qur'an and the Bible have some similar views and yet there is a basic divergence of teaching on the being of God.

A. The Nature of Allah / Lord God

1. The character of Allah / Lord God

What is God like?

The Qur'an	The Bible
1a. Allah	**1b. Lord God**
Surah 1. The opening	**Exodus 34:6–7.** And he [the LORD] passed in
1. In the name of Allah, the Benefi-	front of Moses, proclaiming, "The LORD, the
cent, the Merciful.	LORD, the compassionate and gracious God,
2. Praise be to Allah, Lord of the	slow to anger, abounding in love and faithful-
Worlds:	ness, maintaining love to thousands, and forgiv-
3. The Beneficent, the Merciful:	ing wickedness, rebellion and sin. Yet he does
4. Owner of the Day of Judgement.	not leave the guilty unpunished; he punishes the
5. Thee (alone) we worship; Thee	children and their children for the sin of the fa-
(alone) we ask for help.	thers to the third and fourth generation."
6. Show us the straight path:	**Psalm 145:8–9.** The LORD is gracious and
7. The path of those whom Thou	compassionate, slow to anger and rich in love.
hast favoured; Not (the path) of those	The LORD is good to all; he has compassion on
who earn Thine anger nor of those	all he has made.
who go astray.[1]	

The Qur'an	The Bible
Surah 7:180. Allah's are the fairest names. Invoke Him by them. And leave the company of those who blaspheme His names. They will be requited what they do.[2]	**Psalm 86:15.** But you, O Lord, are a compassionate and gracious God, slow to anger, abounding in love and faithfulness.
Surah 112. The Sincerity *Revealed at Mecca* In the name of Allah, the Beneficent, the Merciful. 1. Say: He is Allah, the One! 2. Allah, the eternally Besought of all! 3. He begetteth not nor was begotten. 4. And there is none comparable unto Him.[3]	**Psalm 139:1.** O LORD, you have searched me and you know me. **Jeremiah 23:24.** "Can anyone hide in secret places so that I cannot see him?" declares the LORD. "Do I not fill heaven and earth?" declares the LORD. **Leviticus 19:2.** [The Lord's words:] "Speak to the entire assembly of Israel and say to them: 'Be holy because I, the LORD your God, am holy.'"
Surah 8. "Allah is Mighty, Wise" (10); "Allah is of Infinite bounty" (29); "Allah is the best of plotters" (30); "Allah is Seer of what they do" (39); "Allah is your Befriender—a transcendent Patron, a transcendent Helper" (40); "Allah is able to do all things" (41); "Allah in truth is Hearer, Knower" (42); "Allah is severe in punishment" (48); "Allah is Forgiving, Merciful" (70).	**Deuteronomy 32:4.** He is the Rock, his works are perfect, and all his ways are just. A faithful God who does no wrong, upright and just is he. **Matthew 6:9.** [Jesus's words:] "This, then, is how you should pray: 'Our Father in heaven, hallowed be your name . . .'" **Romans 11:33.** Oh, the depth of the riches of the wisdom and knowledge of God! **1 Corinthians 8:6.** There is but one God, the Father, from whom all things came and for whom we live; and there is but one Lord, Jesus Christ, through whom all things came and through whom we live. **1 John 4:8.** Whoever does not love does not know God, because God is love.

a. The Qur'an: Allah

■ **How is Allah described in the Qur'an?**

The opening of the Qur'an, in **Surah 1** (which is recited several times in the five daily prayers), describes Allah as "Beneficent," "Merciful," "Lord of the Worlds," "Owner of the Day of Judgement," the one who shows "the straight path," and one who shows favor or anger.

See Surah 5:18: "Allah's is the Sovereignty of the heavens and the earth and all that is between them."

Surah 7:180 encourages Muslims to invoke Allah by his many names. Islam holds that the Qur'an presents ninety-nine names for Allah. **Surah 112** emphasizes the unity of Allah: "He is Allah, the One!" "The corner-stone (of Islam) is belief in the Unity of God (*tauhid*)."[4]

Allah is absolute, independent, unique and sovereign: "He is The First and The Last. He is unique and nothing resembles Him in any respect. He is One and The One. He is self-sustained, does not need anything but everything needs Him. . . . He is the Willer of existing things and the things that will exist, and nothing happens apart from his will. He is the Knower of all that can be known. His knowledge encompasses the whole universe that he has created and he alone sustains. God is completely sovereign over all his creation."[5] Muslims traditionally "insist on learning and remembering the following thirteen attributes specifically: 'Existence, Eternity, Perpetuity, Dissimilarity, Self-Sustenance, Unity, Mighty, Will, Knowledge, Life, Hearing, Sight and Speech.'"[6]

Note the many "names" that describe "Allah" in **Surah 8**: "Mighty," "Wise," of "Infinite bounty," "best of plotters," "Seer," "Befriender," "transcendent Helper," "Hearer," "Knower," "severe in punishment," "Forgiving," and "Merciful."

■ **How does the Qur'an describe Allah's love?**

Allah's love for people is conditional: "If ye love Allah, follow me [Muhammad]; Allah will love you and forgive you your sins" (Surah 3:31). By our love we gain Allah's love. Allah is merciful and loving toward those who "ask pardon of your Lord and then turn unto Him (repentant)" (Surah 11:90); first they must "ask pardon" and "turn unto Him."

In the Qur'an, Allah's love is for those who are good (see Surah 2:195; 2:222; 3:134; 5:13; 9:4; 9:108; 49:9; 60:8). Surah 85:14 speaks of Allah's love—"He is the Forgiving, the Loving"—in the context of "those who believe and do good works" (Surah 85:11). (In contrast, the Lord God loves the "ungodly," "sinners," and "enemies" of God [Rom. 5:6–10]; see "b. The Bible: The Lord God," below.) However, "Allah loveth not the disbelievers" (Surah 3:32); "Allah loveth not wrongdoers" (Surah 3:57).

Allah's love is conditional on obedience:

"Allah loveth those who ward off (evil)" (Surah 3:76).
"Allah loveth the steadfast" (Surah 3:146).
"Allah loveth those who put their trust (in Him)" (Surah 3:159).
"Allah loveth the equitable" (Surah 5:42).

Thus, Allah's love is conditional upon a person being worthy of that love.

■ **Does Islam consider Allah to be our Father?**

Islam rejects the Jewish and especially Christian imagery of God as our Father: "From an Islamic perspective it is degrading for God to be considered a Father. The word is seen to carry with it the idea of a mother and a child."[7]

b. The Bible: The Lord God
■ **How does the Bible describe God?**

The Lord is "compassionate and gracious," "slow to anger, abounding in love and faithfulness," as he tells Moses in **Exodus 34:6–7**. "Yet he does not

Is Allah the Same as the Christian God?

On September 23, 2001, at the gathering hosted by Oprah Winfrey in Yankee Stadium, New York City, "a Christian minister stood at the microphone and began the invocation: 'We pray in the name of our God—the God of Christianity, Judaism and Islam.'"[a] But do Christians, Jews, and Muslims indeed all worship the same God?

Say we meet someone and he asks, "Do you know Tom?" We reply, "Yes, I know Tom. He is friendly, has black hair, lives in Atlanta, and does this and that." The other person says, "Well, I know Tom: he is friendly, and he has blond hair. He lives in Detroit and does this and this." It is obvious that while we both use the name Tom, we are talking about two entirely different people. So while some of the attributes of Allah are similar to those of the Lord God, Allah of the Islamic faith is quite different from the God of the Christian faith revealed in the Bible and in the person of Jesus Christ, the Son of God.

[a] Ergun Mehmet Caner and Fetthi Emir Caner, *Unveiling Islam* (Grand Rapids: Kregel, 2002), 102.

leave the guilty unpunished" if they do not repent. This description of God as compassionate and gracious is often repeated in the Old Testament, for example in **Psalms 145:8–9** and **86:15**.

The Lord is all knowing. He searches and knows us (**Ps. 139:1**). The Lord is all-present, filling heaven and earth (**Jer. 23:24**).

The Lord is holy ("I, the LORD your God, am holy" [**Lev. 19:2**]). He is perfect and just (**Deut. 32:4**). The Bible takes very seriously the justice and holiness of God and the need to meet and "satisfy" the justice of God through sacrifice. (In distinction, in the Qur'an the possibility of ransom for sin is denied and the need for sacrifice and atonement is absent.)

God is Father: "Our Father in heaven . . ." (**Matt. 6:9**).

God's wisdom is celebrated in the Bible: "Oh, the depth of the riches of the wisdom and knowledge of God!" (**Rom. 11:33**).

God is One, according to Deuteronomy 6:4, the Shema (Hebrew "hear") prayer: "Hear, O Israel: The LORD our God, the LORD is one." God's oneness is likewise expressed in **1 Corinthians 8:6**: "There is but one God, the Father, from whom all things came and for whom we live; and there is but one Lord, Jesus Christ, through whom all things came and through whom we live."

More names of the Lord God appear throughout the Bible. Here are some examples: "LORD God" (Gen. 2:4; cf. Gen. 1:1; Isa. 42:5); "God of gods and Lord of lords" (Deut. 10:17); "God Most High" (Gen. 14:19, 22; cf. Num. 24:16; Luke 1:35); "Creator of heaven and earth" (Gen. 14:19, 22; cf. Isa. 54:5); "shield" (Gen. 15:1; Ps. 3:3; 18:2); "strength" (Ps. 18:1); "refuge" (Isa. 25:4);

"very great reward" (Gen. 15:1); "the God who sees me" (Gen. 16:13); "God Almighty" (Gen. 17:1; cf. Num. 24:16); "Lᴏʀᴅ Almighty" (Isa. 1:24; 6:3; 54:5); "Eternal God" (Gen. 21:33); "*Elohe Israel*" (the God of Israel; Gen. 33:20); "*El Bethel*" (God of Bethel; Gen. 35:7); "I ᴀᴍ ᴡʜᴏ I ᴀᴍ" (Exod. 3:14); "banner" (Exod. 17:15); "peace" (Judg. 6:24); "rock" (Ps. 18:2; cf. Isa. 26:4); "King of glory" (Ps. 24:8); "Mighty One of Israel" (Isa. 1:24; cf. Isa. 9:6; 33:21; Luke 1:49); "Everlasting Father" (Isa. 9:6); "Holy One of Israel" (Isa. 43:3; 49:7; 54:5); "Savior" (Isa. 43:3; Luke 1:47); "Redeemer" (Isa. 49:7; 54:5); "God of all the earth" (Isa. 54:5); "Ancient of Days" (Dan. 7:13).

A number of titles are also applied to the second person of the Trinity: "Branch" (Zech. 3:8); "Prince of Peace" (Isa. 9:6); "Wonderful Counselor" (Isa. 9:6); "Jesus" (Matt. 1:21); "Immanuel" (God with us; Matt. 1:23); "Son of the Most High" (Luke 1:32); "Son of God" (Luke 1:35); "Word" (John 1:1; cf. 1 John 1:1; Rev. 19:13); "Savior of the world" (John 4:42); "author of salvation" (Heb. 2:10); "bread of life" (John 6:35); "light of the world" (John 8:12); "good shepherd" (John 10:11); "the resurrection and the life" (John 11:25; cf. 1 John 1:2); "the way and the truth and the life" (John 14:6); "true vine" (John 15:1); "radiance of God's glory" (Heb. 1:3); "the living Stone" (1 Pet. 2:4); "the First and the Last" (Rev. 1:17); "Living One" (Rev. 1:18); "King of kings and Lord of lords" (Rev. 19:16); "the Root and the Offspring of David, the bright Morning Star" (Rev. 22:16).

■ **What does the Bible teach about God's love?**

The Bible says that God *is* love (**1 John 4:8**), in his very essence and in the core of his character. His love is proffered and expressed, before human beings ever respond or can respond. "So loved God the world that he gave his one and only Son" (literal translation from original Greek, John 3:16).

God's love is unconditional, unearned, unmerited, and unexpected: "This is love: not that we loved God, but that he loved us and sent his Son as the atoning sacrifice for our sins" (1 John 4:10). "When we were God's enemies, we were reconciled to him through the death of his Son" (Rom. 5:10).

2. The triune God

Is God Three in One?

The Qur'an	The Bible
2a. Contra the triune God	**2b. The deity of Jesus**
Surah 4:171. *O People of the Scripture! Do not exaggerate in your religion nor utter aught concerning Allah save the truth. The Messiah, Jesus son of Mary, was only a messenger of Allah, and His*	Matthew 28:19. [Jesus's words:] "Therefore go and make disciples of all nations, baptizing them in the name of the Father and of the Son and of the Holy Spirit, and teaching them to obey everything I have

The Qur'an	The Bible
word which he conveyed unto Mary, and a spirit from Him. So believe in Allah and His messengers, and say not "Three"—Cease! (it is) better for you!— Allah is only One God. Far is it removed from His transcendent majesty that He should have a son. His is all that is in the heavens and all that is in the earth. And Allah is sufficient as Defender. [The words italicized here appear inscribed inside the Dome of the Rock in Jerusalem.] **Surah 3:64a.** Say: O people of the Scripture! [note: "Jews and Christians"] Come to an agreement between us and you: that we shall worship none but Allah, and that we shall ascribe no partner unto Him, and that none of us shall take others for Lords beside Allah.	commanded you. And surely I am with you always, to the very end of the age." **2 Corinthians 13:14.** May the grace of the Lord Jesus Christ, and the love of God, and the fellowship of the Holy Spirit be with you all. **John 5:23.** [Jesus's words:] ". . . that all may honor the Son just as they honor the Father. He who does not honor the Son does not honor the Father, who sent him." **John 20:28.** Thomas said to him [Jesus], "My Lord and my God!" **Colossians 2:9.** For in Christ all the fullness of the Deity lives in bodily form. **1 Peter 4:11.** . . . so that in all things God may be praised through Jesus Christ. To him be the glory and the power for ever and ever. Amen.

a. The Qur'an: Contra the triune God

▪ Is Jesus God's Son?

Surah 4:171 states, "The Messiah, Jesus son of Mary, was only a messenger of Allah." While Islam holds that Jesus is the Messiah, it never comes near to professing that Jesus is the Son of God: "Far is it removed from His transcendent Majesty that He should have a son." **Surah 3:64** states that "we shall worship none but Allah, and that we shall ascribe no partner unto Him" (see also 7:173; 10:34–35, 66; 16:86; 30:40; 40:12). It is addressed to "people of the Scripture" and is a clear statement that "no partner," such as Jesus, is to be ascribed to Allah.

Surah 112:3 states, "He begetteth not nor was begotten." This is an obvious objection to the Christian belief stated in the Nicene Creed, professing Jesus to be "the only begotten Son of God, begotten of his Father before all worlds, . . . begotten not made."

b. The Bible: The deity of Jesus

▪ Does Christianity teach that there are three gods?

The Christian faith does not teach the existence of three gods (tritheism). The historic Nicene Creed confesses clearly, "I believe in one God, the Father Almighty. . . . And in one Lord Jesus Christ, the only begotten Son of God. . . . I believe in the Holy Spirit, the Lord and giver of life." The historic Athanasian Creed likewise affirms, "The Father is Lord, the Son is Lord, the Holy Spirit is Lord, and yet there are not three Lords but one Lord." Jesus commanded baptism in "the name [singular] of the Father and of the Son and of the Holy Spirit" (**Matt. 28:19**).

■ What place does Jesus have in the Godhead?

In the Godhead, Jesus is equal in glory with the Father and Holy Spirit: "in the name of the Father and of the Son and of the Holy Spirit" (**Matt. 28:19**) and "the grace of our Lord Jesus Christ, and the love of God, and the fellowship of the Holy Spirit" (**2 Cor. 13:14**).

The Nicene Creed of the Christian faith professes that Jesus is "the only begotten Son of God." Jesus in his high priestly prayer affirms his eternal existence with the Father: "Father, glorify me in your presence with the glory I had with you before the world began" (John 17:5).

Jesus demonstrated his divinity in that even the "wind and the waves" obeyed him (Matt. 8:27); he fed thousands (Mark 6:44; 8:19); changed water into wine (John 2:11); raised three people from the dead (Luke 7:11; 8:41; John 11:43); healed "every disease and sickness" (Matt. 9:35); forgave sins only God can forgive (Luke 5:24); lived a sinless life (John 8:46); and offered himself as a Lamb "without blemish or defect" (1 Pet. 1:19).

Jesus made claims only the Lord God, the great I AM, can make: "I am the bread of life" (John 6:48); "I am the light of the world" (John 8:12); "I am the good shepherd" (John 10:11); "I am the resurrection and the life" (John 11:25); "I am the way and the truth and the life" (John 14:6); and "before Abraham was born, I am!" (John 8:58). See the Hebrew of Exodus 3:14, "I AM sent me to you."

Jesus affirms in John 10:30, "I and the Father are one." Further, in John 14:9–10 he reveals, "Anyone who has seen me has seen the Father. How can you say, 'Show us the Father'? Don't you believe that I am in the Father, and that the Father is in me?" In **John 5:23**, Jesus states that "all may honor the Son just as they honor the Father."

Jesus is worthy of worship: "he [the formerly blind man] worshiped him" (John 9:38). He is worthy of the highest praise: "To him who sits on the throne and to the Lamb be praise and honor and glory and power for ever and ever!" (Rev. 5:13).

Seeing Jesus, Thomas no longer doubts his resurrection and professes that Jesus is "my Lord and my God" (**John 20:28**). **Colossians 2:9** holds unequivocally that in Christ "all the fullness of the Deity lives in bodily form." He is "the image of the invisible God" (Col. 1:15). Through Jesus "all things came," and through him "we live" (1 Cor. 8:6).

As the light of the sun is inseparable from the sun, "the Son is the radiance of God's glory and the exact representation of his being" (Heb. 1:3).

According to **1 Peter 4:11**, God is to be "praised through Jesus Christ." Jesus is the mediator through whom we approach and offer our praise and service to God the Father.

(See also chapter 5, "Jesus.")

3. Summary

Both the Qur'an and the Bible extol the great attributes of Allah and the Lord God such as wisdom, might, mercy, and forgiveness. The strong divergence is that the Qur'an focuses on the unity, sovereignty, and transcendence of Allah, and while the Bible holds to the same, the Bible uniquely reveals that in his essence *God is love*. This love is centered and conveyed to sinful humankind in the person of Jesus, the Son of God, who is the mediator between God and humankind. In his Son the Lord God is not far removed but reaches us personally.

Both the Qur'an and the Bible speak of the unity and oneness of God, but they differ radically in the revelation of this One God. The Qur'an asserts that Jesus was only "a messenger." The New Testament affirms clearly that while God is One, this One God is revealed as Father, Son, and Holy Spirit.

Thus, while both the Islam and Christian faiths are monotheistic, their definitions of God are basically different. The Qur'an denies the teaching of Jesus, who has revealed God as a loving Father. Allah in the Qur'an is loving to those who first are loving and obedient to him. Allah's love is conditional. Thus Allah in his very essence is fundamentally different from the Lord God in the Bible. As the Bible reveals, in his essence God is love, and the expression of this love is revealed in the person of his Son, Jesus. The Lord's love poured out through his Son is *unconditional*.

While the Qur'an denies the deity of Jesus, the Bible teaches that Jesus is the eternal Son of God, the express "image of the invisible God." He revealed his divinity in his words, in his miraculous acts of kindness in healing the sick, feeding the hungry, raising the dead, casting out demons, and offering himself as the perfect Lamb of God for the sins of the world, and in his glorious resurrection. Jesus was the very incarnate expression of God in his love to humankind.

For discussion questions, see study guide 7.

B. The Will of Allah / Lord God

What is God's will toward humankind in his very essence, in his heart of hearts?

The Qur'an	The Bible

1a. The will of Allah
    Surah 9:51. Say: Naught befalleth us save that which Allah hath decreed for us. He is our Protecting Friend. In Allah let believers put their trust!
    Surah 4:79a. Whatever of good befalleth thee (O man) it is from Allah, and whatever of ill befalleth thee it is from thyself.
	2a. The will of the Lord God
	    James 1:13–14. When tempted, no one should say, "God is tempting me." For God cannot be tempted by evil, nor does he tempt anyone; but each one is tempted when, by his own evil desire, he is dragged away and enticed.

The Qur'an	The Bible
1b. Allah sends people away or guides them to himself **Surah 13:27b.** Lo! Allah sendeth whom He will astray, and guideth unto Himself all who turn (unto Him). **Surah 14:4.** And We never sent a messenger save with the language of his folk, that he might make (the message) clear for them. Then Allah sendeth whom He will astray, and guideth whom He will. He is the Mighty, the Wise. **Surah 16:93.** Had Allah willed He could have made you (all) one nation, but He sendeth whom He will astray and guideth whom He will, and ye will indeed be asked of what ye used to do. **Surah 74:31b.** Thus Allah sendeth astray whom He will, and whom He will He guideth. None knoweth the hosts of thy Lord save Him. This is naught else than a Reminder unto mortals.	**2b. God wants all people to be saved** **1 Timothy 2:4.** [God our Savior] wants all men to be saved and to come to a knowledge of the truth. **Ephesians 1:4–7.** For he [God] chose us in him [Christ] before the creation of the world to be holy and blameless in his sight. In love he predestined us to be adopted as his sons through Jesus Christ, in accordance with his pleasure and will—to the praise of his glorious grace, which he has freely given us in the One he loves. In him we have redemption through his blood, the forgiveness of sins, in accordance with the riches of God's grace.

1. The Qur'an

a. The will of Allah

■ **What does the Qur'an state concerning the will of Allah?**

There is a very strong teaching in Islam that Allah is over all things and that Allah's will determines all things: "Naught befalleth us save that which Allah hath decreed for us. He is our Protecting Friend" (**Surah 9:51**). Whatever Allah wills happens, and whatever Allah does not will does not happen.

In **Surah 4:79**, however, the Qur'an states that human beings are responsible for their actions: "whatever of ill befalleth thee is from thyself." The Qur'an's strong emphasis on the final judgment continually impresses upon Muslims that they are responsible and accountable to Allah.

b. Allah sends people away or guides them to himself

■ **What does the Qur'an state concerning predestination?**

Surah 13:27: "Lo! Allah sendeth whom he will astray, and guideth unto Himself all who turn (unto Him)." This might seem to say that the will of Allah predestines a person in view of the fact that people "turn (unto Him)." Maulana Muhammad Ali of the Ahmadiyya group holds that "God's foreknowledge has nothing to do with predestination."[8] Allah gives his decree. Allah is autonomous and is in no way dependent upon human beings.

The Qur'an holds that Allah determines humans' path for both good and evil. **Surah 14:4** states, "Then Allah sendeth whom He will astray, and guideth whom He will." This strong statement is repeated in **Surah 16:93** and **Surah**

Al-Asha'ari (d. 330/942), on the basis of certain texts from the Qur'an, developed the doctrine of "acquisition." He held that "all acts are created and produced by God but attach themselves to the will of man who thus acquires them. . . . The principle that seems to be at work here is that all power is referred to God while responsibility must remain with man. . . . Thus, al-Ash'ari confirmed the absolute Power and Grace of God as orthodoxy had maintained it. All acts take place by the Will and 'Good Pleasure' of God, whether good or evil."[a]

Al-Maturidi (d. 333/945), like al-Ash'ari, "holds that all acts are willed by God, but unlike him, maintains that evil acts do not occur 'with the good pleasure of God.' More important, Maturidism, while emphasizing the Omnipotence of God, allows the efficacy of the human will and, in some of its later developments, the absolutely free human production of acts."[b]

The systematic theology of Islam after al-Ghazaili (d. 505/1111) "was that of an uncompromising determinism and a flat rejection of human freedom. . . . We are not the authors of our acts but God is, on the ground that we are never fully aware of the details and consequences of our actions."[c] This systematic theology was taught in the educational institutions of Islam through the Middle Ages.

In *The Religion of Islam*, Maulana Muhammad Ali (1899–1951) states, "God is recognized by the Qur'an as the first and ultimate cause of all things; but this does not mean that He is the Creator of the deeds of man."[d] Man "is a free agent and responsible for what he does."[e]

[a] Fazlur Rahman, *Islam*, 2nd ed. (Chicago: University of Chicago Press, 1993), 92.
[b] Ibid., 89.
[c] Ibid., 98.
[d] Maulana Muhammad Ali, *The Religion of Islam* (Chelsea, MI: BookCrafters, 1990), 238.
[e] Ibid., 240.

74:31 and throughout the Qur'an. Allah determines the present and eternal destiny for good or ill of human beings. This is his immutable will. "Orthodox Islam teaches the absolute predestination of both good and evil, that all our thoughts, words, and deeds, whether good or evil, were foreseen, foreordained, determined and decreed from all eternity, and that everything that happens takes place according to what has been written for it. This is because God 'is the Irresistible' (6:18)."[9]

As we will see under "Humankind" (chapter 7), some in Islam hold that humans have a free will or at least a limited free will, while most hold to the immutable and determinate will of Allah. In the history of Islam, as chronicled by Fazlur Rahman in his book *Islam* (2nd ed.), the question of predestination and human responsibility has long been a point of struggle. The pendulum has swung between strict determinism and limited free will, with determinism ultimately holding firm.[10]

Geisler and Saleeb summarize the controversy: "There was great discussion among the early Muslim theologians as to free will and predestination, but the free-will parties (al-qadariyya) were ultimately defeated."[11]

It may seem that the Qur'an on sovereignty and free will presents a view somewhat similar to that of the Pharisees of Jesus's day: "On free will and determination, they held a mediating view that made it impossible for either free will or the sovereignty of God to cancel out the other."[12] Nevertheless, it must be said that the strong message of the Qur'an is that the will of Allah dominates and determines all things. The will of Allah determines one's final destiny: "And if We had so willed, We could have given every soul its guidance, but the word from Me concerning evil-doers took effect: that I will fill hell with the jinn and mankind together" (Surah 32:13). (On free will, see "B. The Nature of Humankind" in chapter 7.)

Jen Christiansen in "Predestination and Fatalism" states: "If anyone will take a fair look at the whole Muslim World of today, he will find that, apart from the infinitesimally small percent of modern and secular Muslims, the great masses of ordinary orthodox believers meet all the buffetings of life with an idealistic fatalism. In other words, predestination in the hands of Muhammad's Allah becomes fatalism in the minds and attitudes of the devotees."[13]

Wahhabism is a powerful, radical movement which sees itself as a reformer of Islam. Ergun Mehmet Caner and Fetthi Emir Caner observe: "Adherents insist on a literal interpretation of the Qur'an and a strict doctrine of predestination. . . . Their teaching on *Kismet* (fate) determines their purpose in jihad, being warfare between Islam and all akafir (infidels) who do not worship Allah."[14] David Van Biema and Bruce Crumley in "Wahhabism: Toxic Faith?" conclude, "The new creed (of Wahhabism) had no place for free will or human rights, let alone separation of mosque and state."[15]

2. The Bible

a. The will of the Lord God

■ **What do the Holy Scriptures state concerning the will of God?**

The Bible states clearly in **James 1:13–14** that the Lord God "cannot be tempted by evil, nor does he tempt anyone; but each one is tempted when, by his own evil desire, he is dragged away and enticed." The Lord God is not the author of evil. All things are under his control and pass in his review (see book of Job), and the Lord God "will not let you be tempted beyond what you can bear" (1 Cor. 10:13).

While the Lord God permits evil, he does not cause evil or approve of evil. The devil is the author of sin and evil, and he caused humankind to fall into sin. Human beings are responsible for their actions in that not only do they have the inherited sin of Adam but they repeat the sin of Adam, and "in this way death came to all men, because all sinned" (Rom. 5:12). Every person is

Augustine of Hippo (354–430) "clearly asserts man's total inability to exercise his will favorably before God, and stresses on the other hand that God is absolutely sovereign, indeed irresistible, in His gracious activity."[a]

Martin Luther (1483–1546) approached the mystery of predestination from the perspective of Christ. To those troubled by the mystery and the question whether or not they were elect, Luther writes, "God has given us His Son, Jesus Christ; daily we should think of Him and mirror ourselves in Him. There we shall discover the predestination of God and shall find it most beautiful. For apart from Christ all is danger, death, and devil; but in Him all is pure peace and joy. . . . Therefore avoid and flee such thoughts as temptations that come from the serpent in Paradise. Instead, look at Christ. May God have you in His keeping."[b]

John Calvin (1509–64): "For Calvin God is the Beginning, the Means, the End of everything. This principle prompts 'Calvin to systematize every phase of theology around the "greater glory of God" concept.'[c] This overemphasis on the sovereignty of God becomes most patent in Calvin's doctrine of double election. God is Absolute, subject to no law. In His absolute sovereignty He has predetermined that the salvation of some is to be to the glory of His grace; the reprobation of others likewise to the glory of His name."[d]

Jacobus Arminius (1560–1609) held: "God from all eternity predestined to eternal life those of whom He foresaw that they would remain steadfast in faith to their end." "Christ died for all mankind, not only for the elect." "Man cooperates in his conversion by free will."[e]

[a] Walter W. Oetting, "Augustine of Hippo," in *Lutheran Cyclopedia, A Concise In-Home Reference for the Christian Family*, ed. Erwin L. Lueker (St. Louis: Concordia, 1956), 62.
[b] Martin Luther, quoted in *What Luther Says*, ed. Ewald M. Plass (St. Louis: Concordia, 1959), 1:454.
[c] F. E. Mayer, *The Religious Bodies of America* (St. Louis: Concordia, 1956), 202.
[d] Ibid., 206.
[e] F. E. Mayer, "Arminianism," in *Lutheran Cyclopedia*, ed. Erwin L. Lueker, 49.

accountable to the Lord God; "we must all appear before the judgment seat of Christ, that each one may receive what is due him" (2 Cor. 5:10).

b. God wants all people to be saved

How are we to understand God's choosing?

It cannot be that God is the author of evil and chooses some to condemnation as the Qur'an states, "Allah sendeth whom He will astray" (**Surah 14:4**). Nor can the words of the Bible, "God has mercy on whom he wants to have mercy, and he hardens whom he wants to harden" (Rom. 9:18), be interpreted that God predetermines some to damnation. "God has mercy on whom he wants to have mercy" must be understood in reference to the Old Testament, where these words appear in the context of the hardening of Pharaoh's heart because of Pharaoh's obstinate, persistent rejection and unbelief (Exod. 7:3; 9:12; 14:4, 17; cf. 33:19). In such a case, "God gave them over" (Rom. 1:24, 26, 28) to their rebellious ways and his just judgment. God's judgment is not the predetermined cause of humanity's damnation but rather his just reaction to humankind's rebellion and unbelief (John 3:18; 2 Thess. 1:8–9).

First Timothy 2:4 states clearly that God our Savior "wants all men to be saved." If people are lost, it is due to their own sin and persistent unbelief: "whoever does not believe stands condemned already because he has not believed in the name of God's one and only Son" (John 3:18). "They perish because they refused to love the truth and so be saved" (2 Thess. 2:10).

In Ephesians 1:4–7, believers in Christ are given the assurance that God chose them "before the creation of the world . . . to be adopted as his sons through Jesus Christ." This redounds "to the praise of his glorious grace." The believer in Christ who by faith has received "redemption through his blood, the forgiveness of sins," looks back through the cross and in wonder sees God's love for him or her originating in eternity. It is an eternal love that chose and predestined him or her to be God's very own by his grace through faith in Jesus, the Messiah. This truth is a great comfort to the believer in Christ. (See "B. The Nature of Humankind" in chapter 7.)

3. Summary

The Qur'an sets forth the absolute, determinative power of Allah, so that what he wills will be done. Allah has the absolute power and will to lead astray and to guide aright: "Allah sendeth whom He will astray, and guideth whom He will" (Surah 14:4). This absolute power in his will is over this life and the next.

In the Bible, the Lord God cannot deny his heart of love. His will and heartfelt desire is that all people should be saved. His will and purpose are fulfilled in the giving of his Son. The believer knows this to be true when he looks at the cross and sees that "God is for us," in that he "did not spare his own Son, but gave him up for us all" (Rom. 8:31–32). It is the believer's comfort that he or she was chosen to be saved by grace through faith in Christ from eternity. Since that is true, God the Father does not lead his child astray in this life or the next. He does not "tempt anyone" to evil or predestine anyone to damnation. If they are lost it is because of their own sin and unbelief. While this is a great mystery and questions remain, the believer in Christ knows the heart of God.

For discussion questions, see study guide 8.

C. Allah / Lord God as Creator

What are the teachings of the Qur'an and the Bible with regard to creation? Are they similar?

The Qur'an	The Bible
1a. Creation Surah 35:11. Allah created you from dust, then from a little fluid, then He made you pairs (the male and female). No female beareth or bringeth forth save with His knowledge. And no one groweth old who groweth old nor is aught lessened of his life, but it is recorded in a Book. Lo! that is easy for Allah.	**2a. Creation** Genesis 1:31. God saw all that he had made, and it was very good. And there was evening, and there was morning—the sixth day. Psalm 33:6. By the word of the LORD were the heavens made, their starry host by the breath of his mouth.
1b. God's time and ours Surah 57:4a. He it is Who created the heavens and the earth in six Days. Surah 22:47b. But lo! a Day with Allah is as a thousand years of what ye reckon. Surah 70:4. (Whereby) the angels and the Spirit ascend unto Him in a Day whereof the span is fifty thousand years.	**2b. God's time and ours** 2 Peter 3:8. But do not forget this one thing, dear friends: With the Lord a day is like a thousand years, and a thousand years are like a day. Exodus 20:8–11. Remember the Sabbath day by keeping it holy. Six days you shall labor and do all your work, but the seventh day is a Sabbath to the LORD your God. . . . For in six days the LORD made the heavens and the earth.

1. The Qur'an

a. Creation

■ **What does the Qur'an teach about the creation of the world and humankind?**

Surah 35:11 states that "Allah created you from dust, then from a little fluid, then He made you pairs (the male and female)." He gives us birth and determines the length of our days. The length of our life is "recorded in a Book."

According to the Qur'an, Allah is the creator and "Lord of the Worlds" (Surah 1:2).

Surah 6:101 acknowledges Allah as the "Originator of the heavens and the earth." All life comes from him and is dependent upon him. Man is his vice regent on earth (see Surah 2:30).

b. God's time and ours

■ **How long did it take Allah to create the heavens and the earth?**

Surah 57:4 states that Allah created the heavens and the earth "in six Days." The account in Surah 41:9–12 adds up to eight days. Footnotes in various renditions of the Qur'an clarify that the time is not in human terms, for "a Day with Allah is as a thousand years of what ye reckon" (Surah 22:47) and as "fifty thousand years" (Surah 70:4). What is emphatic is that Allah is the absolute Creator.

2. The Bible

a. Creation

■ **What does the Bible teach concerning creation?**

Throughout the Bible, the Lord God is presented as the Creator of the heavens and the earth. See Genesis 1 to observe the Lord God creating the sea and the dry land, the birds of the air, the fish of the sea, all creeping things, and animals, culminating in the creation of humankind and declaring that it was "very good" (**Gen. 1:31**). There is nothing he did not create by his almighty wisdom and power. He created the "starry host" by his "word" and "the breath of his mouth" (**Ps. 33:6**). The Creator declares, "I am God Almighty" (**Gen. 17:1**). "In his hand is the life of every creature and the breath of all mankind" (Job 12:10). The Lord God placed the first man as the caretaker of his creation (Gen. 2:15).

The Lord God is the Creator and sustainer of every human being. He planned our personal creation. He has a purpose for each of us: "The LORD will fulfill his purpose for me" (Ps. 138:8). "All the days ordained for me were written in your book before one of them came to be" (Ps. 139:16). The length of our days is in his hand: "I trust in you, O LORD; I say, 'You are my God.' My times are in your hands" (Ps. 31:14–15).

b. God's time and ours

■ **How long did it take God to create the heavens and the earth?**

According to the Bible, the Lord God created all things in six days (**Gen. 1:31**). While to the eternal Lord God a day is "like" a thousand years (**2 Pet. 3:8**), it is clear from **Exodus 20:8–11** that the time of his creation was six days.

3. Summary

Both the Qur'an and the Bible have Allah and the almighty Lord God creating the world in six days. In Surah 41:9–12, however, creation adds up to eight days.

In the Qur'an, a day of creation "is as a thousand years" or a span of "fifty thousand years." The length of a human life is "recorded in a Book."

In the Bible, a day before the Lord God is "like" a thousand years. The institution of a seven-day week is based on the fact that the world was created in six days and that the Lord God rested on the seventh day. The Lord God is the Creator of all things and of every human being. The length of days of each person is written in God's book. He provides, preserves, and protects each of us in his fatherly grace and goodness.

In both the Qur'an and the Bible, humankind is responsible for the care of God's creation.

For discussion questions, see study guide 9.

5

Jesus

A. The Person of Jesus

What is the assessment of the person of Jesus in the Qur'an and the Bible?

The Qur'an	The Bible

1a. No son of God
    Surah 6:101. The Originator of the heavens and the earth! How can He have a child, when there is for Him no consort, when He created all things and is Aware of all things?
	2a. Jesus the Son of God
	    Matthew 3:17. And a voice from heaven said, "This is my Son, whom I love; with him I am well pleased."
	    Matthew 16:15–16. "But what about you?" he asked. "Who do you say I am?" Simon Peter answered, "You are the Christ, the Son of the living God."
	    Mark 14:61–62. The high priest asked him, "Are you the Christ, the Son of the Blessed One?" "I am," said Jesus. "And you will see the Son of Man sitting at the right hand of the Mighty One and coming on the clouds of heaven."

1b. Jesus and Mary are not gods
    Surah 5:116a. And when Allah saith: O Jesus, son of Mary! Didst thou say unto mankind: Take me and my mother for two gods beside Allah? he saith: Be glorified! It was not mine to utter that to which I had no right.
	2b. Mary is a humble servant of God
	    Luke 1:38a. "I am the Lord's servant," Mary answered.
	    Luke 1:46–48a. And Mary said: "My soul glorifies the Lord and my spirit rejoices in God my Savior, for he has been mindful of the humble state of his servant."

The Qur'an	The Bible
1c. Jesus was created like Adam **Surah 3:59.** Lo! the likeness of Jesus with Allah is as the likeness of Adam. He created him of dust, then He said unto him: Be! and he is.	**2c. The Son was with God from the beginning** **John 1:1–4, 14.** In the beginning was the Word, and the Word was with God, and the Word was God. He was with God in the beginning. Through him all things were made; without him nothing was made that has been made. In him was life, and that life was the light of men. . . . The Word became flesh and made his dwelling among us. We have seen his glory, the glory of the One and Only, who came from the Father, full of grace and truth.

1. The Qur'an

a. No son of God

■ **What does the Qur'an declare concerning the person of Jesus?**

The Qur'an asks in **Surah 6:101,** "How can He [Allah] have a child, when there is for Him no consort?" Allah has no wife, so how can he have a son? Jesus is the "son of Mary" (**Surah 5:116**), but he is not the Son of God.

The Qur'an holds Jesus in high regard. He is called the "slave of Allah" (Surah 19:30), the "messenger" (Surah 19:19), the "mercy" (Surah 19:21), a "word [Rodwell: the Word]" (Surah 3:45), and "only a messenger" (Surah 4:171). He is among the prophets (Surah 19:30). While Jesus is called Messiah, he is denied and rejected as the Son of God. In the Qur'an the name Jesus or Isa occurs twenty-five times, while Jesus as "son of Mary" appears twenty-three times. The use of all names and titles for Jesus adds up to thirty-five times.

b. Jesus and Mary are not gods

■ **What view does the Qur'an address concerning Mary and Jesus?**

Somehow Muslims received the false impression that Jesus and Mary were being worshiped as "two gods beside Allah" (**Surah 5:116**). Was this a conclusion from the veneration of icons at the time? Was it because of the increasingly exalted position of Mary in the Christian church? Did the designation "Mother of God" (Council of Ephesus, AD 431) lend itself to supporting the false concept among non-Christians of Mary's being divine? "It appears that Muhammad adopted his heretical ideas from a 'Christian sect' in Mecca called the Miriamites. They 'had made Mary a goddess, Jesus her son, and God Almighty her husband.'"[1]

c. Jesus was created like Adam

Surah 3:59 states that Jesus is created by God's command, "Be! and he is." He was created pure and sinless like Adam. The Qur'an does not teach that Jesus is the incarnate Son of God, the Word become flesh (**John 1:14**).

2. The Bible

a. Jesus the Son of God

■ **What is the witness of the Bible to the person of Jesus?**

The New Testament calls Jesus the son of Mary once, in Mark 6:3, and the son of Joseph twice, in Luke 3:23 and John 6:42. In the book of Daniel the "son of man" is "worshiped" by all nations (Dan. 7:14). Jesus is referred to as the "Son of Man" or "Son of God" over forty times in the Gospel of Matthew. He is the "Son of God" some sixty times in the Gospel and Epistles of John. In all, Jesus is referred to as "Son of God" 121 times in the New Testament.

In **Matthew 3:17** and 17:5, God the Father twice exclaims, "This is my Son, whom I love."

In Matthew 14:33, after Jesus walked on water and stilled the sea, the disciples "worshiped him, saying, 'Truly you are the Son of God.'"

In **Matthew 16:15–16**, Peter professes that Jesus is the "Son of the living God."

In Mark 3:11, evil spirits cry out, "You are the Son of God."

In **Mark 14:61–62**, to the question "Are you the Christ, the Son of the Blessed One?" Jesus responds, "I am" (consider the resonance of this with the Old Testament name of God, "I AM").

In fact, Jesus's enemies recognized his claim when they said, "He said, 'I am the Son of God'" (Matt. 27:43; see also 26:63–64).

While the Bible steadfastly applies the designation "Son of God" to the person of Jesus, it is clear that he is not the Son by means of sexual relations between God and Mary.

(See "2a. Jesus Is the Son of God" under "C. Be Fortified with Biblical Truth" in chapter 15.)

b. Mary is a humble servant of God

■ **What is the status of Mary in the Bible?**

The Mary of the Scriptures is a devout, humble, obedient, and blessed woman of faith. In her own words, "I am the Lord's servant" (**Luke 1:38**). Her spirit "rejoices in God my Savior" (**Luke 1:47**). She is submissive and obedient to her son, "Do whatever he tells you" (John 2:5). Her song of praise in Luke

1:46–56 reveals that she as a young person was saturated with the Scriptures. She is held in respect as the mother of our Lord and a woman of great faith. The Bible does not hold Mary to be divine or a god. She is a sinful human being who trusts in God as her "Savior" (**Luke 1:47**). She is an example of piety, humility, and faith; however, she is never revered as part of the Godhead.

c. The Son was with God from the beginning

In **John 1:1–4**, Jesus is identified as the eternal Word who was "in the beginning" and "was with God"—indeed the Word through whom "all things were made." He "was God." Jesus clearly states, "Before Abraham was born, I am!" (John 8:58). And the people take up stones to kill him for blasphemy.

Jesus himself testifies to his being the Son of God from eternity: "Father, glorify me in your presence with the glory I had with you before the world began" (John 17:5). When Philip says, "Lord, show us the Father and that will be enough for us," Jesus answers, "Don't you know me, Philip . . . ? Anyone who has seen me has seen the Father. How can you say, 'Show us the Father'?" (John 14:8–9).

3. Summary

While the Qur'an states that Jesus is the Messiah, it repeatedly denies that Jesus is the son of Allah. Jesus cannot be Allah's son, since Allah has no wife. The Qur'an teaches that Jesus is as sinless as Adam in his creation, however, and a great messenger, word, slave, mercy, and prophet of Allah.

The Bible states emphatically many times that Jesus is the Son of God and the promised Messiah. All things were made through him. Through him God reconciled all things unto himself (Col. 1:20). Jesus is the incarnate Word. He is God's very life and light and love come into this world, become flesh. He is the embodiment of God's grace and truth for the salvation of humankind. He is the Son of God, our Savior and the Savior of the world.

The Qur'an's strong rejection of Jesus as the Son of God is a great chasm between Islam and Christianity. Islam answers the basic question "What do you think of Christ—whose son is he?" with a distressing denial of Jesus as the Son of God.

For discussion questions, see study guide 9.

B. The Nativity

How do the accounts of the conception and birth of Jesus differ in the Qur'an and the Bible? Are there some similarities?

1. The Annunciation

What does the angel announcing Jesus's conception say about Jesus's identity in the Qur'an and in the Bible?

The Qur'an	The Bible
1a. Illustrious Messiah **Surah 3:45.** (And remember) when the angels said: O Mary! Lo! Allah giveth thee glad tidings of a word from Him [Rodwell: God announceth to thee the Word from Him], whose name is the Messiah, Jesus, son of Mary, illustrious in the world and the Hereafter, and one of those brought near (unto Allah).	**1b. God's Son, Messiah, Israel's king** **Luke 1:30–33.** But the angel said to her, "Do not be afraid, Mary, you have found favor with God. You will be with child and give birth to a son, and you are to give him the name Jesus. He will be great and will be called the Son of the Most High. The Lord God will give him the throne of his father David, and he will reign over the house of Jacob forever; his kingdom will never end."

a. The Qur'an: Illustrious Messiah

■ **How does the angel announce to Mary the good news?**

In **Surah 3:45**, the angel brings Mary "glad tidings" concerning the child she is to bear. Jesus is described as "a word from Him." (Rodwell renders this "*the* Word from Him.") He is "the Messiah, Jesus, son of Mary." He is acknowledged as the promised Messiah throughout the Qur'an and as "illustrious in the world and the Hereafter." He is not recognized as the Son of God or the King of Israel.

b. The Bible: God's Son, Messiah, Israel's king

■ **How does the Bible's account of the annunciation differ from the Qur'an's?**

In **Luke 1:32**, the angel Gabriel states that Jesus will "be great and will be called the Son of the Most High." He will be the promised Messiah. He will be given "the throne of his father David," to whom the promise was given (2 Sam. 7:16). He will be a king who will "reign over the house of Jacob forever," and "his kingdom will never end" (**Luke 1:33**). Jesus is "the holy one" and "the Son of God" (Luke 1:35), the King of Israel, whose reign is eternal.

2. Miraculous Conception

What do the Qur'an and the Bible say about Jesus's conception?

The Qur'an	The Bible
2a. Special creation **Surah 3:47.** She said: My Lord! How can I have a child when no mortal hath touched me? He said: So (it will be). Allah createth what He will. If He decreeth a thing, He saith unto it only: Be! and it is.	**2b. Conceived by the Spirit** **Luke 1:34.** "How will this be," Mary asked the angel, "since I am a virgin?"

The Qur'an	The Bible
Surah 19:19. He [Gabriel] said: I am only a messenger of thy Lord, that I may bestow on thee a faultless son. **20.** She said: How can I have a son when no mortal hath touched me, neither have I been unchaste? **21.** He said: So (it will be). Thy Lord saith: It is easy for Me. And (it will be) that We may make of him a revelation for mankind and a mercy from Us, and it is a thing ordained. **22.** And she conceived him, and she withdrew with him to a far place.	**35.** The angel answered, "The Holy Spirit will come upon you, and the power of the Most High will overshadow you. So the holy one to be born will be called the Son of God."

a. The Qur'an: Special creation

▪ **What does the Qur'an say about the conception of Jesus?**

According to **Surah 3:47**, Mary is informed that the conception of Jesus would be a special creation of Allah. He says, "Be! and it is." This will be "easy" for Allah. Jesus will be created as Adam by fiat. However, Jesus will be "only a messenger" (Surah 4:171), nothing more. He will be a "faultless son" of Mary (**Surah 19:19**), but nothing more. **Surah 19:21** proclaims that Jesus will be "a revelation for mankind" and "a mercy" from Allah, but nothing more.

b. The Bible: Conceived by the Holy Spirit

▪ **What is the unique revelation of Gabriel to Mary in the Bible?**

The Bible in **Luke 1:34–35** presents Mary as a virgin who will miraculously conceive a child by the Holy Spirit and "the power of the Most High." Mary's child will be "the holy one" and "the Son of God" (**Luke 1:35**). The Holy Spirit specifically, not just "spirit" generically, is the creative instrument of God in conceiving Jesus. He is not conceived through the Father's engaging in sexual relations with Mary. Matthew 1:22 also emphasizes that Mary is a virgin by quoting Isaiah 7:14: "The virgin will be with child and will give birth to a son."

Gabriel says that "The power of the Most High will overshadow you" (**Luke 1:35**), even as "the cloud" of the presence of the Lord God "covered the Tent of Meeting, and the glory of the LORD filled the tabernacle" (Exod. 40:34). The child is not just holy or "faultless" as a prophet, but is called "the Son of the Most High" (Luke 1:32), "the Son of God" (**Luke 1:35**), and the "beloved Son" of the Father (Matt. 3:17 RSV). He is a "revelation to the Gentiles" (Luke 2:32) and the expression of God's mercy (Luke 1:72) and grace (Titus 2:11).

3. The birth of Jesus

How is Jesus's birth described in the Qur'an and the Bible?

The Qur'an	The Bible
3a. Born under a palm tree	**3b. Born in a Bethlehem stable**
Surah 19:23. And the pangs of childbirth drove her unto the trunk of the palm tree. She said: Oh, would that I had died ere this and had become a thing of naught, forgotten! 24. Then (one) cried unto her from below her, saying: Grieve not! Thy Lord hath placed a rivulet beneath thee, 25. And shake the trunk of the palm-tree toward thee; thou wilt cause ripe dates to fall upon thee. 26. So eat and drink and be consoled. And if thou meetest any mortal, say: Lo! I have vowed a fast unto the Beneficent, and may not speak this day to any mortal. 27. Then she brought him to her own folk, carrying him. They said: O Mary! Thou hast come with an amazing thing.	Luke 2:1–20. In those days Caesar Augustus issued a decree that a census should be taken of the entire Roman world. (This was the first census that took place while Quirinius was governor of Syria.) And everyone went to his own town to register. So Joseph also went up from the town of Nazareth in Galilee to Judea, to Bethlehem the town of David, because he belonged to the house and line of David. He went there to register with Mary, who was pledged to be married to him and was expecting a child. While they were there, the time came for the baby to be born, and she gave birth to her firstborn, a son. She wrapped him in cloths and placed him in a manger, because there was no room for them in the inn. And there were shepherds living out in the fields nearby, keeping watch over their flocks at night. An angel of the Lord appeared to them, and the glory of the Lord shone around them, and they were terrified. But the angel said to them, "Do not be afraid. I bring you good news of great joy that will be for all the people. Today in the town of David a Savior has been born to you; he is Christ the Lord. This will be a sign to you: You will find a baby wrapped in cloths and lying in a manger." Suddenly a great company of the heavenly host appeared with the angel, praising God and saying, "Glory to God in the highest, and on earth peace to men on whom his favor rests." When the angels had left them and gone into heaven, the shepherds said to one another, "Let's go to Bethlehem and see this thing that has happened, which the Lord has told us about." So they hurried off and found Mary and Joseph, and the baby, who was lying in the manger. When they had seen him, they spread the word concerning what had been told them about this child, and all who heard it were amazed at what the shepherds said to them. But Mary treasured up all these things and pondered them in her heart. The shepherds returned, glorifying and praising God for all the things they had heard and seen, which were just as they had been told.

a. The Qur'an: Born under a palm tree

▪ Where is Jesus born, according to the Qur'an?

Surah 19 describes how Mary is suddenly overtaken by birth pangs. She is troubled. The Lord comforts her and provides a "rivulet beneath" her (**Surah 19:24**) and a palm tree with ripe dates to strengthen her. She brings forth her child there.

▪ Who heralds the birth of Jesus?

Mary brings the newborn Jesus to "her own folk," and they exclaim that she has "come with an amazing thing" (**Surah 19:27**).

b. The Bible: Born in a Bethlehem stable

■ **Where is Jesus born, according to the Bible?**

Luke 2:1 records the birth of the Messiah as taking place in a specific time and place, under the reign of Caesar Augustus. The Roman Empire is God's instrument to make certain that the Messiah is born in Bethlehem, "the town of David," as foretold. Mary gives birth in a stable and lays the baby in a manger, because "there was no room for them in the inn."

■ **Who heralds the birth of Jesus?**

The baby's location "in a manger" serves as a sure and certain "sign" to the shepherds to whom the holy birth is announced by an angel. Thus there would be no doubt that this baby is indeed the promised Messiah and Savior from sin, as the angel announced. The message is first proclaimed to despised and lowly shepherds as an act of grace. The baby is proclaimed to be "a Savior" for "all the people." He is "Christ [Messiah] the Lord." The shepherds, upon seeing the child, "spread the word . . . about this child." The people of Bethlehem are "amazed" at their witness. The shepherds' lives are changed, and they return, "glorifying and praising God for all the things they had heard and seen."

4. The infancy of Jesus

What do the Qur'an and the Bible tell us about Jesus's infancy?

The Qur'an	The Bible

4a. Speaking from the cradle
    Surah 3:46. He will speak unto mankind in his cradle and in his manhood, and he is of the righteous.
	4b. Speaking from the cradle?
	    No record in the Bible of Jesus speaking from the cradle.

a. The Qur'an: Speaking from the cradle

■ **What mention does the Qur'an make of Jesus's infancy?**

One of the unusual elements of the Qur'an is that it presents the infant Jesus talking from the cradle as a baby boy (**Surah 3:46**; Surah 19:29). Muhammad was perhaps influenced in his revelation of the infant Jesus speaking from the cradle (as well as Jesus's creating birds from clay; see Surah 3:49; Surah 5:110) by the pseudo-apocryphal writings *The Gospel of Thomas the Israelite* and the Arabic *Gospel of Infancy*.

b. The Bible: Speaking from the cradle?

■ **What does the Bible say about Jesus's infancy?**

There is no record in the Bible of Jesus speaking from the cradle. The only other accounts of Jesus's infancy in the Bible are his circumcision when he was eight days old and his presentation in the temple on the fortieth day (see Luke 2:21–24), and the visit of the Magi, the threat from Herod, and his family's flight to Egypt (see Matt. 2:1–15).

5. Summary

There are some hints of similarity between the Qur'an and the Bible and significant differences concerning the annunciation, conception, birth, and infancy of Jesus.

In the Qur'anic version of the annunciation, Jesus is called the "son of Mary." In the Bible, Jesus is miraculously born of Mary but called "the Son of the Most High." The Qur'an designates Jesus as the "Messiah" but does not say that he will be given the "throne of his father David" and will "reign over the house of Jacob forever."

In the Qur'an, the conception is by Allah's decree. In the Bible, the Holy Spirit comes upon Mary and "overshadows" her, even as "the cloud" of the glory of the presence of the Lord God "covered" the tabernacle. The biblical account of the conception conveys an immanence that the Islamic faith would find inconsistent with Allah's transcendence.

While the Qur'an designates Jesus as "of the righteous," in the Bible, in the words of the angel Gabriel, Jesus is the "Son of the Most High," the "holy one," and "the Son of God."

In the Qur'an, the birth of Jesus takes place under a palm tree that provides sustenance for Mary. In the Bible, Jesus is born in Bethlehem, the city of David. To bring this about, the Lord God moves the Roman emperor to decree a census requiring Joseph and his betrothed to go to Bethlehem. The birth of the Messiah must take place in "the town of David," as the prophet foretold. The Bible provides both a historical and a universal dimension in the account of the birth of Jesus.

In the Bible, the Messiah humbles himself and is born in a stable and laid in a manger. The angel announces to lowly shepherds the good news of a Savior for all people. Jesus is not just another prophet, as in the Qur'an. He is the Son of God coming as Savior to the whole world. This is "good news of great joy that will be for all the people." Jesus is the gracious gift of the Lord God to Jews, Arabs, and all people. It is a message to be "spread" immediately. It is a life-changing message that moves the heart to praise and glorify the Lord God with the shepherds in one's everyday life.

For discussion questions, see study guide 10.

C. The Mission of Jesus

How do the Qur'an and the Bible describe the mission of Jesus differently?

1. Jesus, the slave/servant/Savior

Is Jesus a slave, servant, or Savior?

The Qur'an	The Bible
1a. Slave and prophet of Allah Surah 19:29. Then she pointed to him. They said: How can we talk to one who is in the cradle, a young boy? 30. He spake: Lo! I am the slave of Allah. He hath given me the Scripture and hath appointed me a Prophet, 31. And hath made me blessed wheresoever I may be, and hath enjoined upon me prayer and almsgiving so long as I remain alive, 32. And (hath made me) dutiful toward her who bore me, and hath not made me arrogant, unblest. 33. Peace on me the day I was born, and the day I die, and the day I shall be raised alive!	**1b. Slave/servant/Savior** Philippians 2:7–8. Taking the very nature of a servant [literally, slave] . . . he humbled himself and became obedient to death—even death on a cross! Matthew 1:21. [An angel of the Lord:] "She will give birth to a son, and you are to give him the name Jesus, because he will save his people from their sins."

a. The Qur'an: Slave and prophet of Allah

■ **What does the Qur'an say about Jesus being a "slave of Allah?"**

According to the Qur'an, the child Jesus, from the cradle, declares, "Lo! I am the slave of Allah" (**Surah 19:30**). "Slave of Allah" is a common designation applied to Muhammad and all Muslims. The child Jesus also proclaims that he will be "a Prophet." He will be "dutiful" toward Mary. He will be given to prayer and almsgiving. He will not be "arrogant" (**Surah 19:32**). He will be born and he will die (**Surah 19:33**). According to the Qur'an, all people must die, and Jesus is no exception—but as we shall see, his death is not by crucifixion. **Surah 19:33** also states that he "shall be raised alive." This does not mean he will rise again "on the third day" but rather that he "shall be raised alive" to Allah, or that he will be raised on the final day of the resurrection.

b. The Bible: Slave/servant/Savior

■ **Does the Bible call Jesus "a slave"?**

The Bible states that Jesus took "the very nature of a servant" (Greek: slave; **Phil. 2:7**). Indeed, in his washing of the disciples' feet Jesus acts the part of the lowliest slave and calls all his followers to be the lowliest of slaves to one another (John 13). He is likewise described as being "obedient" to Mary and Joseph as a child (Luke 2:51). Jesus is the obedient Son who does the Father's will. He is such a servant and person of prayer that the disciples implore him, "Lord, teach us to pray" (Luke 11:1). He was not arrogant but "humbled himself and became obedient to death—even death on a cross" (**Phil. 2:8**), the death of a slave. The Bible clearly states that Jesus was put to death on a cross and that "on the third day" (Matt. 16:21) "God raised him from the dead" (Acts 2:24).

■ What does the Bible say about Jesus as Savior?

Matthew 1:21 states that Jesus is not just a great servant whose example is to be followed, but indeed our Savior, for he will "save his people from their sins."

2. Jesus the Righteous One

What does it mean that Jesus was righteous?

The Qur'an	The Bible
2a. Jesus among the righteous Surah 6:85. And Zachariah and John and Jesus and Elias. Each one (of them) was of the righteous.	**2b. Righteous for the unrighteous** 1 Peter 3:18. For Christ died for sins once for all, the righteous for the unrighteous, to bring you to God. 1 John 2:1–2. My dear children, I write this to you so that you will not sin. But if anybody does sin, we have one who speaks to the Father in our defense—Jesus Christ, the Righteous One. He is the atoning sacrifice for our sins, and not only for ours but for the sins of the whole world.

a. The Qur'an: Jesus among the righteous

■ Does the Qur'an call Jesus "righteous"?

The Qur'an does not have a problem calling the prophets, including Jesus, "righteous." Jesus is listed with the prophets Zechariah, John (the Baptizer), and Elijah (**Surah 6:85**). However, Muhammad is the greatest of all prophets.

b. The Bible: Righteous for the unrighteous

■ What does the Bible say about Jesus as "righteous"?

Peter states in **1 Peter 3:18**, "For Christ died for sins once for all, the righteous for the unrighteous, to bring you to God." Not only is Jesus, the Christ, the Righteous One, but far more, he offers himself, "the righteous for the unrighteous." He performs the great exchange of taking our sin and giving us his righteousness. Thus he brings us to God. Jesus is "the Righteous One" who "is the atoning sacrifice for our sins" (1 John 2:1–2).

3. Summary

In the Qur'an, Jesus is a slave of Allah. Muhammad and all Muslims call themselves "slaves of Allah." In the Qur'an, Jesus is a great "prophet." He is a righteous one. The Qur'an rejects Jesus as Savior and takes strong exception to his being recognized as the Son of God or as dying in our stead.

In the Bible, however, Jesus is given the name Jesus because it means "Yahweh saves." His name signifies that "he will save his people from their sins." He is "the Righteous One." Jesus is the Son of God and more than a prophet. He humbles himself and takes the form of a slave (servant) and is obedient to the point of death on a cross. That is how great his obedience is to the Father and how great his love is for all humankind. Thus he shows himself to be the righteous Savior. He is the Messiah who died for our sins, "the righteous for the unrighteous," to bring us and all people back to the Lord God.

For discussion questions, see study guide 10.

D. The Crucifixion

Do the Qur'an and the Bible differ over such a basic question as whether Jesus was really crucified?

The Qur'an	The Bible
1a. Jesus was not crucified; it only appeared as if he were Surah 4:157. And because of their saying: We slew the Messiah Jesus son of Mary, Allah's messenger—They slew him not nor crucified, but it appeared so unto them; and lo! those who disagree concerning it are in doubt thereof; they have no knowledge thereof save pursuit of a conjecture; they slew him not for certain. 158. But Allah took him up unto Himself. Allah was ever Mighty, Wise. **1b. The Ahmad messenger** Surah 61:6. And when Jesus son of Mary said: O Children of Israel Lo! I am the messenger of Allah unto you, confirming that which was (revealed) before me in the Torah, and bringing good tiding of a messenger who cometh after me, whose name is the Praised One [Rodwell: Ahmad].	**2a. Jesus was crucified** Matthew 16:21–23. From that time on Jesus began to explain to his disciples that he must go to Jerusalem and suffer many things at the hands of the elders, chief priests and teachers of the law, and that he must be killed and on the third day be raised to life. Peter took him aside and began to rebuke him. "Never, Lord!" he said. "This shall never happen to you!" Jesus turned and said to Peter, "Get behind me, Satan! You are a stumbling block to me; you do not have in mind the things of God, but the things of men." Matthew 27:31. After they [soldiers] had mocked him, they took off the robe and put his own clothes on him. Then they led him away to crucify him. **2b. The risen Christ shows the marks of his crucifixion** Luke 24:36, 40. While they [the disciples] were still talking about this, Jesus himself stood among them and said to them, "Peace be with you.". . . . When he had said this, he showed them his hands and feet.

1. The Qur'an

a. Jesus was not crucified; it only appeared as if he were

■ **Does the Qur'an teach that Jesus was crucified?**

The Qur'an clearly states that "the Messiah Jesus son of Mary, Allah's messenger" was not crucified; rather, it only "appeared so." In fact, he was not killed at all. As the Qur'an states, "They slew him not for certain" (**Surah 4:157**). According to Islam, Jesus was too great a prophet for Allah to allow him to be crucified. The three most popular views are: (1) Jesus hid while one of his companions died in his place; (2) Allah made Judas Iscariot to appear like Jesus and to take his place; (3) Simon of Cyrene replaced Jesus before the crucifixion. There is also the view that Satan was substituted and punished for disobedience.[2]

There are many different explanations concerning the crucifixion of Jesus in Islam. Helmut Gatje avers that "the Jews came to an agreement to kill Jesus. Then God informed Jesus that he would raise him up to heaven; so Jesus said to his disciples: 'Who among you will agree to take a form similar to mine and die (in my place) and be crucified and then go (straight) to paradise?' A man among them offered himself, so God changed him into a form to look like Jesus, and he was killed and crucified."[3]

The *Gospel of Barnabas* is often cited to corroborate the Qur'an. In it Judas is mistaken as Jesus. Jesus by his magic has transformed Judas into his own likeness. Judas frantically tries to persuade the chief priests, Herod, Pilate, and the soldiers that he is not Jesus—to no avail. And so Judas is crucified in the place of Jesus.[4] Scholars today consider the *Gospel of Barnabas* to be a medieval forgery.[5] It contains obvious anachronisms, such as using the Roman Catholic Latin Vulgate for its biblical quotations. The *Gospel of Barnabas* is purported to have been written in the first century, whereas the Vulgate was translated in the fourth. There are also medieval terms used for New Testament times. Please note that the *Gospel of Barnabas* is to be distinguished from the *Epistle of Barnabas* (between AD 70 and 165). The *Gospel of Barnabas*, however, is "a best seller in Muslim countries."[6]

Jesus is held to be too great a prophet to die such an ignominious death as crucifixion; thus Christ only "appeared" to be crucified (Dawood notes: "Literally, 'He was made to resemble another for them'"). One is reminded of the Gnostic view that Christ "only seemed to suffer."[7]

While there are different theories in Islam as to how a substitute was arranged for Jesus, there is no doubt that according to the Qur'an and the teaching of Islam Jesus was not actually crucified or put to death. There are some conjectures as to whether Jesus died a natural death and to what age he lived.

"The generally accepted Muslim view affirms that Jesus did not die, but that Allah raised him (*rafa'u*) to himself."[8] Jesus was raised to Allah without death. Allah rescued Jesus from death by crucifixion (**Surah 4:157**) "and took him up unto Himself" (**Surah 4:158**).

Further, Islamic tradition holds that since Jesus did not die, his ministry cannot be complete. He must return to complete his ministry and die at the end of time. He must be buried as all men are, so that he might be raised on the final day. "Tradition explains that he will appear to all just before the final judgment. He then will battle the Antichrist, defeat him, confess Islam, kill all pigs, break all crosses, and establish a thousand years of righteousness. Some expand on this notion and explain that Jesus will subsequently die and be buried beside the prophet Muhammad."[9]

b. The Ahmad messenger

▪ **According to the Qur'an, did Jesus foretell the coming of Muhammad?**

Yes, Jesus is but "the messenger of Allah" (**Surah 61:6**), as the Qur'an states many times. He came to confirm the Torah and to bring the "good tiding" of a "messenger who cometh after me, whose name is the Praised One [Rodwell: Ahmad]." Thus Islamic scholars say that the original Greek in John 14:16 should be *periklytos*, rendered as "praised one." Jesus would then be foretelling one greater than he, namely Muhammad.[10]

However, in thousands of Greek manuscripts of the Gospel of John there is not one *periklytos*. Rather, the original Greek reads *paraklētos* (literally "Paraclete"), which means "one called to one's side," "helper," or "counselor." It is clear that Jesus is referring to the Holy Spirit as the *paraklētos* (John 14:16–17, 26).

2. The Bible

a. Jesus was crucified

▪ **What does the Bible say about Jesus being crucified?**

The fact that Jesus would be and was crucified and killed is affirmed frequently and repeatedly in the Bible.

Jesus himself foretells that he will "be killed" (**Matt. 16:21–23**; see also Matt. 17:22; Mark 8:31; 10:34; Luke 9:22; 18:31), indeed "mocked and flogged and crucified" (Matt. 20:19). Peter rejects and strongly opposes the notion that Jesus would be killed and asserts emphatically, "This shall never happen to you!" Jesus rebukes Peter and states that his objection comes from Satan himself: "Get behind me, Satan!" A denial of Jesus's crucifixion and death came not from "the things of God, but the things of men" (**Matt. 16:21–23**). The strong witness of the Bible is that soldiers "led him away to crucify him" (**Matt. 27:31**).

b. The risen Christ shows the marks of his crucifixion

▪ **How did Jesus's body attest to the crucifixion?**

Jesus was undeniably crucified. On the third day afterward, the risen Lord "showed them his hands and feet," which still bore nail marks (**Luke 24:40**). This demonstrates irrefutably that the One crucified for our sins had triumphed over death. His atoning sacrifice is acceptable and sufficient for all humankind.

Where Islamic scholars believe it would have been a travesty for the Messiah to be crucified and also proof of weakness, we can see that Abraham's willingness to sacrifice his son, and his son's willingness to be sacrificed, was no evidence of weakness but of obedience, strength, and love. The resurrection likewise certifies that Jesus's crucifixion was a demonstration not of weakness but of great strength, obedience, and love.

The crucifixion of Jesus is central and crucial. If there is no crucifixion, then there is no atonement for sin, and if there is no atonement for sin, either humankind is condemned or human beings are not by nature sinful and need no atonement. However, the Bible teaches that salvation is not by works but a gift by grace through faith to sinful human beings "through the redemption that came by Christ Jesus" (Rom. 3:24).

Secular Corroborating Testimony to the Crucifixion

Along with the eyewitness accounts in the Bible, the record of history confirms the literal crucifixion of Jesus, as a number of modern apologists point out.

Lee Strobel cites Josephus, the Jewish historian, in the *Testimonium Flavianum*, in words he considers to be genuine: "About this time there lived Jesus. . . . When Pilate, upon hearing him accused by men of the highest standing among us, had condemned him [Jesus] to be crucified . . ."[a] Paul L. Maier affirms that the fact of the crucifixion of Jesus is substantiated by the recent discovery of an Arabic manuscript of Josephus's *Antiquities*: "Pilate condemned him to be crucified. . . . His disciples . . . reported that he had appeared to them three days after his crucifixion."[b]

Strobel appeals to Tacitus, the Roman historian of the first century, who writes: "Christus, from whom the name [Christian] had its origin, suffered the extreme penalty during the reign of Tiberius at the hand of one of our Procurators, Pontius Pilate. . . ."[c]

Crucifixion was "the extreme penalty" of the time. Norman Geisler and Abdul Saleeb give evidence: "According to Julius Africanus (c. A.D. 221), the first-century historian, Thallus (c. A.D. 52), 'when discussing the darkness which fell upon the land *during the crucifixion of Christ*,' spoke of it as an eclipse.[d] The second-century Greek writer, Lucian, speaks of Christ as '*the man who was crucified in Palestine* because he introduced a new cult into the world.'"[e]

[a] Lee Strobel, *The Case for Christ* (Grand Rapids: Zondervan, 1998), 103, citing Josephus, *Jewish Antiquities* 18.63–64.
[b] Paul L. Maier, *In the Fulness of Time* (Grand Rapids: Kregel, 1991), 200.
[c] Strobel, *Case for Christ*, 107, citing Tacitus, *Annals* 15.44.
[d] F. F. Bruce, *The New Testament Documents: Are They Reliable?* (Chicago: InterVarsity, 1968), 113.
[e] Norman L. Geisler and Abdul Saleeb, *Answering Islam* (Grand Rapids: Baker Books, 2002), 236, citing Julius Africanus, *Chronography* 18.1 and Lucian, *On the Death of Peregrine* 11 (italics original).

3. Summary

The difference between the Qur'an and the Bible is most stark when the Qur'an denies the actual crucifixion of Jesus and his death. Islam rejects the crucifixion of Jesus so completely that its tradition states that when Jesus returns he will destroy all crosses. The Bible unequivocally states that Jesus was crucified, that he died, and that he was buried. His willingness to die as an atoning sacrifice on the despised cross shows the depth of his love. His resolve to endure this most humiliating of all deaths demonstrates his yearning for all human beings to be saved. Jesus predicted his crucifixion again and again. He was resolute and unwavering in his mission to go to the cross. The clear witness of the Bible to the crucifixion of Jesus is attested to by the testimony of secular historians.

The crucifixion of Jesus is central to the Christian belief in his atoning sacrifice as the Lamb of God offered for the sins of the world, as we shall see. The Qur'an holds, however, that human beings are born without sin and that one is able to pass the test of life and the final judgment on the basis of one's belief in Allah and one's good works, "As for those who believe and do good works, We shall make them enter Gardens underneath which rivers flow to dwell therein for ever" (Surah 4:57). Hence in Islam there is no need for sacrifice. However, according to the Qur'an, Allah saw the need to ransom Ishmael: "Then We [Allah] ransomed him [Ishmael] with a tremendous victim [Dawood: a noble sacrifice]" (Surah 37:107; see "E. Ransom and Sacrifice for Sin," below).

If there is no crucifixion, there is no atoning sacrifice. If Jesus was crucified, an atoning sacrifice has been made. The fact of Jesus's crucifixion is irrefutable, given the eyewitness accounts in the Bible and the testimony of secular history.

For discussion questions, see study guide 11.

E. Ransom and Sacrifice for Sin

Is there found in the Qur'an, as in the Bible, a ransom and sacrifice for sin?

The Qur'an	The Bible
1a. No ransom or sacrifice for sin Surah 3:91. Lo! those who disbelieve, and die in disbelief, the (whole) earth full of gold would not be accepted from such a one if it were offered as a ransom (for his soul). Theirs will be a painful doom and they will have no helpers.	**2a. Ransom for sin** Matthew 20:28. [Jesus's words:] "The Son of Man did not come to be served, but to serve, and to give his life as a ransom for many."
1b. Ransom for Ishmael Surah 37:107. Then We [Allah] ransomed him [Ishmael] with a tremendous victim [Dawood: a noble sacrifice].	**2b. Sacrifice for sin** Leviticus 4:32–33. If he brings a lamb as his sin offering, he is to bring a female without defect. He is to lay his hand on its head and slaughter it for a sin offering.

The Qur'an	The Bible
	Leviticus 16:15–16. He shall then slaughter the goat for the sin offering for the people and take its blood behind the curtain and do with it as he did with the bull's blood: He shall sprinkle it on the atonement cover and in front of it. In this way he will make atonement for the Most Holy Place because of the uncleanness and rebellion. **Isaiah 53:7–8.** He was led like a lamb to the slaughter. . . . For the transgression of my people he was stricken. **Matthew 26:27–28.** [Jesus's words:] "Drink from it, all of you. This is my blood of the covenant, which is poured out for many for the forgiveness of sins." **John 1:29.** The next day John saw Jesus coming toward him and said, "Look, the Lamb of God, who takes away the sin of the world!" **Hebrews 7:26–27.** Such a high priest meets our need—one who is holy, blameless, pure, set apart from sinners, exalted above the heavens. Unlike the other high priests, he does not need to offer sacrifices day after day, first for his own sins, and then for the sins of the people. He sacrificed for their sins once for all when he offered himself.

1. The Qur'an

a. No ransom or sacrifice for sin

■ **Does the Qur'an allow no way for sins to be expiated?**

In the Qur'an, there is no ransom for sin for "those who disbelieve, and die in disbelief" (**Surah 3:91**). Surah 10:54 states that when each soul sees its awaiting punishment, the soul "would seek to ransom itself," but it is too late. Surah 13:18 holds that there is no ransom that can be offered "for those who answered not His call."

However, the issue goes deeper: Is there a ransom provided, and is it applied to those who repent and believe in the ransom? The Qur'an mentions only nine plagues or "tokens unto Pharaoh" of God's judgment when the Hebrews escaped their enslavement in Egypt (Surah 27:12), thus omitting the ransom sacrifice of the Passover lamb. There is no need for ransom sacrifice. Humankind is not so sinful that it needs to be freed from the slavery of sin by a ransom. Allah is "Forgiving [and] Merciful" (Surah 4:110). In the Qur'an, Allah diminishes his demands in the words "We tax not any soul beyond its scope" (Surah 7:42). Allah does not demand more than a person is able to perform.

b. Ransom for Ishmael

■ **What about the story of Ishmael's ransom?**

It should be noted that in the story of Abraham and his son, **Surah 37:107** says, "Then We [Allah] ransomed him [Ishmael] with a tremendous victim [Dawood: a noble sacrifice]." Here even Allah recognizes the need for ransom.

In its references to the Old Testament the Qur'an fails to make any acknowledgment of sacrifice other than here, in Abraham's willingness to sacrifice his son. The assertion of Islam is that the Qur'an is a testimony and confirmation of the Torah, the Psalms, and the Prophets, yet the Qur'an makes no mention of the all-important practice of sacrifice throughout the Old Testament.

2. The Bible

a. Ransom for sin

■ **What does the Bible say about ransom?**

The Bible, like the Qur'an, affirms that no sinful human being can offer himself or herself as a ransom for another (Ps. 49:7–8). However, Jesus is the *sinless* Son of God. He presented his mission clearly: "The Son of Man did not come to be served, but to serve, and to give his life as a ransom for many" (**Matt. 20:28**). In the Bible's account of the Hebrews' liberation from Egyptian slavery, there were ten plagues, and it was the tenth, the sacrifice and ransom of the Passover lamb, that set the people of God free. Christ is the Passover lamb who frees his people from the slavery of sin (Mark 10:45; 1 Tim. 2:6; Heb. 9:15). All humankind was ransomed and set free from sin not with "silver or gold" but "with the precious blood of Christ, a lamb without blemish or defect" (1 Pet. 1:18–19).

b. Sacrifice for sin

■ **Are the Old and New Testaments unified in calling for sacrifice for sin?**

The Bible depicts the crucifixion as not only a ransom for all but an *atoning* sacrifice for all. To understand the crucifixion as an act of atonement, one must go to the Hebrew Scriptures, which strongly set forth the need for sacrifice for the remission of sins. In Leviticus 17:11 God tells his people, "The life of the creature is in the blood, and I have given it to you to make atonement for yourselves on the altar." These Old Testament passages display a strong emphasis on the need for sacrifice:

> Leviticus 4:32–33: A person shall offer "a lamb as his sin offering," and the transfer of guilt shall be by laying "his hand on its head."

Leviticus 16:15: On the Day of Atonement the high priest shall "slaughter the goat for the sin offering for the people."

Isaiah 53:7–8: Speaking of the suffering of the Messiah, Isaiah prophesied, "He was led like a lamb to the slaughter." As a sacrificial lamb he would be stricken "for the transgression of my [the Lord's] people."

On the basis of the Old Testament teaching, the New Testament writer of Hebrews states, "Without the shedding of blood there is no forgiveness" (Heb. 9:22). These New Testament texts clearly proclaim that Jesus was sacrificed for sin:

Matthew 26:28: Jesus on the night of his betrayal announced that he would shed his blood "for the forgiveness of sins."

John 1:29: John the Baptist declared Jesus to be "the Lamb of God, who takes away the sin of the world."

Hebrews 7:26–27: Jesus was the "holy, blameless, pure" high priest, who was "sacrificed for their [the people's] sins once for all when he offered himself."

The sacrifice of the Messiah and Son of God is the greatest demonstration of God's love for all people: "This is love: not that we loved God, but that he loved us and sent his Son as an atoning sacrifice for our sins" (1 John 4:10). "He is the atoning sacrifice for our sins, and not only for ours but also for the sins of the whole world" (1 John 2:2).

3. Summary

The Qur'an holds that it is impossible for one person to ransom another. While this is true for two sinful human beings, the Bible declares that the sinless Christ offered his life as a ransom "to free" human beings from the guilt and power of sin.

It is significant that the Qur'an makes no mention of sacrifice for sin from the Torah, the Psalms, and the Prophets. While Islam accepts these Jewish scriptures as being revelation from God (with inaccuracies), it passes over the large portions that speak of the need for sacrifice and provision for sacrifices. The Qur'an holds that the revelation given to Muhammad reaches back to the faith of Abraham, who was willing to "offer his son" as a sacrifice—but it does not address the necessity of atonement in satisfying the justice of God.

Rather, it states that no person can ransom another. As to the question of divine justice, Allah qualifies his demands by saying, "We tax not any soul beyond its scope" (Surah 7:42). Thus the strict demands of divine justice are accommodated to human ability. For whatever shortcoming, Allah is ever forgiving and merciful (Surah 4:110). The denial of ransom and sacrifice is so complete that in the Qur'an there are only nine plagues by which Allah shows his power to free the Hebrew people. The Bible lists ten plagues; deliverance from the tenth plague came through the blood of a Passover lamb.

The Hebrew Scriptures of the Old Testament clearly set forth the necessity of sacrifice and point toward the ultimate sacrifice of Jesus the Messiah. The justice of the Lord God cannot be pushed aside or diminished. It must be taken seriously. Sin must be atoned for. To say that it can simply be forgiven does not reckon with the seriousness of sin or the holiness and justice of the Lord God. The demands of the Lord God's holy law are not adjusted down to human limitations. Jesus did not say, "Try your best to love your enemies." As the Son of God he presented God's immutable law in all of its righteousness and holiness in perfect love toward the Lord God and our neighbor (Matt. 22:37, 39). Sinful human beings cannot meet such demands for perfection. Humankind is helpless to fulfill the standard of perfect love toward God and fellow human beings.

The Lord God, with a love that cannot bear to see the sinner condemned, finds a way to deal seriously with sin and meet his own just demands. He does it by sending his Son to be an "atoning sacrifice for our sins." Thus sin is not just overlooked; it is dealt with. Sin is not softened. The Lord God's condemnation of sin is not dampened. Sin is paid for. The sacrifice of Jesus was sufficient "once for all" when he willingly offered up himself as the Lamb of God for the sins of the whole world (Heb. 7:27). This is the Lord God's great act of grace. By the atoning sacrifice of his Son, the Lord God restores friendship and fellowship with human beings whom he loves.

For discussion questions, see study guide 12.

F. Grace and Faith

What is the concept of grace and faith in the Qur'an compared with the Bible?

The Qur'an	The Bible
1. Not by grace through faith—forgiveness without atonement	**2a. By grace through faith—forgiveness with atonement**
Surah 3:193. Our Lord! Lo! we have heard a crier calling unto Faith: "Believe ye in your Lord!" So we believed. Our Lord! Therefore forgive us our sins, and remit from us our evil deeds, and make us die the death of the righteous.	Romans 3:23–27. For all have sinned and fall short of the glory of God, and are justified freely by his grace through the redemption that came by Christ Jesus. God presented him as a sacrifice of atonement, through faith in his blood. He did this to demonstrate his justice, because in his forbearance he had left the sins committed beforehand unpunished—he did it to demonstrate his justice at the present time, so as to be just and the one who justifies those who have faith in Jesus. Where, then, is boasting? It is excluded. On what principle? On that of observing the law? No, but on that of faith.
Surah 3:135. And those who, when they do an evil thing or wrong themselves, remember Allah and implore forgiveness for their sins—Who forgiveth sins save Allah only?—and will not knowingly repeat (the wrong) they did.	

The Qur'an	The Bible
136. The reward of such will be forgiveness from their Lord, and Gardens underneath which rivers flow, wherein they will abide for ever—a bountiful reward for workers! **Surah 3:195b.** So those who fled and were driven forth from their homes and suffered damage for My cause, and fought and were slain, verily I shall remit their evil deeds from them and verily I shall bring them into Gardens underneath which rivers flow—A reward from Allah. And with Allah is the fairest of rewards. **Surah 39:53b.** Despair not of the mercy of Allah, Who forgiveth all sins. Lo! He is the Forgiving, the Merciful. **Surah 3:31.** Say, (O Muhammad, to mankind): If ye love Allah, follow me; Allah will love you and forgive you your sins. Allah is Forgiving, Merciful. **Surah 4:124.** And whoso doth good works, whether of male or female, and he (or she) is a believer such will enter Paradise.	**2b. Promise to Abraham by grace through faith** **Romans 4:13.** It was not through law that Abraham and his offspring received the promise that he would be heir of the world, but through the righteousness that comes by faith. **2c. Christ our Passover lamb** **1 Corinthians 5:7.** Get rid of the old yeast that you may be a new batch without yeast—as you really are. For Christ, our Passover lamb, has been sacrificed. **2d. God sympathizes with us** **Hebrews 4:15–16.** For we do not have a high priest who is unable to sympathize with our weaknesses, but we have one who has been tempted in every way, just as we are—yet was without sin. Let us then approach the throne of grace with confidence, so that we may receive mercy and find grace to help us in our time of need. **John 11:34–35.** "Where have you laid him?" he [Jesus] asked. "Come and see, Lord," they replied. Jesus wept.

1. The Qur'an: Not by grace through faith—forgiveness without atonement

■ How does forgiveness come, according to the Qur'an?

In **Surah 3:193**, Allah as Lord calls people "unto Faith: 'Believe ye in your Lord!' So we believed. Our Lord!" Therefore, the plea is that Allah forgive sins. Only Allah is able to forgive sins (**Surah 3:135**). Forgiveness is a "reward" for those who ask and do "not knowingly repeat (the wrong) they did," and Paradise is "a bountiful reward for workers" (**Surah 3:135–36**).

Surah 3:195 promises that those who "suffered damage for My cause, and fought and were slain" will have remission of their evil deeds and they will be brought to gardens in Paradise. This will be "a reward from Allah." Thus forgiveness is not a gift of unconditional love. It is earned by those who "suffered damage" for the cause of Allah.

Allah "forgiveth all sins. Lo! He is the Forgiving, the Merciful" (**Surah 39:53**). Since Allah is able to forgive sins, there is no need for a Mediator or a Savior.

Surah 3:31 exhorts humankind to love Allah. "If ye love Allah, follow me [Muhammad]; Allah will love you and forgive you your sins." The 2007 "Open Letter" by world Islamic leaders to world Christian leaders states, "Thus in the Holy Qur'an God enjoins Muslims who truly love God to follow this example, in order in turn to be loved by God: *Say, (O Muhammad, to mankind): If ye love God, follow me; God will love you and forgive you your sins. God is Forgiving, Merciful (Aal 'Imran, 3:31)*."[11] Thus by loving Allah, one earns the love of Allah.

It is clear from **Surah 4:124** that one enters Paradise if one "doth good works" and is "a believer." Faith plus works in Allah assures one of Paradise. (See Surah 2:177 on the righteous person.)

In the Qur'an, there is no concept of becoming righteous before God by grace alone through faith alone in the Savior. As we have seen in the lives of Abraham, Ishmael, Isaac, and Jacob, they are said to be righteous and acceptable based on their belief in Allah *and* their piety of life and good deeds (Surah 19:55). There is no need for proffered grace to the sinner, for humanity is basically good. There is no concept of being saved through faith alone in a Savior, for Jesus is "a messenger," a great prophet, but not the Savior.

2. The Bible

a. By grace through faith—forgiveness with atonement

■ **Why does not God just forgive sins? Why is sacrifice necessary?**

Romans 3:23 sets forth the truth that "all have sinned and fall short of the glory of God," and so we could not be justified by our works or our own efforts. It is impossible for sinful human beings to meet the demands of the Lord God's law (Rom. 3:20). Rather, we "are justified freely by his grace through the redemption that came by Christ Jesus" (Rom. 3:23). As the sacrifices of old were presented as means of atonement, so "God presented him as a sacrifice of atonement" (**Rom. 3:25**). This is a blood atonement, for "the life . . . is in the blood" (Lev. 17:11). Through sacrifice one life was offered in the place of another. Christ offered his life in our stead. We are therefore justified "through faith in his [Jesus's] blood" (**Rom. 3:25**).

This is not like the pagan sacrifices where a vengeful God demands the blood of his victims. This is a sacrifice "offered" not by human beings but by God himself. Jesus, the victim, also willingly "offered himself" in love (Heb. 9:14). The Father and the Son were of one will and one love for humankind. Jesus prayed, "Not my will, but yours be done" (Luke 22:42). Thus, while it is a sacrifice, it is very different from a pagan sacrifice.

The sacrifice demonstrated not only God's great love but also his justice (**Rom. 3:25**). God's justice had to be met and satisfied. God could not just be lenient, "overlook" sin, and pretend that it was not so serious. Justice expressed in God's holy law requires that the debt of sin be paid. Even human justice objects to leaving those guilty of criminal offense unpunished. Justice must be done. God in grace, in undeserved love, found a way to meet and satisfy his just requirements. God himself was in Christ "reconciling the world to himself" through an atoning sacrifice for all time. Now on the basis of that sacrifice, "on Christ's behalf," God willingly and out of immeasurable grace and love does not count "men's sins against them" (2 Cor. 5:19–21).

This forgiveness of sins is ours by grace "through faith in his blood" (**Rom. 3:25**). It is through faith in the Lamb of God that God appropriates this atonement to us personally and we are justified—that is, declared just and righteous before God.

b. Promise to Abraham by grace through faith

■ **Is the way of salvation in the New Testament different from the Old Testament?**

As **Romans 4:13** reveals, God's way of accepting people as righteous has always been "not through law," or works, but "through the righteousness that comes by faith." It is by faith that Abraham believed the promise, and God "credited it to him as righteousness" (Gen. 15:6). Thus, God makes it possible for all humankind to be saved from their sins. It was not possible by works, as Psalm 143:2 states, "no one living is righteous before you," but it is possible by God's grace through faith in his Son, the Messiah, the offspring of Abraham.

c. Christ our Passover lamb

■ **What is the connection between Jesus's death and the Passover?**

Christ "our Passover lamb" has "been sacrificed" for us (**1 Cor. 5:7**). Even as the people of Israel were saved from the wrath of God in the tenth plague of death by the sacrifice of a lamb, so we have been saved by the sacrifice of the Passover lamb Jesus, the Christ. The Lamb's blood has saved us from the wrath of God and eternal death. As Israel was freed from the bondage of slavery, so we have been rescued from the slavery of sin. Therefore we ought to "get rid of the old yeast" of sin in our lives and become like new unleavened bread.

d. God sympathizes with us

■ **Does God care about our suffering?**

Through the sacrifice of Christ we are "brought near" to God" (Eph. 2:13). We learn the heart of God. We learn that God not only suffers for us but suffers *with* us. He is able to "sympathize with our weaknesses." He was tested and tempted "in every way, just as we are." Therefore we can "approach the throne of grace with confidence" (**Heb. 4:15–16**). Jesus, our high priest, understands our struggles in times of testing and temptation. He was truly human and experienced our struggles and our sorrows, yet "without sin."

When we come to Christ in times of distress, he is touched by our predicament. He weeps with us (**John 11:34–35**). He is not a God who is far off. He is not a God who is so high and lofty that he cannot be touched by our feelings. No, he was "a man of sorrows, and familiar with suffering" (Isa. 53:3). Now we "may receive mercy and find grace to help us in our time of need" (**Heb. 4:16**).

The Qur'an lists only nine plagues at the end of the Hebrews' captivity in Egypt. The tenth, which is the plague of death and the deliverance through the ransom and sacrifice of the Passover lamb, is omitted (see "E. Ransom and Sacrifice for Sin," above). The Jews of Medina actually broke off their association with Muhammad when they learned how different his revelations were from those of the biblical prophets. Muhammad in turn ceased to observe the Day of Atonement with them. He instructed that henceforth his followers were no longer to face Jerusalem but Mecca in prayer.

3. Summary

In the Qur'an, Allah destines people and calls them to faith in him as Lord. To those who repent and do not repeat their evil deeds, he promises Paradise as "a reward." Forgiveness is for "all sins" with no mediator needed. Forgiveness is not a gift but "a bountiful reward for workers." It is given to those who "suffer damage" for Allah's cause. It is by loving Allah that we are loved by Allah. "If ye love Allah . . . Allah will love you and forgive you your sins" (Surah 3:31). One enters Paradise if one does good works and is a believer in Allah.

The Bible teaches that since "all have sinned and fall short of the glory of God," the Lord God in grace—that is, undeserved love—freely declares human beings just through redemption in Christ Jesus. The Lord God loves us in Christ before we ever love him. In love he offers Christ as a sacrifice of atonement to show his love and to demonstrate his justice.

The just condemnation of God's law is not softened, nor is his immeasurable love denied. In love the Lord God satisfies his holy standards through the sacrifice of his Son. Now through our faith in the blood of the Passover lamb, sin is covered. The angel of death "passes over" the sinner and frees him or her from the slavery of sin and the doom of eternal death. All this is the Lord God's doing. It is an act of grace. It is not by works or human merit but by faith in the Passover lamb that a person is righteous before the Lord God, just as Abraham was righteous by faith.

In his suffering Jesus not only died for us but suffered *with us*, and so he is able to "sympathize with our weaknesses." We are now able to "approach the throne of grace" and find "grace to help us in our time of need." Since he lived in flesh and blood and suffered as our brother as well as our Savior, he understands our trials, testings, and temptations. In time of distress he is able to help us. He is able to grant us grace that "is sufficient" for us (2 Cor. 12:9) in all circumstances of life.

For discussion questions, see study guide 13.

G. Rebirth

Is there a concept of rebirth in the Qur'an? What does the Bible teach about rebirth, and what does "rebirth" mean?

The Qur'an	The Bible
1. No rebirth The Qur'an does not speak of rebirth.	**2. Rebirth** **John 3:3, 5.** [Jesus's words:] "I tell you the truth, no one can see the kingdom of God unless he is born again. . . . I tell you the truth, no one can enter the kingdom of God unless he is born of water and the Spirit." **Titus 3:4–5.** But when the kindness and love of God our Savior appeared, he saved us, not because of righteous things we had done, but because of his mercy. He saved us through the washing of rebirth and renewal by the Holy Spirit. **2 Corinthians 5:17.** Therefore, if anyone is in Christ, he is a new creation; the old has gone, the new has come! **Galatians 2:20.** I have been crucified with Christ and I no longer live, but Christ lives in me. The life I live in the body, I live by faith in the Son of God, who loved me and gave himself for me.

1. The Qur'an: No rebirth

■ **What does the Qur'an say about the necessity of being born again?**

The Qur'an does not speak of rebirth. To be saved one must "submit" and sincerely profess in the presence of two witnesses the Shahada (the creed), "I testify that there is no god but Allah and I testify that Muhammad is the Messenger of Allah." Rebirth is not necessary since human beings are basically born without sin. It is through profession of the Shahada and the keeping of the Five Pillars (belief in Allah, prayer, fasting, almsgiving, and pilgrimage to Mecca) that one is a Muslim and assured of paradise.

In the Islamic faith, Allah is transcendent. While he cares for his creation and knows an individual's inner thoughts, "what his soul whispereth," and is nearer than "his jugular vein" (Surah 50:16), Allah remains totally independent of his creation. Allah does not have an intimate relationship with Muslims, nor does he dwell in them.

2. The Bible: Rebirth

■ **What does rebirth mean in the Bible?**

Jesus spoke of the necessity of rebirth to Nicodemus: "I tell you the truth, no one can see the kingdom of God unless he is born again" (**John 3:3**). Since human beings are born sinful (Ps. 51:5), rebirth is necessary if one is to enter the kingdom of God. "No one can enter the kingdom of God unless he is born of water and the Spirit" (**John 3:5**). Each of us has already been "born of flesh"; now we need to be "born of the Spirit" (**John 3:8**) from above.

We are reborn when by the Holy Spirit we come to faith in Jesus as the Messiah: "Everyone who believes that Jesus is the Christ is born [literally 'begotten'] of God" (1 John 5:1). To be reborn means to become a child of

God. Just as we cannot accomplish our own natural begetting or conception, nor our own birth, so we become a child of God not by "natural descent, nor of human decision or a husband's will," but we are "born [begotten] of God" (John 1:13).

■ How is one reborn into the kingdom of God?

St. Paul states in **Titus 3:5**: "He saved us through the washing of rebirth and renewal by the Holy Spirit." One is reborn by "water and the Spirit" (**John 3:5**). In the Nicene Creed the historic church professes "one baptism for the remission of sins." Christ gave himself for the church and cleansed it "by the washing with water through the word" (Eph. 5:26).

Likewise, faith is created when the Holy Spirit convicts us of sin and calls us to embrace the good news that Christ died for us so that we might have forgiveness and eternal life. "Faith comes from hearing the message, and the message is heard through the word of Christ" (Rom. 10:17).

■ How is spiritual rebirth in Christianity distinctive?

In the Christian faith, while God is transcendent, God becomes personally identified with his human creation in the incarnation of his Son, who "became flesh" (John 1:14). Furthermore, the Lord God comes into personal relationship with us through baptism and the Word and calls us into a faith relationship. When we come to such faith we are reborn as children of God: "Everyone who believes that Jesus is the Christ is born of God" (1 John 5:1).

■ What difference does it make in a person's life to be "born of God"?

Second Corinthians 5:17 tells us that "if anyone is in Christ, he is a new creation." He or she is "in Christ"—that is, in intimate union with Christ. The new believer has been grafted into Christ through baptism, and now Christ dwells in his or her heart "through faith" (Eph. 3:17). By God's grace through faith, the believer is "a new creation" with a new start. The old is gone; "the new has come!" (**2 Cor. 5:17**).

The new life in Christ is filled with a sense of forgiveness, peace, and hope and the certainty of eternal life. Christ brings a new perspective, a new attitude, a new lifestyle, and a new purpose of no longer living for self "but for him who died for [us] and was raised again" (2 Cor. 5:15).

Galatians 2:20 states that Christ has so identified himself with each believer that we are "crucified with Christ." Being "baptized into Christ" and "into his death," and being "buried with" Christ "through baptism," we rise with Christ to a new life (Rom. 6:1–4). By grace through faith we share in all the blessings of Christ's death and resurrection.

Now we have new life and a new way of living, not by works, not in guilt and fear, but "by faith in the Son of God." Now we have a new inner motivation and power by the Holy Spirit. That motivation is not self-justification or hope of reward but the Son of God, "who loved me and gave himself for me" (Gal. 2:20).

3. Summary

In the Qur'an, Allah remains transcendent. He cares for his people, but he does not give "rebirth." Rebirth is not necessary, in fact, since human beings are not basically sinful. Allah's followers are not referred to as his "children," nor does he dwell in their hearts by faith. It is by submission to Allah, beginning with the Shahada and the keeping of the Five Pillars, thus tipping the scales of judgment in one's favor, that one enters Paradise.

In the Christian faith, "God is love" (1 John 4:8). The heart of God yearns for us to come to him and for us to have an intimate friendship and fellowship with him (Luke 15). This love of God reaches out to us in the person of his Son. The sacrificial love of Jesus as the Lamb of God acts as a magnet, drawing us to himself as our personal Savior (John 12:32), saving us from the curse of the law (Gal. 3:13). Thus, by God's grace, as we hear the good news of God's grace in Jesus, we are "called" to a personal faith in him as our Savior (Gal. 1:1, 15).

It is by the "rebirth of the Spirit" that the Father's love reaches its destination in our hearts, moving us to repentance, cleansing us from sin, bringing us into a faith fellowship with him through Jesus, and making us his children and heirs of eternal life. This new faith relationship with Christ becomes visible in a new life. The love of God in Christ becomes "complete" when through us it touches the lives of others (1 John 4:12). The Lord God is a very personal and intimate God, pursuing that kind of close friendship with each of us.

For discussion questions, see study guide 14.

6

Angels and Jinn

A. Angels

Both the Qur'an and the Bible assume the existence of angels. How does their teaching differ?

The Qur'an	The Bible
1a. All angels prostrated before man at his creation, except the devil **Surah 38:71.** When thy Lord said unto the angels: lo! I am about to create a mortal out of mire, **72.** And when I have fashioned him and breathed into him of My spirit, then fall down before him prostrate, **73.** The angels fell down prostrate, every one. **74.** Saving Iblis; he was scornful and became one of the disbelievers. **1b. Angels pray for believers' forgiveness** **Surah 40:7.** Those who bear the Throne, and all who are round about it, hymn the praises of their Lord and believe in Him and ask forgiveness for those who believe (saying): . . . forgive those who repent and follow Thy way: Ward off from them the punishment of hell! **Surah 42:5b.** The angels hymn the praise of their Lord and ask forgiveness for those on the earth. Lo! Allah is the Forgiver, the Merciful.	**2a. Angels worship and praise God and the Lamb** **Revelation 5:11–12.** Then I looked and heard the voice of many angels, numbering thousands upon thousands, and ten thousand times ten thousand. They encircled the throne and the living creatures and the elders. In a loud voice they sang: "Worthy is the Lamb, who was slain, to receive power and wealth and wisdom and strength and honor and glory and praise!" **2b. Angels serve believers** **Hebrews 1:14.** Are not all angels ministering spirits sent to serve those who will inherit salvation?

The Qur'an	The Bible
1c. Angels aid Muslims	**2c. Jesus returns with angels**
Surah 8:9. When ye sought help of your Lord and He answered you (saying): I will help you with a thousand of the angels, rank on rank.	**Matthew 25:31–32.** [Jesus's words:] "When the Son of Man comes in his glory, and all the angels with him, he will sit on his throne in heavenly glory.
Surah 6:61b. He sendeth guardians over you until, when death cometh unto one of you, Our messengers receive him, and they neglect not.	All nations will be gathered before him, and he will separate the people one from another as a shepherd separates the sheep from the goats."
1d. Angels guard hell	
Surah 74:30. [Dawood: I will surely cast him into the Fire. Would that you knew what the Fire is like! It leaves nothing, it spares no one; it burns the skins of men. It is guarded by nineteen keepers.]	
31a. We have appointed only angels to be wardens of the fire, and their number have We made to be a stumbling-block for those who disbelieve.	

1. The Qur'an

a. All angels prostrated before man at his creation, except the devil

■ **What does the Qur'an teach about angels at the creation of humankind?**

In **Surah 38:71–74**, Allah announces to the angels that he will create "a mortal out of mire." Allah will breathe "into him of My spirit," and then all angels are to "fall down before him prostrate."

Islamic scholars explain that the angels were not really to "fall down" to worship Adam but were to bow in honor of the great creation wrought by Allah.

Muhammad seems to be influenced by Jewish traditions. "The Talmudists also enlarge on the honour paid to Adam. 'Adam sat in the garden and the Angels brought him flesh and cooling wine.'"[1] All the angels fell prostrate before Adam except Iblis, the devil (**Surah 38:74**). "*Eblis* is used in the Arabic version of the New Testament" for the devil.[2]

b. Angels pray for believers' forgiveness

■ **Do angels pray for people?**

One of the unique teachings of the Qur'an is that angels pray for Muslims and "ask forgiveness for those who believe" (**Surah 40:7**), and "forgiveness for those on the earth" (**Surah 42:5**).

c. Angels aid Muslims

■ **How else do angels help the faithful?**

The Qur'an teaches that angels help Muslims (**Surah 8:9**). They are their "guardians" until death comes, and then they receive them for Allah (**Surah 6:61**).

Muslims believe in guardian angels. The angels carry people's souls to Paradise upon death.

d. Angels guard hell

■ **What is the angels' duty in regard to hell?**

The Qur'an teaches in **Surah 74:30–31** that nineteen angels, or "keepers," guard hell. The number of them is chosen to confound "those who disbelieve," who may wonder, "Why nineteen?"

2. The Bible

a. Angels worship and praise God and the Lamb

■ **What does the Bible teach about angels?**

The Bible reveals that "thousands upon thousands" of angels praise God and the Lamb saying, "Worthy is the Lamb, who was slain, to receive power and wealth and wisdom and strength and honor and glory and praise!" (**Rev. 5:11–12**). There is no statement that angels are to worship the creation of humankind. In fact, the angels forbid any worship except to God himself (Rev. 22:9).

■ **Do angels pray for believers?**

The Bible does not present angels "praying for our forgiveness" as in the Qur'an, nor does it encourage belief in the angels praying for us. Angels do not act as mediators between God and human beings. Jesus, the Son of God, is the only Mediator "between God and men" (1 Tim. 2:5). He "is able to save completely those who come to God through him, because he always lives to intercede for them" (Heb. 7:25). Angels are powerful, but they are not to be prayed to or worshiped (Rev. 19:10), since they too are creations of the Lord God.

b. Angels serve believers

■ **Do angels serve God's people? How?**

Hebrews 1:14 reveals that angels are God's "ministering spirits," whom the Lord God sends to serve the heirs of salvation. Jesus taught that angels at the death of Lazarus "carried him to Abraham's side" (Luke 16:22). The angels of little children "in heaven always see the face" of the Father and are zealous to defend his little ones (Matt. 18:10). An angel fed Elijah (1 Kings 19:5–6), delivered Daniel from the "mouths of the lions" (Dan. 6:22), and "opened the doors of the jail" for imprisoned apostles (Acts 5:19). Angels announced the birth of the Messiah, ministered to him in time of temptation, proclaimed his glorious resurrection, and promised his return in glory.

c. Jesus returns with angels

▪ What will the role of angels be at the consummation of all things?

Angels, who worship and serve God and the Lamb continually, will return with Jesus on the final judgment day (**Matt. 25:31–32**). Jesus will sit as judge on his throne. Angels will gather the people before him for the public judgment (**Matt. 13:39**). Jesus will then separate the righteous from the unrighteous as a "shepherd separates the sheep from the goats."

3. Summary

In both the Qur'an and the Bible angels are real.

The Qur'an gives to angels the task of interceding for humankind, imploring forgiveness. Nineteen angels guard hell. Angels guard and aid Muslims and "receive" their souls back to Allah at time of death.

In the Bible, angels were active in the life of Jesus, his birth, his temptation, his agony in the garden, his resurrection, and his ascension. They will be prominent in his return and in the final judgment. They protected the apostles (Acts 5:19). Angels serve believers in Christ, protect them from harm and the evil one, and carry their souls to paradise. They are not to be worshiped.

For discussion questions, see study guide 15.

B. Jinn and Satan

What do the Qur'an and the Bible teach concerning the spirit world?

The Qur'an	The Bible
1. Jinn (Djinn) **Surah 15:27.** And the Jinn did We create aforetime of essential fire. **Surah 72:1.** Say (O Muhammad): It is revealed unto me that a company of the Jinn gave ear, and they said: Lo! it is a marvellous Qur'an. **Surah 32:13b.** I will fill hell with the jinn and mankind together. **Surah 18:50a.** And (remember) when We said unto the angels: Fall prostrate before Adam, and they fell prostrate, all save Iblis. He was of the Jinn. **Surah 16:98.** And when thou recitest the Qur'an, seek refuge in Allah from Satan the outcast. **99.** Lo! he hath no power over those who believe and put trust in their Lord.	**2. Satan and evil spirits** **Genesis 3:4–5.** "You will not surely die," the serpent said to the woman. "For God knows that when you eat of it your eyes will be opened, and you will be like God, knowing good and evil." **1 John 3:8.** He who does what is sinful is of the devil, because the devil has been sinning from the beginning. The reason the Son of God appeared was to destroy the devil's work. **2 Peter 2:4.** For if God did not spare angels when they sinned, but sent them to hell, putting them into gloomy dungeons to be held for judgment . . . **1 Peter 5:8–9.** Be self-controlled and alert. Your enemy the devil prowls around like a roaring lion looking for someone to devour. Resist him, standing firm in the faith, because you know that your brothers throughout the world are undergoing the same kind of sufferings.

1. The Qur'an: Jinn (Djinn)

▪ Who are the Jinn?

Jinn are mentioned frequently in the Qur'an. There is a wide variety of opinions about the identity of the Jinn. **Surah 15:27** states that the Jinn were created by Allah "of essential fire." Norman Geisler and Abdul Saleeb state: "There has been much speculation concerning the identity and nature of *jinn*, but it is commonly believed that they are powerful, intelligent creatures who possess freedom of choice. Therefore, some are good and some are evil (cf. 72:11). They seem to be halfway between men and angels."[3]

Surah 72 is titled "The Jinn." According to **Surah 72:1**, some of the Jinn "gave ear" and overheard the revelation of the Qur'an and exclaimed, "Lo! it is a marvellous Qur'an." In Surah 72:14, it is revealed that "there are among us [the Jinn] some who have surrendered (to Allah) and there are among us some who are unjust."

Jinn, like human beings, can "choose between obedience and disobedience, faith and disbelief. . . . At scores of places in the Quran, it has also been stated that Iblis at the very creation of Adam had resolved to misguide mankind, and since then the Satanic jinn have been persistently trying to mislead man, but they do not have the power to overwhelm him and make him do something forceful. However, they inspire him with evil suggestions, beguile him and make evil seem good to him."[4] **Surah 32:13** states that Allah "will fill hell with the jinn and mankind together."

Surah 18:50 teaches that Iblis or the devil "was of the Jinn." Rodwell points out, "Muhammad appears, according to this text [Surah 18:50], to have considered Eblis not only as the father of the Djinn, but as one of their number. The truth appears to be that Muhammad derived his doctrines of the Genii from the Persian and Indian mythology, and attempted to identify them with the Satan and demons of the Semitic races. Both the Satans and Djinn represent in the Koran the principle of Evil."[5]

Reading the Qur'an, one encounters a sense of fear and apprehension concerning these mysterious beings—the Jinn and Iblis, or the devil. Surah 35:6 says, "Lo! the devil is an enemy for you, so treat him as an enemy." The devil in the Qur'an is a Jinn who tempts, leads astray, and has as his aim to divert humankind from allegiance to Allah.

The Jinn have unusual powers, evidenced, for example, when Solomon enlisted "a stalwart of the Jinn" to bring the throne of Queen Candice of Sheba to his palace. Candice (Balqis in Islamic tradition) was so impressed that she converted to Islam (Surah 27:39, 44). The Jinn or genie were popular in traditional Middle Eastern literature, as in the *Tales from the Thousand and One Nights*.

Surah 16:98–99 assures those who recited the Qur'an and seek refuge in Allah that they need have nothing to fear. Satan has "no power over those who believe and put trust in their Lord."

2. The Bible: Satan and evil spirits

▪ What is the teaching of the Bible concerning Satan and evil spirits (demons)?

Genesis 3:4–5 reveals to us that the serpent (Satan), "the father of lies" (Jesus's term in John 8:44), deceived the original man and woman. "The devil has been sinning from the beginning," says John; the reason the Son of God came "was to destroy the devil's work" (1 John 3:8).

Satan was a good angel who rebelled against God and misled other angels and humankind. The Lord God "did not spare angels when they sinned" but put them into "gloomy dungeons to be held for judgment" (2 Pet. 2:4). They still, however, have ability to tempt and entice human beings away from God, as Adam and Eve were tempted. In fact, there is a cosmic warfare between good and evil angels in which the evil angels seek to involve human beings in rebellion against God; therefore we are to "put on the full armor of God" (Eph. 6:13). Jesus resisted the temptations of the devil by saying "It is written that . . ." (see Matt. 4:4–10)—that is, by speaking scriptural truth. Believers in Christ likewise are to take "the sword of the Spirit, which is the word of God" (Eph. 6:17), to overcome the evil one.

In 1 Peter 5:8–9, Peter exhorts us to be "self-controlled and alert" because our "enemy the devil prowls around like a roaring lion looking for someone to devour. Resist him, standing firm in the faith." It is only through faith in the victorious Lamb of God that we have power to overcome the evil one and his angels.

3. Summary

The Qur'an has a persistent and mysterious focus on the Jinn. The Jinn fill the Muslim with fear and apprehension. The devil is the chief Jinn. He is the great tempter and misleader. The Jinn entice and influence people to deny Allah.

The Bible is clear on the devil being the angel that fell into sin and caused the fall of humankind into sin. Along with his evil angels, the devil continues to mislead humankind into unbelief and despair. Christ, the Son of God and the Lamb of God, came in human flesh and blood to destroy the works of the devil. Jesus resisted the devil with the words "It is written." The armor of Christ and the Word of God, which is the sword of the Spirit, are sufficient to overcome the temptations of the devil and his evil angels. Those who believe in Christ are secure and need not fear.

For discussion questions, see study guide 15.

7

Humankind

A. The Creation of Humankind

How do the Qur'an and the Bible describe the creation of human beings and humans' special relationship with Allah / Lord God?

The Qur'an	The Bible
1a. Humans' creation by Allah Surah 75:37. Was he not a drop of fluid which gushed forth? 38. Then he became a clot; then (Allah) shaped and fashioned 39. And made of him a pair, the male and female. 40. Is not He (Who doth so) able to bring the dead to life? Surah 15:26. Verily We created man of potter's clay of black mud altered. **1b. Viceroy of Allah** Surah 2:30. And when thy Lord said unto the angels: Lo! I am about to place a viceroy in the earth, they said: Wilt Thou place therein one who will do harm therein and will shed blood, while we, we hymn Thy praise and sanctify Thee? He said: Surely I know that which ye know not.	**2a. Humans' creation by God** Genesis 2:7. The Lord God formed the man from the dust of the ground and breathed into his nostrils the breath of life, and the man became a living being. **2b. Image of God** Genesis 1:27. God created man in his own image, in the image of God he created him; male and female he created them.

1. The Qur'an

a. Humans' creation by Allah

■ **What does the Qur'an teach concerning the creation of humankind?**

According to **Surah 75:37–40**, Allah created man from a "drop of fluid." This formed into a clot that Allah shaped and fashioned. He created a pair, "male and female." Allah "created man of potter's clay of black mud altered" (Surah 15:26). Woman was not created of a rib. Allah created man and woman out of clay by his almighty power, since he is "able to bring the dead to life."

b. Viceroy of Allah

■ **Does the Qur'an say that human beings bear Allah's image?**

Chawkat Moucarry states: "The creation of human beings in the image of God is not a concept found in the Qur'an. The Qur'an does, however, describe humanity as God's *caliph* on earth ([Surah] 2:30). The Arabic word *khalifa* is used to refer to the men who succeeded Muhammad at the head of the Muslim nation. When it is applied to people in general, it indicates that the Creator has entrusted us with the responsibility of representation and of stewardship (cf. [Surah] 38:26)."[1] Human beings, then are the vice regents of Allah on earth. Muslims, however, do not focus attention on human creation in the likeness of God. Rather, they concentrate on the unique sovereignty of Allah.

In the Hadith (the tradition of the teaching and practice of Muhammad and somewhat of his companions), "the Prophet declares that 'God created Adam in His [or his] image.'"[2] There are different interpretations whether "his" refers to Allah, or to Adam, or to humankind, or in a spiritual sense to Adam's high dignity as the vice regent of Allah. A Muslim, when fighting his Muslim brother, "should avoid his face for God created Adam [or man] in his image."[3]

Islam struggles to interpret Muhammad's statement regarding the "image of God," since the Qur'an allows no image to be made of Allah. Allah has no "likeness" to himself. If human beings were, in the strict sense, in the "image" of Allah, it would mean that they would possess and reflect the attributes of Allah. They would see Allah face to face and reflect the being of Allah in human form. This kind of intimacy and communion with God and his human creation is unthinkable in Islam.

2. The Bible

a. Humans' creation by God

■ **What is the biblical view of the creation of humankind?**

According to the Bible, the Lord God "formed the man from the dust of the ground and breathed into his nostrils the breath of life" (Gen. 2:7). Later the Lord God "made a woman from the rib he had taken out of the man and he brought her to the man" (Gen. 2:22). In the Bible, the Lord God has a personal touch. He not only shapes the first man from dust but also breathes "into his nostrils the breath of life." He not only creates woman but creates her from the rib of the man.

The Lord God creates in Adam an awareness that "it is not good for the man to be alone" (Gen. 2:18). Adam has been made aware of an incompleteness as the animals pass before him and he finds "no suitable helper" among them (Gen. 2:20). When God himself brings Eve to Adam, he is filled with great ecstasy: "This is now bone of my bones and flesh of my flesh" (Gen. 2:23). Eve will complement and complete him, will understand him; she is someone with whom he can communicate, who will "tune in to him," and he to her. Together they will have a sense of being complete and whole. This sense of "completeness" will cause a man to "leave his father and mother and be united to his wife" (Gen. 2:24).

b. Image of God

■ **How were human beings to represent God?**

On the image of God important differences exist between the Qu'ran and the Bible.

In the biblical account of creation, "God created man in his own image" (**Gen. 1:27**). Adam and Eve are the highest of creation and are assigned to "take care" of creation (Gen. 2:15). Made in the image of God, they reflect in human degree the holiness, the goodness, the wisdom, the love, and the creativity of their Creator. Because they are made in his image, the Lord God is able to have an intimate relationship with man and woman and to walk and talk with them (Gen. 3:8).

Since the fall, human beings have lost the spiritual and moral qualities of the image, but they retain unique intelligence, creative and imaginative powers, and a high status and position in creation. They retain the responsibility of being stewards and "rulers" of God's creation (Ps. 8:6). And through faith in Christ, the Son of God, human beings are able to have fellowship with their Creator once again. The image of God is being renewed in them: "[You] have put on the new self, which is being renewed in knowledge in the image of its Creator" (Col. 3:10). This image of God will be totally restored when the believer in Christ, in the life to come, beholds God face to face (Ps. 17:15; 1 John 3:2).

3. Summary

In the Qur'an, Allah took at "drop of fluid" and formed a clot and fashioned male and female. He also created man of "potter's clay." They were not created in the image of God, since the Qur'an allows no image to be made of Allah. This kind of intimacy and communion with Allah is unthinkable.

In contrast, in the Bible the Lord God personally and specially forms man from the dust of the ground. God personally and intimately breathes into his nostrils the breath of life. He specially creates woman from the rib of man and personally brings her to Adam. Man and woman complement and complete one another. They delight in one another. Man and woman are created in "the image of God."

Since the fall, the Bible teaches, human beings have lost the spiritual and moral qualities of God's image and are sinful. By God's grace through faith in His Son, human beings are able to have fellowship with their Creator and the image of God is being renewed in them. It will be completely restored in eternity when they behold God "face to face" (1 Cor. 13:12; see also Ps. 17:15; 1 John 3:2.)

For discussion questions, see study guide 16.

B. The Nature of Humankind

Is every person sinful from birth? Do we have free will? Do our works earn us merit before God? How do the Qur'an and the Bible differ in their understanding of the nature of humankind?

The Qur'an	The Bible
1a. Humankind is created upright Surah 30:30a. So set thy purpose (O Muhammad) for religion as a man by nature upright—the nature (framed) of Allah, in which He hath created man.	**2a. Humankind is sinful** Romans 5:12. Sin entered the world through one man, and death through sin, and in this way death came to all men, because all sinned.
1b. Humankind is created weak Surah 4:28. Allah would make the burden light for you, for man was created weak.	**2b. Humankind is responsible, but not righteous by works** Romans 3:19–20. Now we know that whatever the law says, it says to those who are under the law, so that every mouth may be silenced and the whole world held accountable to God. Therefore no one will be declared righteous in his sight by observing the law.
1c. Humans believe only by Allah's permission Surah 10:100. It is not for any soul to believe save by the permission of Allah. He hath set uncleanness upon those who have no sense.	
1d. Personal responsibility and ability Surah 6:164b. Each soul earneth only on its own account, nor doth any laden bear another's load. Then unto your Lord is your return and He will tell you that wherein ye differed.	**2c. Spiritually, humans have no free will** 1 Corinthians 2:14. The man without the Spirit does not accept the things that come from the Spirit of God, for they are foolishness to him, and he cannot understand them, because they are spiritually discerned. Romans 8:7. The sinful mind is hostile to God.
1e. Free will and Allah Surah 81:28. Unto whomsoever of you willeth to walk straight. 29. And ye will not, unless (it be) that Allah, the Lord of Creation, willeth.	John 3:6. [Jesus's words:] "Flesh gives birth to flesh, but the Spirit gives birth to spirit."

1. The Qur'an

a. Humankind is created upright

■ **What is the state of humans "by nature" in the Qur'an?**

According to **Surah 30:30**, "man by nature [is] upright." Since Allah's creation cannot be changed, humankind was and is created good and sinless. Thus each person is born good, upright, sinless, and righteous. "For Muslims, there was no original sin. Everybody is born as a child of God and as a sinless and pure spirit."[4] The Qur'an holds that humankind is not sinful in the heart. Humans are pure but can be tempted and led astray by outside influences.

Some passages in the Qur'an refer to human beings as sinners: "Man is verily a wrong-doer, an ingrate" (Surah 14:34); "verily man is rebellious" (Surah 96:6). However, the vast majority of Muslim scholars do not believe in "inherited sin."

b. Humankind is created weak

■ **What is the result of human weakness?**

According to the Qur'an, while people are pure and sinless by nature, because they were created of clay they are weak (**Surah 4:28**). Human beings are subject to temptation, to being enticed, to being misled, to being forgetful of the goodness of Allah and in need of his forgiveness.

c. Humans believe only by Allah's permission

■ **Can humans believe of their own volition?**

Surah 10:100 states, "It is not for any soul to believe save by the permission of Allah." Thus Muslims believe in Allah through the "permission of Allah." As we have seen under section B.1.a, "The will of Allah," in chapter 4, "Allah sendeth astray whom He will, and whom He will He guideth" (Surah 74:31). Allah finally determines each person's destiny.

What about unbelievers? According to Surah 2:6–7, "As for the disbelievers, whether thou warn them or thou warn them not it is all one for them; they believe not. Allah hath sealed their hearing and their hearts, and on their eyes there is a covering. Theirs will be an awful doom." According to this passage, Allah "seals" their fate. Some Islamic teachers such as Maulana Muhammad Ali interpret that this "seal" or "hardening" is only upon those who of their own free will have hardened their hearts and persistently refused to hear and heed the warnings of the prophets: "They refuse to open their hearts to receive the truth."[5]

d. Personal responsibility and ability

■ **Do Muslims then bear responsibility for their choices?**

The Qur'an emphasizes that every person will be judged and earn reward "only on its own account" (**Surah 6:164**). Each will return to their Allah, and he will tell how one person's reward or punishment differs from that of another (**Surah 6:164**).

e. Free will and Allah

■ **How do the will of Allah and human will interact?**

Surah 81:28–29 clearly states Allah wills a person "to walk straight." He or she cannot "walk straight" unless "Allah, the Lord of Creation, willeth." Yet some in Islam hold that each human being has a free will to choose right from wrong. If one heeds the guidance of Allah and his prophets and chooses the course of righteousness, that person will be rewarded in this life and the next. If one who has free will chooses the course of sin and wickedness, that person will experience corruption and frustration in this life and pain and misery in hell.[6]

Human beings must not think of themselves as "totally free." Human beings have the responsibility of caring for planet earth. This is a testing period, and in due time a person will return to his Lord to be judged "according to the way he has spent that period."[7]

Allah has given his revelation to every person. Each person can choose right from wrong. He is responsible. Yet finally it is "Allah, the Lord of Creation" who "willeth" a person "to walk straight" (**Surah 81:28–29**).

Fazlur Rahman, comparing the view of the Shi'a with the Sunni, states: "The Shi'a have imbibed a more rational spirit which they inherited from the Mu'tazila School: the majority of them reject the 'official' Sunni predestinarianism and believe in the freedom of human choice. Also, they have left open the door of *ijtihad*—individual creative thinking and interpretation of the dogma and the law—at least theoretically, whereas the Sunni door of *ijtihad* has been at least theoretically closed since the 4th/10th century."[8]

Moucarry observes about the Sunni, "Ash'ari (320/930), the most representative of Sunni Islam, takes the view that all human actions, good or evil, are created and willed by God (cf. [Surah] 6:102; 13:16). This often turns into fatalism in Islam because humans are seen primarily as God's servants."[9]

Geisler and Saleeb record that in the Hadith, Muhammad takes a strong stand for Allah's determining evil as well as good. In fact, Allah creates the devil and evil:

> While we were sitting in company with the Apostle of Allah upon whom be Allah's blessing and peace—a group of his Companions, Abu Bakr and Umar entered through one of the gates of the mosque. With them was quite a large body of people disputing with loud voices, the one contradicting the other, till they came to the Apostle of Allah. . . . Said he: "What is it you are disputing about that causes you to raise your voices so and make such a clamor?" "It is

about the decree," they answered. "Abu Bakr asserts that Allah decrees good but does not decree evil, but Umar says that He decrees both alike."

Muhammad replied:

> "The decree necessarily determines all that is good and all that is sweet and all that is bitter, and that is my decision between you." Then he slapped Abu Bakr on the shoulder, and said: "O Abu Bakr, if Allah Most High had not willed that there be disobedience, He would not have created the Devil." Abu Bakr replied: "I seek pardon from Allah. I slipped and stumbled, O Apostle of Allah, but never again will I fall into error about this matter."[10]

The Qur'an presents the fate of humankind as subject to the determinate will of Allah. The Qur'an presents on the one hand the sovereignty of Allah and on the other hand the free will, or limited free will, of man. As stated previously under "Predestination," it may seem that the Qur'an presents a view somewhat similar to the Pharisees in Jesus's day: "On free will and determination, they held a mediating view that made it impossible for either free will or the sovereignty of God to cancel out the other." [11] A person has free will to perform good works, prayer rituals, fasting, purifications, and pilgrimages so as to tip the scales of justice in his or her favor. However, the dominant teaching of the Qur'an is that the will of Allah determines all thoughts, words, deeds, events, and one's final destiny. The highly respected Muslim theologian Al Ghazali states, "He [God] willeth also the unbelief of the unbeliever and the irreligion of the wicked, without that will, there would neither be unbelief nor irreligion. All we do we do by His will: what He willeth not does not come to pass."[12]

2. The Bible

a. Humankind is sinful

■ **What is the Bible's view of "human nature"?**

The Bible presents a view of human nature that is quite different from that of the Qur'an. Humanity was created good in the image of God. However, by the fall of Adam and Eve "sin entered the world" (**Rom. 5:12**). This fall has affected all of humankind, so that "out of the heart come evil thoughts, murder, adultery, sexual immorality, theft, false testimony, slander" (Matt. 15:19).

Humankind, while a precious creation, after the fall is by nature sinful, or infected fully with sin and inclined to sin. The Bible holds that the problem begins in the heart of man. Sin may also come from Satan and other sinful human beings, but the fact remains, "out of the heart come evil thoughts" (Matt. 15:19); and "surely I was sinful at birth" (Ps. 51:5).

b. Humankind is responsible, but not righteous by works

■ **Are human beings answerable for what they do?**

Every person is responsible to God. No human beings live up to their human understanding of the living God revealed to them in creation and natural knowledge. "What may be known about God is plain to them, because God has made it plain to them . . . so that men are without excuse. For although they knew God, they neither glorified him as God nor gave thanks to him" (Rom. 1:19–21).

As Romans declares, human beings are "without excuse" (1:20). Every mouth is "silenced" and "the whole world (is) held accountable to God"; therefore, "no one will be declared righteous in his sight by observing the law" (**Rom. 3:19–20**).

c. Spiritually, humans have no free will

■ **Does the Bible depict human beings as having free will?**

While a person has the ability to choose in human matters such as whether to go here or there, human beings do not have free will in spiritual matters.

First Corinthians 2:14 states that "the man without the Spirit does not accept the things that come from the Spirit of God, for they are foolishness to him, and he cannot understand them, because they are spiritually discerned." In fact, "the sinful mind is hostile to God" (**Rom. 8:7**). This hostility may manifest itself not only in open rebellion but in passive indifference and neglect. "They are darkened in their understanding and separated from the life of God because of the ignorance that is in them due to the hardening of their hearts" (Eph. 4:18). This hostility may take the form of apathy toward things spiritual

---

When the Christian faith teaches that we are born sinful, this does not mean that the way humans are created is evil. God's creation is good. Sin was not created in humans by God but came from the evil source, Satan. Satan was not created by God as the Slanderer and Adversary. He was a good angel who led a rebellion against the Lord God of his own free will (1 John 3:8; 2 Pet. 2:4; Jude 6.). Also, "Original sin is not the nature itself."[a] Rather, the human being has been so infected with the disease of sin and so corrupted that he or she is "full" of sin, or "sinful," with a natural inclination to sin. Thus, sin permeates a person's being, and as Jesus said, "Out of the heart come evil thoughts." If human beings were sin itself, they would be beyond redemption. A man who is sick with cancer is not cancer itself; he is *infected with* cancer. If he were cancer, there would be no hope of a cure. Humankind is sinful, but not sin itself. Human beings are redeemable in Christ.

[a] F. Bente and W. H. T. Dau, eds., *Concordia Triglotta* (St. Louis: Concordia Publishing House, 1921), 877.

and delight in things sinful. They "invent ways of doing evil" (Rom. 1:30). Jesus said, "Everyone who sins is a slave to sin" (John 8:34). Each human being needs to be liberated from the guilt and power of sin by the Son of God, who sets the individual free for a new, full life (John 8:36).

According to **John 3:6,** "flesh gives birth to flesh," so that each person by birth is sinful and needs to be born again from above by the Spirit. Thus, human beings "by nature" are inclined to sin. Human beings do not need to be taught how to sin. From early childhood on, the human person just does "what comes naturally." One need not think, "Now I am going to think a selfish and hurtful thought"; such thoughts just pop into one's mind. We say this is "human nature." Introspection, human experience, interpersonal relationships, history, and current events attest to the fact that human beings are sinful.

3. Summary

The Qur'an and the Bible present different views of humankind. While both teach that human beings are precious in their creation, the Qur'an speaks of their being born upright or sinless even after the disobedience of Adam. But since a person is made from clay, he or she is weak and susceptible to temptation from without. The Qur'an holds that human beings have a problem, but they can resist the temptations from without. Their nature is basically good. Allah gives guidance and warning by his messengers. A person has the free will to choose what is right, to resist temptation, and to earn paradise by surrendering to Allah and doing good works. But this leaves one wondering, "What is sufficient to tip the scales of judgment in my favor? What has Allah willed for my destiny?" Such uncertainty can last all one's life.

The Bible recognizes that since the fall of Adam and Eve human beings have been born sinful. It is not just that they are as "weak" as clay: they are born with the propensity to sin. This sinful condition is passed on from one generation to the next. Because of this inherent sinfulness, humans are not able to offer works that can merit the favor of God. People need redemption. They need the righteousness of Christ in order to be declared acceptable to a holy God. They need God's grace in Christ. They need a personal faith in Jesus as Lord and Savior.

Believers in Christ see fellow human beings as precious by creation and doubly precious because they are redeemed by the blood of Christ. The merciful and gracious Lord God has answered our basic need in the person of his beloved Son, who set us free from the curse and slavery of sin to live a new purposeful life in him. "God our Savior . . . wants all men to be saved" (1 Tim. 2:3–4). Through the good news of Christ's life, death, and resurrection the Holy Spirit calls us into a personal faith relationship with Jesus Christ as Lord and Savior.

Because human beings remain sinful to their dying day, eternal life is always a gift by God's grace through faith in his Son. "It is by grace you have been saved, through faith—and this not from yourselves, it is the gift of God—not by works, so that no one can boast" (Eph. 2:8–9). Through faith in Christ a person has the certainty of eternal security and knows the loving will of the gracious Lord God.

For discussion questions, see study guide 16.

C. The Fall of Humankind

Do both the Qur'an and the Bible tell of a fall into sin?

The Qur'an	The Bible
1a. Fall of humankind **Surah 2:35.** And We said: O Adam! Dwell thou and thy wife in the Garden, and eat ye freely (of the fruits) thereof where ye will; but come not nigh this tree lest ye become wrongdoers. **36.** But Satan caused them to deflect therefrom and expelled them from the (happy) state in which they were; and We said: Fall down, one of you a foe unto the other! There shall be for you on earth a habitation and provision for a time.	**2a. Fall of humankind** **Genesis 2:17.** [God's words:] "You must not eat from the tree of the knowledge of good and evil, for when you eat of it you will surely die." **Romans 5:12.** Therefore, just as sin entered the world through one man, and death through sin, and in this way death came to all men, because all sinned. **Matthew 15:19–20.** [Jesus's words:] "For out of the heart come evil thoughts, murder, adultery, sexual immorality, theft, false testimony, slander. These are what make a man 'unclean.'"
1b. Allah shows mercy **Surah 2:37.** Then Adam received from his Lord words (of revelation), and He relented toward him. Lo! He is the Relenting, the Merciful.	**2b. Promise of a Savior** **Genesis 3:15.** [God's words:] "And I will put enmity between you and the woman, and between your offspring and hers; he will crush your head and you will strike his heel." **Genesis 3:21.** The Lord God made garments of skin for Adam and his wife and clothed them.

1. The Qur'an

a. Fall of humankind

How does the fall of humankind take place?

In the Qur'an (**Surah 2:35**), Allah warns Adam and Eve they may eat freely, but they are not to come "nigh this tree lest ye become wrongdoers. But Satan caused them to deflect therefrom and expelled them from the (happy) state in which they were." (The Qur'an does not speak of the "tree of life" in the garden.)

b. Allah shows mercy

■ **How does Allah show mercy at the time of Adam's fall into sin?**

In the Qur'an, Allah shows mercy to Adam and Eve after they are misled by Satan, for Allah "is the Relenting, the Merciful" (**Surah 2:37**). But the Qur'an offers no promise of a Savior.

2. The Bible

a. Fall of humankind

■ **How does the fall of humankind take place?**

In the Bible (**Gen. 2:17**), the Lord God warns Adam and Eve they "must not eat from the tree of the knowledge of good and evil, for when you eat of it you will surely die." Death and separation from God will be the result. The result of the fall of Adam and Eve was that "sin entered the world . . . and death through sin," and so death and sin were passed on to future generations of sinners (**Rom. 5:12**). The very heart of each human being was infected. Now "out of the heart come evil thoughts" and all manner of evil (**Matt. 15:19–20**).

See "B. The Nature of Humankind," above, especially its discussion of free will, for more on the significance of the fall of humankind.

b. Promise of a Savior

■ **How does God promise to respond to the fall?**

In **Genesis 3:15**, the Lord God shows his mercy in giving the promise of a Savior. The "offspring" of the woman (the Promised One, Jesus) will "crush" the head of the serpent (Satan). However, the serpent will "strike his heel"— that is, wound the "offspring" but not overcome him. With this promise of the Lord God, Adam and Eve must be filled with an assurance of forgiveness and a hope that not all is lost. A champion, the seed of the woman, will come who will overcome the one who has overcome them.

In the Bible's account, the Lord God shows personal tenderness and care for Adam and his wife by clothing them with "garments of skin" (**Gen. 3:21**). This means that the Lord God had to sacrifice the life of animals to clothe them. This first sacrifice is performed so as to clothe Adam and Eve physically, but for Adam and Eve this personal touch has a deeper significance. It is a sign that the Lord God in lovingkindness has covered their guilt and their shame with the sacrifice. They are forgiven. The Lord God will not abandon them. The sacrifice prefigures the great sacrifice of the Son of God and the promise of the Savior to fallen humankind.

3. Summary

The Qur'an presents the temptation of Satan, who casts Adam and Eve out of the garden. They do not "fall" into sin; the devil leads them astray. Allah is forgiving and merciful to them.

The Bible depicts an intimate and tender creation of man and woman; a close personal relationship between God and Adam and Eve; the Lord God's warning not to eat fruit of a particular tree; his calling them, "Where are you?"; his judgment; his promise of the seed of the woman who will crush the head of the serpent; his sacrifice of animals to clothe Eve and Adam with garments; and his protecting them from the tree of life that they may not forever remain in their sinful state. The whole account reveals intimacy and loving concern for the redemption and restoration of humankind through the seed of the woman, Jesus the Christ.

For discussion questions, see study guide 16.

8

Women and Marriage

A. Women

What do the Qur'an and the Bible teach with regard to the dignity and status of women?

The Qur'an	The Bible

1. Women are subject to men
    Surah 4:34a. Men are in charge of women, because Allah hath made the one of them to excel the other, and because they spend of their property (for the support of women). So good women are the obedient, guarding in secret [Dawood: unseen parts] that which Allah hath guarded. As for those from whom ye fear rebellion, admonish them and banish them to beds apart, and scourge them.
	2. Women are equal to men
	    Genesis 1:27. So God created man in his own image, in the image of God he created him; male and female he created them.
	    Galatians 3:26–29. You are all sons of God through faith in Christ Jesus, for all of you who were baptized into Christ have clothed yourselves with Christ. There is neither Jew nor Greek, slave nor free, male nor female, for you are all one in Christ Jesus. If you belong to Christ, then you are Abraham's seed, and heirs according to the promise.

1. The Qur'an: Women are subject to men

■ **What is the status of women in the Qur'an?**

The Qur'an teaches that man and woman are equal in human dignity, "Ye (proceed) one from another" (Surah 4:25; Pickthall adds a footnote that explains, "This expression, which recurs in the Qur'an, is a reminder to men that women are of the same human status as themselves"). However, "men are in charge of women" (**Surah 4:34**). That is, men in general are in charge of women. A wife is to be admonished if she is given to "rebellion." Then

In Saudi Arabia, unlike in other Muslim countries, women are generally not allowed to drive cars; in rural areas, however, driving is tolerated. Women customarily take taxis, driven by men. All females must have a legal male guardian, typically a father or husband. Most offices, banks, and universities have separate entrances for men and women. Public transportation is segregated by sex.

But recent years have also brought some changes for women in Saudi Arabia. Since 2005 women have had the right to vote.[a] In September 2009, King Adullah opened the nation's first coeducational university, appointed the first female cabinet member, and passed laws against domestic violence. Yet not all changes have opened more opportunities for women. For example, the board of Islamic clerics "has endorsed a fatwa that calls for a ban on female vendors because it violates the kingdom's strict segregation of the sexes."[b]

Even when living in the United States, Muslims often adhere to Islamic practices, which sometimes conflict with American law. A New Jersey judge ruled that a Muslim husband who engaged in nonconsensual sexual acts with his wife "was operating under his belief that it is, as the husband, his desire to have sex when and whether he wanted to, was consistent with his practices and was something that was not prohibited." The appellate court reversal on July 23, 2010, states, "The judge [Joseph Charles Jr.] determined to except defendant from the operation of the state's statutes as the result of his religious belief. In doing so, the judge was mistaken."[c] On April 16, 2011, an Iraqi immigrant was sentenced to over thirty-four years in an Arizona prison for running over and killing his twenty-year-old daughter in an "honor killing" because she became "too westernized."[d]

It is noteworthy that four Muslim countries have been led by women: Pakistan, Bangladesh, Indonesia, and Turkey.

[a] *Wikipedia*, s.v. "Women's Rights in Saudi Arabia," accessed April 18, 2011, http://en.wikipedia.org/wiki/Women%27s_rights_in_Saudi_Arabia.
[b] "Saudi Clerics Ban Female Cashiers," *Daily Herald* (Arlington Heights, IL), November 7, 2010.
[c] Michelangelo Conte, "Court: Religion Is No Defense in Couple's Non-consensual Sex," *Jersey Journal* (New Jersey), August 2, 2010.
[d] "'Honor Killing' Dad Sentenced," *Daily Herald* (Arlington Heights, IL), April 16, 2011.

she may be banished to a separate bed and finally scourged or beaten for her disobedience (**Surah 4:34**).

All women are to be obedient and modest, guarding their "adornment," namely their hair, bosom, and ankles (Surah 24:31; see "D. Veil and Modesty," below). With regard to inheritance, the man is to receive twice as much as his sister: "to the male the equivalent of the portion of two females" (Surah 4:11).

In Islamic tradition, it is the husband who determines the religion of the children of his household. Three times in the Hadith, Muhammad says, "I was shown the Hellfire and that the majority of its dwellers are women."[1]

2. The Bible: Women are equal to men

■ **What is the biblical view of women?**

In **Genesis 1:27**, women are given worth and dignity equal to those of men, being created in the "image of God."

While the fall into sin wrecked the moral and spiritual aspects of the image of God in members of both genders, in Christ Jesus men and women are given equal status as "sons of God" (**Gal. 3:26**). In Christ, they are children of Abraham and heirs of the promise: "For all of you who were baptized into Christ have clothed yourselves with Christ. There is neither Jew nor Greek, slave nor free, male nor female, for you are all one in Christ Jesus" (**Gal. 3:27–28**).

3. Summary

While women have dignity through creation by Allah, the Qur'an makes them subject to men in general, not just their husbands. Islamic women as a whole suffer under Sharia or Islamic law. Under strict Islamic law they can be held in extreme subjection.

The Bible gives equal and high dignity to women as being created in the image of God. In Christ there is no distinction between male and female, since they are "one in Christ Jesus." Jesus in his ministry raised the status of women. He welcomed their service. He showed concern and compassion to the woman caught in adultery (John 8:1–11). Women were the last to leave at the cross and the first to arrive at the tomb (Matt. 27:55; 28:1; Luke 24:10; John 19:25–26; 20:1). The love of Christ gave them new status and godly dignity. Women and men are equal children of God in Christ Jesus.

For discussion questions, see study guide 17.

B. Marriage

Marriage is the basic divine institution of human society. What does the Qur'an teach concerning marriage? How many wives may a Muslim have? What is the teaching of the Bible with regard to marriage?

The Qur'an	The Bible

1a. Polygamy permitted
    Surah 4:3b. Marry of the women, who seem good to you, two or three or four; and if ye fear that ye cannot do justice (to so many) then one (only) or (the captives) that your right hands possess. Thus it is more likely that ye will not do injustice.
	2a. Two become one
	    Matthew 19:4–6. "Haven't you read," [Jesus] replied, "that at the beginning the Creator 'made them male and female,' and said, 'For this reason a man will leave his father and mother and be united to his wife, and the two will become one flesh'? So they are no longer two, but one. Therefore what God has joined together, let man not separate."

The Qur'an	The Bible
1b. Sexual relations in marriage Surah 2:223a. Your women are a tilth [field] for you (to cultivate) so go to your tilth as ye will, and send (good deeds) before you for your souls, and fear Allah.	**1 Corinthians 7:3–4.** The husband should fulfill his marital duty to his wife, and likewise the wife to her husband. The wife's body does not belong to her alone but also to her husband. In the same way, the husband's body does not belong to him alone but also to his wife.
1c. Adultery Surah 24:2. The adulterer and the adulteress, scourge ye each one of them (with) a hundred stripes. And let not pity for the twain withhold you from obedience to Allah, if ye believe in Allah and the Last Day. And let a party of believers witness their punishment.	**2b. Submitting to one another** Ephesians 5:21–23. Submit to one another out of reverence for Christ. Wives, submit yourselves to your husbands as to the Lord. For the husband is the head of the wife as Christ is the head of the church. 25. Husbands, love your wives, just as Christ loved the church and gave himself up for her.

1. The Qur'an

a. Polygamy permitted

■ **What does the Qur'an teach about how many wives a man may have?**

As **Surah 4:3** states, in marriage a man may have up to four wives provided that he is able to provide for them and to "do justice" to them. Abraham Sarker writes: "Islam considers marriage a civil contract between a man and his wife. Traditionally, marriages are arranged by the families of the man and woman; but modern Muslims often make their own choice in a mate, and then the two parties negotiate. A dowry is customarily an important part of the marriage process."[2]

John Bowker states, "Men are allowed to marry up to four wives, but women are not allowed to marry four husbands; men are allowed to beat their wives (Surah 4:34, 38), the reverse is not true; Muslim men are allowed to marry women who come from the People of the Book. Muslim women are forbidden

Muhammad had eleven wives and two concubines. Aishah was six years old when she was betrothed to Muhammad, and when she was nine their marriage was consummated. Muhammad received special dispensation for more wives "if she give herself unto the Prophet and the Prophet desire to ask her in marriage—a privilege for thee only, not for the (rest of) believers" (Surah 33:50). In 2001 the Iranian Council of Guardians ruled that girls as young as nine can be married with parental permission. On July 31, 2009, Hamas in Gaza sponsored a mass wedding for 459 couples: most of the grooms were in their mid to late twenties, while most of the brides were under ten years of age.

to marry men from *ahl al-Kitab* ['the People of the Book,' Jews and Christians]."[3] The man determines the religion of the children.

b. Sexual relations in marriage

▥ **What does the Qur'an teach about sexual relations between a husband and wife?**

Husbands can expect sexual relations from their wives: "Your women are a tilth [field] for you (to cultivate) so go to your tilth as ye will, and send (good deeds) before you for your souls, and fear Allah" (**Surah 2:223**). Wives are the fields of their husband, to be cultivated.

"The so-called 'marriage of enjoyment' allowed by the Shi'ites is a temporary marriage that one enters for a stipulated period of time. A businessman, for instance, who is spending a month in a large city, such as Teheran, can go to the mosque and arrange for a temporary marriage of so-and-so many days."[4]

c. Adultery

▥ **What punishment does the Qur'an prescribe for adulterers?**

In the Qur'an, adultery for both the man and the woman is punished with "a hundred stripes": "The adulterer and the adulteress, scourge ye each one of them (with) a hundred stripes" (**Surah 24:2**). This is usually interpreted as to be performed upon the unmarried who have committed premarital sex.

Married men and women who have been convicted of adultery are to be stoned. The practice of stoning is based on very strong early tradition and Islamic Sharia (law and jurisprudence) going back to Muhammad. Stoning is a legal punishment in Saudi Arabia, Somalia, Sudan, Pakistan and Nigeria.[5] The sentence to stoning for adultery has been reported from time to time by news publications. The international outcry against stoning has usually resulted in some suspension or delay to the sentence, except in the tribal areas of Afghanistan.

(For the Bible's teaching on adultery, see "C. Divorce," below.)

2. The Bible

a. Two become one

▥ **What does the Bible teach about God's design for marriage?**

In **Matthew 19:4–6**, Jesus restores God's original design for marriage. God's idea was a union and a love that was permanent. Their love for each other is expressed mutually in sexual union: "The husband should fulfill his marital duty to his wife, and likewise the wife to her husband" (**1 Cor. 7:3**). No other person is to "separate" a married couple, whom God has "joined together" (**Matt. 19:6**). Christ is the Redeemer and restorer of marriage relationships. In his forgiveness there is power for reconciliation and healing.

b. Submitting to one another

In the biblical relationship of husband and wife, the Lord is central. Christian spouses are to have love and respect for each other, just as all believers are called to "submit to one another out of reverence for Christ" (**Eph. 5:21**).

The believing husband loves his wife "just as Christ loved the church and gave himself up for her" (**Eph. 5:25**). He is not abusive or harsh but tender, caring, and self-giving. Such Christlike love "drives out fear" (1 John 4:18) from their relationship.

The believing wife in turn loves and respects her husband and submits to him "as to the Lord" (**Eph. 5:22**). She is not disrespectful but loyal and loving as the believer is toward the Lord, who is the Bridegroom of the church.

> One should note that **Ephesians 5:22–23** urges wives to be submissive to "your" husbands, not to men in general. Both husband and wife and all Christians are to "submit to one another out of reverence for Christ" (**Eph. 5:21**).

Christ and his bride, the church, are the model and the motive for both the believing husband and the believing wife in their relationship with each other. They are to "be kind and compassionate to one another, forgiving each other, just as in Christ God forgave you" (Eph. 4:32).

3. Summary

The Qur'an allows a man to marry as many wives as he can afford, up to four wives at a time. Not so for a woman. The Qur'an gives the husband the right to banish his wife to a separate bedroom and to "scourge" or beat her if she is rebellious. The woman may not marry from any "People of the Book," as a man may. The husband determines the religion of the children.

In the Bible, Jesus takes us back to God's original beautiful design of an unbroken bond between one man and one woman in marriage. Marriage is the Lord God's good gift to one man and one woman. A believing husband and wife pattern their relationship after Christ and his relationship with his bride the church. There is no thought of either coercion or rebellion, since both have experienced the love of Christ. Christ is the Savior and Lord of both husband and wife. This makes a unique difference in their relationship with one another.

For discussion questions, see study guide 17.

C. Divorce

Under what circumstances may a marriage be severed? Are the restrictions on divorce in the Qur'an and the Bible similar?

The Qur'an	The Bible
1. Divorce is easy	**2. Divorce not God's original design**
Surah 2:228. Women who are divorced shall wait, keeping themselves apart, three (monthly) courses. And it is not lawful for them that they should conceal that which Allah hath created in their wombs if they are believers in Allah and the Last Day. And their husbands would do better to take them back in that case if they desire a reconciliation. And they (women) have rights similar to those (of men) over them in kindness, and men are a degree above them. Allah is Mighty, Wise. (cf. Surah 65:1–2)	Matthew 5:31–32. [Jesus's words:] "It has been said, 'Anyone who divorces his wife must give her a certificate of divorce.' But I tell you that anyone who divorces his wife, except for marital unfaithfulness, causes her to become an adulteress, and anyone who marries the divorced woman commits adultery."
229a. Divorce must be pronounced twice and then (a woman) must be retained in honour or released in kindness. And it is not lawful for you that ye take from women aught of that which ye have given them.	Matthew 19:3–6, 9. Some Pharisees came to him to test him. They asked, "Is it lawful for a man to divorce his wife for any and every reason?" "Haven't you read," he [Jesus] replied, "that at the beginning the Creator 'made them male and female,' and said, 'For this reason a man will leave his father and mother and be united to his wife, and the two will become one flesh'? So they are no longer two, but one. Therefore what God has joined together, let man not separate. . . . I tell you that anyone who divorces his wife, except for marital unfaithfulness, and marries another woman commits adultery."
230a. And if he hath divorced her (the third time), then she is not lawful unto him thereafter until she hath wedded another husband. Then if he (the other husband) divorce her it is no sin for both of them that they come together again if they consider that they are able to observe the limits of Allah. These are the limits of Allah.	1 Corinthians 7:15. But if the unbeliever leaves, let him do so. A believing man or woman is not bound in such circumstances; God has called us to live in peace.

1. The Qur'an: Divorce is easy

■ **What does the Qur'an allow in divorce?**

Surah 2:228 states that in divorce a woman must keep herself "apart, three (monthly) courses," to make sure that she is not pregnant: "it is not lawful for them that they should conceal that which Allah hath created in their wombs." In case of pregnancy special consideration is given to the mother and child. The husband would do well "to take them back in that case if they desire a reconciliation."

According to **Surah 2:229**, the divorced wife is to be given her possessions: "And it is not lawful for you that ye take from women aught of that which ye have given them." If divorce is initiated before consummation there is no waiting period (Surah 33:49).

The husband may pronounce, "I wish to divorce you," three times over a period of three months in front of a witness, to divorce his wife (**Surah 2:230**). The wife is no longer "lawful" unto the man "if he hath divorced her (the

Muhammad married Zainab, the divorced wife of his adopted son Zaid. There had been an attraction between the two, and Zaid actually divorced his wife so that Muhammad might marry her. The fact that Zainab was the wife of Muhammad's adopted son caused a scandal in the Muslim community, as such a marriage was considered incestuous. But Muhammad received the revelation that adopted sons are not really sons, "nor hath he made those whom ye claim (to be your sons) your sons." And so "there is no sin for you in the mistakes that ye make unintentionally" (Surah 33:4, 5). Thus, this divorce and marriage were allowed by a special revelation from Allah. As noted elsewhere, by special revelation Muhammad was allowed to marry eleven women and take two others as concubines.

third time)." He may not marry her again until she has married and been divorced by another husband. Bowker observes that, "the practice of repeating the threefold formula all on one occasion is strongly repudiated by many Muslims, but it has nevertheless become a practice in some areas of Islam."[6]

Men may divorce their wives, but the Qur'an does not grant wives an explicit right of divorce. According to Bowker, wives may get a divorce by going to a judge and saying that "for these reasons she would like a divorce, and he can give the divorce—though he [the judge] too must try to get them to discuss their problems. . . . Many Muslim women do not know that they have the right to divorce."[7] "Divorce is easy in Islam. The door is wide open for a woman or a man who wants to come out of marriage."[8]

2. The Bible: Divorce not God's original design

■ **What does the Bible teach about divorce?**

Matthew 5:31–32 records the strong stand Jesus takes for the permanence of marriage. He speaks forcefully against divorce, "except for marital unfaithfulness."

In Jesus's day it was possible for a man to divorce his wife for inconsequential reasons. Jesus elevates marriage by bringing it back to the Lord God's original institution and design of a lifelong, loving union (see Mark 10:11; Luke 16:18). Thus he strengthens greatly the position and security of the woman in a marriage relationship.

Jesus takes the Pharisees, who wanted to justify their loveless practice, back to God's design "at the beginning" (**Matt. 19:3–6**). Husband and wife "become one flesh," with all that this implies of intimacy, completeness, love, and loyalty. This divinely designed union has the blessing of the Lord God. "Therefore what God has joined together, let man not separate."

Jesus adds that for a husband to divorce his wife, "except for marital unfaithfulness," and to marry another woman is to commit adultery (**Matt. 19:9**).

When a Christian believer experiences divorce, he or she should recognize that the Lord God's design for marriage has been broken and agree with the assessment of the Lord, "I hate divorce" (Mal. 2:16). Often a person is shattered by the experience of divorce and needs to seek refuge in the grace of a merciful Father and forgiveness, healing, and restoration in the Lord Jesus Christ.

Jesus's example of forgiveness to the woman caught in adultery (John 8:3–11) is an example of how God desires for the sinner to be forgiven and "leave [their] life of sin" (8:11), and how we are to recognize our own sinfulness and need for forgiveness: "If any one of you is without sin, let him be the first to throw a stone at her" (8:7).

In **1 Corinthians 7:15**, St. Paul allows divorce "if the unbeliever leaves." That is, in the case of desertion—which some hold may include intolerable abuse—the believer is not to be bound, for "God has called us to live in peace."

Christ is the Redeemer and healer of the marriage relationship. In his love for the church, he gives to husbands and wives a noble motive and model in their love for each other.

3. Summary

The difference between the Qur'an and the Bible with regard to marriage and divorce is significant. While reconciliation is encouraged, the Qur'an makes it relatively easy to divorce one's spouse.

In the Bible, Jesus transports us back to the Garden of Eden and the original design and will of the Lord God. Marriage is not to be entered into lightly but reverently and in accordance with the Lord God's institution and design. It is not to be dissolved except when the union of "one flesh" has been violated in adultery or the marriage is abandoned by desertion.

For discussion questions, see study guide 18.

D. Veil and Modesty

How do the Qur'an and the Bible view the virtues of purity and modesty?

The Qur'an	The Bible
1. Modesty and the veil Surah 24:31a. And tell the believing women to lower their gaze and be modest, and to display of their adornment only that which is apparent, and to draw their veils over their bosoms, and not to reveal their adorn-	**2. Modesty and purity** Ephesians 5:3–4. But among you there must not be even a hint of sexual immorality, or of any kind of impurity, or of greed, because these are improper for God's holy people. Nor should there

The Qur'an	The Bible
ment save to their own husbands or fathers or husbands' fathers, or their sons or their husbands' sons, . . . or their women, or their slaves. . . . And let them not stamp their feet so as to reveal what they hide of their adornment. **Surah 33:59a.** O Prophet! Tell thy wives and thy daughters and the women of the believers to draw their cloaks [Dawood: veils] close round them (when they go abroad). That will be better, so that they may be recognised and not annoyed [Dawood: molested].	be obscenity, foolish talk or coarse joking, which are out of place, but rather thanksgiving. **Ephesians 5:8.** For you were once darkness, but now you are light in the Lord. Live as children of light. **1 Corinthians 6:18–20.** Flee from sexual immorality. . . . Do you not know that your body is a temple of the Holy Spirit, who is in you, whom you have received from God? You are not your own; you were bought with a price. Therefore honor God with your body.

1. The Qur'an: Modesty and the veil

■ **Why do Muslim women wear the veil?**

The headdress or veil is a sign of humility and modesty for Muslim women. Girls begin to wear the headdress at age ten or at puberty. Preparation for the wearing of the headdress begins at the age of seven. Some women wear the headdress only for prayer. Difference in interpretation of doctrine determines the practice. The burka in Afghanistan is one form of headdress.

According to **Surah 24:31**, Muslim women are to "lower their gaze and be modest," "draw their veils over their bosoms," and not "reveal their adornment"—such as their bosoms, hair, and (in Afghanistan) ankles—except to their husbands and immediate members of their household in their homes. **Surah 33:59** gives the reason for such modesty: so that they may "not [be] annoyed" or molested.

Muslim men are likewise to be modest. "Tell the believing men to lower their gaze and be modest. That is purer for them" (Surah 24:30).

2. The Bible: Modesty and purity

■ **What does the Bible teach about purity and modesty?**

In the Bible, the injunction for purity and modesty applies equally to men and women.

Ephesians 5:3–4 states that believers in Christ, both men and women, are not to give "a hint of sexual immorality, or of any kind of impurity. . . . Nor should there be obscenity, foolish talk or coarse joking, which are out of place, but rather thanksgiving." Thus, in their actions, speech, and appearance believers are not to give "a hint of sexual immorality."

The reason for sexual purity is that "you were once darkness, but now you are light in the Lord. Live as children of light" (**Eph. 5:8**). The believer is in union with Christ (1 Cor. 6:15–17), and his or her body is the "temple of the

Holy Spirit" (**1 Cor. 6:19**). How could believers think of uniting in an intimate way with an immoral person when they are united with Christ and their body is the temple of the Holy Spirit? Furthermore, we were "bought" with the precious blood of Christ. We now belong to him. We are, therefore, compelled by his redeeming love to honor God with our bodies (**1 Cor. 6:18–20**).

3. Summary

Both the Qur'an and the Bible have statements enjoining purity. The Qur'an focuses especially on modesty for women; it demands the covering of "adornment" (bosom, hair, ankles), so as to encourage modesty and prevent molestation.

The approach of the Bible is that believers, both men and women, have been redeemed and cleansed by the blood of Christ from an immoral lifestyle to live in purity as "children of light." The appeal is inwardly compelling. The believer in Christ has been cleansed. He or she is now attached to Christ. His or her body is the temple of the Holy Spirit. How then can a Christ-follower become attached to an immoral person in an act of sexual immorality? Believers have been bought with a price. They are to glorify God with their bodies.

For discussion questions, see study guide 18.

9

Ethical Teachings

A. Homosexuality

How to respond to homosexual behavior is a burning issue in our society. What does the Qur'an teach? What does the Bible teach?

The Qur'an	The Bible
1. Homosexual acts an abomination **Surah 27:54.** And Lot! when he said unto his folk: will ye commit abomination knowingly? **55.** Must ye needs lust after men instead of women? Nay, but ye are folk who act senselessly. **Surah 29:28.** And Lot! (Remember) when he said unto his folk: Lo! ye commit lewdness such as no creature did before you. **29.** For come ye not in unto males, and cut ye not the road (for travellers), and commit ye not abomination in your meetings? But the answer of his folk was only that they said: Bring Allah's doom upon us if thou art a truth-teller!	**2. Homosexual acts detestable** **Genesis 19:5.** They [the men of the city of Sodom] called to Lot, "Where are the men who came to you tonight? Bring them out to us so that we can have sex with them." **Judges 19:22.** While they were enjoying themselves, some of the wicked men of the city surrounded the house. Pounding on the door, they shouted to the old man who owned the house, "Bring out the man who came to your house so we can have sex with him." **Leviticus 18:22.** Do not lie with a man as one lies with a woman; that is detestable. **Romans 1:26–27.** Because of this, God gave them over to shameful lusts. Even their women exchanged natural relations for unnatural ones. In the same way the men also abandoned natural relations with women and were inflamed with lust for one another. Men committed indecent acts with other men, and received in themselves the due penalty for their perversion.

The Qur'an	The Bible
	1 Corinthians 6:9–11. Do you not know that the wicked will not inherit the kingdom of God? Do not be deceived: Neither the sexually immoral nor idolaters nor adulterers nor male prostitutes nor homosexual offenders nor thieves nor the greedy nor drunkards nor slanderers nor swindlers will inherit the kingdom of God. And that is what some of you were. But you were washed, you were sanctified, you were justified in the name of the Lord Jesus Christ and by the Spirit of our God.

1. The Qur'an: Homosexual acts an abomination

■ **What is the teaching of the Qur'an on homosexuality?**

Surah 27:54 takes a clear stand against homosexuality and calls it an "abomination."

Surah 29:28 cites the example of Lot, who warned the people not to "commit lewdness." But the people of Sodom were hardened and taunted Lot to "bring Allah's doom upon us" if he were telling the truth (**Surah 29:29**).

The practice of homosexuality is repulsive to the Muslim: "People are told to keep away from it. It is unnatural, it is wrong, it is something disgusting."[1]

2. The Bible: Homosexual acts detestable

■ **What does the Bible say about homosexual behavior?**

In both the Old and New Testaments the Bible speaks against the practice of homosexuality.

In **Genesis 19:5**, Sodom is cited as an example of God's wrath on homosexual practice. According to Judges 19–21, the homosexual lust of the people of Gibeah, along with their ravaging of a concubine servant girl, was so abhorrent to Israel that the other tribes of Israel almost destroyed the tribe of Benjamin.

From the days of Moses through the centuries of Christian influence until recent time, homosexual behavior was considered "detestable" (**Lev. 18:22**) and "an abomination" (Lev. 20:13 RSV). Only recently have some in Christian circles begun to hedge on this judgment.

The New Testament strongly condemns homosexual practice (**1 Cor. 6:9–11**; see also **Rom. 1:26–27**) but holds out hope for the "homosexual offender," stating, "That is what some of you were. But you were washed, you were sanctified, you were justified in the name of the Lord Jesus Christ and by the Spirit of our God."

3. Summary

The practice of homosexual behavior is repugnant and an abomination in the Qur'an. It is unnatural and it is wrong.

The practice of homosexual behavior is "unnatural" and a "perversion" (Rom. 1:26–27) and "detestable" (Lev. 18:22) in the Bible. While the behavior is abhorrent, the Bible holds out hope to the homosexual to be "washed . . . sanctified . . . [and] justified in the name of the Lord Jesus Christ and by the Spirit of our God" (1 Cor. 6:11). Christ has paid the ransom of his precious blood to set people free from the bondage of this practice so that they might live a pure life. Christ offered his precious body on the cross so that we might "honor God" with our bodies (1 Cor. 6:20). The believer in Christ has concern that the homosexual might find new life in Christ.

For discussion questions, see study guide 19.

B. Murder, Suicide, Abortion

Do the Qur'an and the Bible have the same views of suicide? What is the value of human life?

The Qur'an	The Bible

1. The sacredness of life
   Surah 5:32a. For that cause We decreed for the Children of Israel that whosoever killeth a human being for other than manslaughter or corruption in the earth, it shall be as if he had killed all mankind.
   Surah 4:29. O ye who believe! Squander not your wealth among yourselves in vanity, except it be a trade by mutual consent, and kill not one another. Lo! Allah is ever Merciful unto you.
   [Rodwell: And commit not suicide:—of a truth God is merciful to you.]
   [Dawood: Do not kill yourselves. God is merciful to you.]
   30. Whoso doth that through aggression and injustice, We shall cast him into Fire, and that is ever easy for Allah.
	2. The sacredness of life
	   Exodus 20:13. [The Lord God's commandment:] "You shall not murder."
	   Psalm 139:13–14. For you created my inmost being; you knit me together in my mother's womb. I praise you because I am fearfully and wonderfully made.

1. The Qur'an: The sacredness of life

■ How is life valued in the Qur'an?

Surah 5:32 states "whosoever killeth a human being. . . it shall be as if he had killed all mankind." One person's life is inseparably linked with the lives of all humankind.

Surah 4:29 forbids Muslims to "kill . . . one another." This may refer to mutual assisted suicide, since Rodwell translates the verse "And commit not suicide," while Dawood renders it "Do not kill yourselves." Only Allah gives life. Only Allah can take life. Whatever applies to the crime of murder likewise applies to committing suicide. "Whoever takes his life by any means whatsoever has unjustly taken a life which Allah has made sacred. Since a person did not create himself, not even so much as a single cell of his or her body, the life of an individual does not belong to him; it is a trust given to him by Allah. He is not allowed to diminish it, let alone to harm or destroy it."[2] Surah 6:151 states: "Slay not the life which Allah hath made sacred, save in the course of justice." According to Sharia law, soul-life begins with "four months in the womb."[3] "There are those in Islam who oppose all abortions. . . . The scholars all agree that abortion is forbidden after the first four months of pregnancy, since by this time the soul has entered the embryo."[4] For any abortion to be permissible, the life of the mother must be threatened.

For the justification of jihad and the taking of human life in that context, see "C. Aggression and Jihad," below.

2. The Bible: The sacredness of life

■ **What does the Bible say about the sacredness of life?**

The Bible teaches that life is a sacred gift from the Lord God, who is the Creator and giver of life. **Psalm 139:13–14** praises God, marveling that "you created my inmost being; you knit me together in my mother's womb." The Lord God preserves and sustains life. And human life is doubly precious because it has been redeemed by the blood of Christ, the Lamb of God.

A person has identity and personhood from conception, as we see in the conceptions of Jesus, John the Baptizer, and Jeremiah (Luke 1:35, 41; Jeremiah 1:5).

The Bible forbids the taking of another person's life in murder or the taking of one's own life in self-murder: "You shall not murder" (**Exod. 20:13**). Only the Lord God, the giver of life, has the prerogative to take life: "The LORD gave and the LORD has taken away" (Job 1:21).

Abortion is not a possible option except to prevent the death of the mother. *The Didache* (a Christian text of ca. AD 150) instructs, "You shall not murder a child by abortion, or kill one when born" (2:2).[5] Indeed, early Christians rescued abandoned infants from refuse heaps.

The Bible strongly upholds the sanctity of life, the gift and creation of the Lord God.

3. Summary

Both the Qur'an and the Bible teach the sanctity of life. Life is not to be taken or shortened but rather to be nurtured and cared for. In the Qur'an only Allah, and in the Bible only the Lord God, has the authority to give and to take human life.

In the Bible, since human life is a gift of the Lord God, it is immeasurably precious, and since it is redeemed by the precious blood of the Lamb of God, it is doubly precious. Human life is therefore to be valued, nurtured, and protected from the womb to the tomb.

For discussion questions, see study guide 19.

C. Aggression and Jihad

What does the Qur'an teach concerning jihad, and specifically physical aggression? What does the Bible, in the words of Jesus, teach concerning aggression?

The Qur'an	The Bible
1a. Aggression and jihad	**2a. Blessed are the peacemakers**
Surah 2:190. Fight in the way of Allah against those who fight against you, but begin not hostilities. Lo! Allah loveth not aggressors.	**Matthew 5:9.** [Jesus's words:] "Blessed are the peacemakers, for they will be called sons of God."
Surah 9:5. Then, when the sacred months have passed, slay the idolaters wherever ye find them, and take them (captive), and besiege them, and prepare for them each ambush. But if they repent and establish worship and pay the poor-due, then leave their way free. Lo! Allah is Forgiving, Merciful.	**Luke 6:27–29, 31.** [Jesus's words:] "But I tell you who hear me: Love your enemies, do good to those who hate you, bless those who curse you, pray for those who mistreat you. If someone strikes you on one cheek, turn to him the other also. . . . Do to others as you would have them do to you."
Surah 9:29a. Fight against such of those who have been given the Scripture as believe not in Allah nor the Last Day.	**Matthew 5:43–45.** [Jesus's words:] "You have heard that it was said, 'Love your neighbor and hate your enemy.' But I tell you: Love your enemies and pray for those who persecute you, that you may be sons of your Father in heaven."
Surah 48:16a. Say unto those of the wandering Arabs who were left behind: Ye will be called against a folk of mighty prowess, to fight them until they surrender. [Dawood: Say to the desert Arabs who stayed behind: "You shall be called upon to fight a mighty nation, unless they embrace Islam. . . ."]	**Luke 23:34.** Jesus said, "Father, forgive them, for they do not know what they are doing."
Surah 48:29a. Muhammad is the messenger of Allah. And those with him are hard against the disbelievers and merciful among themselves. [Dawood: Muhammad is God's apostle. Those who follow him are ruthless to the unbelievers but merciful to one another.]	**2b. Two kingdoms** **John 18:36.** Jesus said, "My kingdom is not of this world. If it were, my servants would fight to prevent my arrest by the Jews. But now my kingdom is from another place."
Surah 66:9. O Prophet! Strive against the disbelievers and the hypocrites, and be stern with them. Hell will be their home, a hapless journey's end. [Dawood: Prophet, make war on the unbelievers and the hypocrites, and deal sternly with them. Hell shall be their home, evil their fate.]	**2c. Christians are not to retaliate** **Matthew 26:52.** "Put your sword back in its place," Jesus said to him, "for all who draw the sword will die by the sword." **Romans 12:17, 21.** Do not repay anyone evil for evil. . . . Do not be overcome by evil, but overcome evil with good.
1b. Pardon for those who die in Allah's way **Surah 3:157.** And what though ye be slain in Allah's way or die therein? Surely pardon from Allah and mercy are better than all that they amass.	**2d. Example in the Acts of the Apostles** **Acts 7:59–60.** While they were stoning him, Stephen prayed, "Lord Jesus, receive my spirit." Then he fell on his knees and cried out, "Lord, do not hold this sin against them." When he had said this, he fell asleep.

1. The Qur'an

a. Aggression and jihad

■ **What does the Qur'an teach concerning aggression and jihad?**

Jihad can mean strive, struggle, or fight. It is perhaps similar to the German *Kampf*, which can be translated "struggle" or "fight" (as in Hitler's *Mein Kampf*).

According to John Bowker, "A Muslim is in a state of jihad all the time." Further, "The greater jihad is the fight within yourself, the lesser jihad is the warfare outside."[6] John L. Esposito writes, "Jihad, 'to strive or struggle' in the way of God, is sometimes referred to as the sixth pillar of Islam, although it has no such official status. In its most general meaning, it refers to the obligation incumbent on all Muslims, as individuals and as community, to exert themselves to realize God's will, to lead a virtuous life, and to extend the Islamic community through preaching, education and so on. As discussed earlier, a related meaning is the struggle for or a defense of Islam, holy war."[7]

James Beverley, in the article "Is Islam a Religion of Peace?" writes, "In reference to the Qur'an, many have drawn attention to the famous passage in Surah 2:256: 'Let there be no compulsion in religion.' This verse fits well with other Qur'an verses in which *Jihad* means personal and communal spiritual struggle or striving. But the Qur'an also uses *Jihad* to mean 'holy war,' and the language can be extreme."[8] The Caner brothers, Ergun and Emir, both former Muslims, state, "Despite the explanation of Islamic apologists after the terrorist attacks, Jihad does not primarily refer to a 'struggle of personal piety.' Jihad is combat on the fronts of politics, warfare, and culture."[9]

Surah 2:190 instructs Muslims to "fight [jihad] in the way of Allah against those who fight against you." They, however, are not to be the "aggressors." A few passages later the Qur'an commands, "Fight them until persecution is no more, and religion is for Allah. But if they desist, then let there be no hostility except against wrongdoers" (Surah 2:193). Still later in the surah the Qur'an states, "There is no compulsion in religion" (Surah 2:256).

Is mere opposition to Islam sufficient cause for preemptive aggression? Muhammad's teaching was resisted by the people of Mecca, and his life was threatened. It was during this time that Muhammad received his first revelation of jihad, giving him permission to wage war against his persecutors. As Surah 22:39 states, "Sanction is given unto those who fight because they have been wronged; and Allah is indeed Able to give them victory."

Surah 9:5 (Surah 9 is Muhammad's "last word" of revelation in the Qur'an) was quoted by five Islamic caliphates in a fatwa (religious decree) declaring war against the United States, signed February 23, 1998: "Then, when the sacred months have passed, slay the idolaters wherever ye find them." The only exception is if "they repent" and become Muslim.[10] Further, Surah 9:123

urges, "Fight those of the disbelievers who are near to you, and let them find harshness in you."

As we see from **Surah 9:29**, Christians and Jews are subject to jihad as well: "Fight against such of those who have been given the Scripture [Christians and Jews] as believe not in Allah nor the Last Day" (see also Surah 98:6).

Muhammad was criticized by the pagan Arabs of Medina after raids on the commercial caravans of Mecca in 624 resulted in one person being killed and two being taken captive. These Arabs were shocked that this had taken place during a sacred month for them. Muhammad, however, received a revelation that defended his right to fight and divide up the booty: "Warfare therein is a great (transgression), but to turn (men) from the Way of Allah, and to disbelieve in Him and in the Inviolable Place of Worship, and to expel its people thence, is a greater (transgression) with Allah" (Surah 2:217). In other words, the greater sin would be not to fight for the cause of Allah.

In **Surah 48:16**, Muslims are exhorted by Muhammad to fight the people of Mecca "until they surrender" (Dawood: "unless they embrace Islam").

Surah 48:29 states the attitude that Muslims are to have toward "disbelievers." Followers of Muhammad are to be "hard against the disbelievers and merciful among themselves." See Surah 8:15, 39: "O ye who believe! When ye meet those who disbelieve in battle, turn not your backs to them. . . . Fight them until persecution is no more, and religion is all for Allah." **Surah 66:9** expresses the same: "Strive [Dawood: make war] against the disbelievers and the hypocrites, and be stern with them."

Fellow Muslims are not exempt from jihad. Esposito, after tracing the course of Islamic revivalism in the nineteenth century, concludes, "The struggle [jihad] to reassert the rightful place of Islam in society requires moral self-discipline, and where necessary, armed struggle, and . . . those Muslims who resist are no longer to be regarded as Muslim but numbered among the enemies of God."[11]

Even members of one's own family who are unbelievers are to be treated with hostility, as Abraham and those with him "told their folk . . . We have done with you. And there hath arisen between us and you hostility and hate for ever until ye believe in Allah" (Surah 60:4). In fact, Abraham "disowned" his father when it became clear that he did not believe and was "an enemy to Allah" (Surah 9:114).

Jihadists apply the rule of "abrogation," holding that the militant verses given later in time "abrogate," or nullify, the more conciliatory verses toward Jews and Christians given earlier in the revelation of the Qur'an. Other Muslims may question this assumption.

b. Pardon for those who die in Allah's way

■ **What rewards are promised to jihadist martyrs?**

Forgiveness and pardon are promised in the Qur'an to those who are slain in Allah's way: "And what though ye be slain in Allah's way or die therein? Surely pardon from Allah and mercy are better than all that they amass" (Surah 3:157). A "vast reward" is assured those who fight "in the way of Allah," whether they are slain or victorious (Surah 4:74).

The Prophet Muhammad has been cited as a model for the suicide terrorists of September 11, 2001. On September 28, 2001, the *Washington Post* published excerpts of a letter found in the luggage of Muhamed Atta, who was alleged to be the leader of the suicide bombers: "Think about what God has promised the good believers and the martyrs. Remember the battle of the prophet . . . against the infidels, as he went on building the Islamic state. . . . You will be entering paradise if you have not had a major problem."[12]

While the Qur'an teaches that human life is sacred and one is not to take one's own life, in the case of jihad it is not only justifiable but rewarded.

The Prophet Muhammad set a precedent for physical jihad. Esposito observes: "Muhammad initiated a series of raids against Meccan caravans, threatening both the political authority and the economic power of the Quraysh [Meccan tribe]."[13] Before the first battle of Badr in 624, Muhammad took three hundred men and attacked a large caravan of great wealth (fifty thousand dinars' worth) returning from Syria. In response, the Meccans sent troops to protect their property. The devout, conservative Muslim Mohammed Marmaduke Pickthall, states in his introduction: "The number of the campaigns which he [Muhammad] led in person during the last years of his life is twenty-seven, in nine of which there was hard fighting. The number of the expeditions which he planned and sent out under other leaders is thirty-eight. He personally controlled every detail of organization."[14]

Bowker points out that the vision of Islam is for Umma, a community united in Islam under Sharia. "Every true Muslim is always a missionary. So we try to convert the world. Our concept of the world and of the end of the world (in the sense of the objective) is to have one state, one religion and one umma—the umma being the religious community. So we want to convert the world. That is our objective."[15] The hope is for universal Umma ruled by Sharia. "The way forward for Islam is the way back to Sharia" (Islamic law and jurisprudence).[16] Islam makes no distinction between earthly governments and Allah's realm. The Qur'an, Sharia law, and jihad may be used with physical force to establish the Umma, a theocratic kingdom on earth.

Esposito observes that today many Muslims feel their faith and values threatened by the secularism, materialism, and promiscuity of Western influence.[17] Islamic fundamentalists feel justified in their use of jihad against such assaults upon Islam.

The Qur'an speaks strongly against those who "make war upon Allah and His messenger and strive after corruption in the land." They "will be killed or crucified, or have their hands and feet on alternate sides cut off, or

> After Muhammad's death, Islam spread by military might and message. Islam conquered and converted, or subjected, within two years Syria; within four years Iraq; within five years Jerusalem; within seven years Egypt; and within ten years Persia (Iran). Muhammad was asked, "What is most loved by Allah?" His answer was first, to offer prayers, second, to be good and dutiful to one's parents, and third, "to participate in Jihad for Allah's Cause."[a]
>
> [a] Ergun Mehmet Caner and Fetthi Emir Caner, *Unveiling Islam* (Grand Rapids: Kregel, 2002), 192.

will be expelled out of the land. Such will be their degradation in the world, and in the Hereafter theirs will be an awful doom" (Surah 5:33). The Caner brothers state, "In both the Qur'an and the Hadith, the infidel (kafir) must be converted or conquered."[18]

Since the bombings in London on July 7, 2005, some Islamic groups, especially in the West, have condemned terrorism and declared that suicide bombings against civilians are not permissible in Islam, basing it upon Surah 5:32: "Whosoever killeth a human being . . . , it shall be as if he had killed all mankind" (see "B. Murder, Suicide, Abortion," above). However, the full text reads, "Whosoever killeth a human being *for other than manslaughter or corruption in the earth* [italics added], it shall be as if he had killed all mankind." Thus, personal revenge and killing for "corruption" are justified. Extremist Muslims who wish to find reason for aggressive action against infidels and those who spread "corruption in the earth" will find sufficient justification in the Qur'an for their actions.

Fazlur Rahman holds that Islam "regarded itself as the repository of the Will of God which had to be worked on earth through a political order. From this point of view, Islam resembles the Communist structure which, even if it does not oblige people to accept its creed, nevertheless insists on the assumption of the political order."[19] This desire to create an Islamic state under Sharia motivates the radical Islamists in their aggressive behavior.

Is one who commits jihad assured of Paradise?

Esposito explains that "these holy warriors (*mujahidin*) will be rewarded in this life with victory and the spoils of war. Those who fall in battle will be rewarded with eternal life as martyrs (*shahid*, witness) for the faith."[20]

Beverley writes, "The prophet is quoted as saying, 'The sword is the key of heaven and hell; a drop of blood shed in the cause of Allah, a night spent in arms, is of more avail than two months of fasting or prayer; whosoever falls in battle, his sins are forgiven, and at the day of judgment his limbs shall be supplied by the wings of angels and cherubim.'"[21] Muhammad ibn Ismail al-Bukhari records, "Our Prophet has informed us that our Lord says: 'Whoever amongst us is killed as a martyr shall go to Paradise.'"[22]

On the other hand, a young man once asked Muhammad what he would have if he died in jihad, a martyr's death. Muhammad answered, "Paradise," but then as the man got up to go, the Prophet added, "Unless you have some debts to pay. Gabriel has informed me about it just now."[23] Even in jihad the assurance of Paradise is uncertain; there still may be "debts to pay."

2. The Bible

a. Blessed are the peacemakers

■ **What does the Bible teach about aggression and peace?**

Jesus's words in **Matthew 5:9** are "Blessed are the peacemakers, for they will be called sons of God." God is a peacemaker. He was "reconciling the world to himself in Christ" (2 Cor. 5:19), "making peace through his blood, shed on the cross" (Col. 1:20). Those who know God's peace in Christ become peacemakers. They are truly blessed.

Whereas the Qur'an sets forth Abraham as an example of one who "disowned" his father as "an enemy of Allah" (Surah 9:114), the words of Jesus are very different: "Love your enemies, . . . bless those who curse you" (**Luke 6:27–28**). We are compelled by the love of Christ to love our enemies and to do good to those who hate us (**Luke 6:27–29**). We are moved not only to avoid harming others but positively to "do to others as [we] would have them do to [us]" (**Luke 6:31**).

Christ calls us not only passively not to do the negative but also actively to do the positive. His love compels us not only not to rob and beat others (as in the parable of the good Samaritan) but indeed to go "the extra mile" (see Matt. 5:41) for the man who "fell among thieves"—to bind up his wounds and care for him. The good Samaritan "put the man on his own donkey, took him to an inn and took care of him," and promised to reimburse the innkeeper "for any extra expense" (Luke 10:34–35). The call of Christ is more than to avoid evil; it is to be active in doing good to all people.

Christ's words in **Matthew 5:43–44** call us to "love your enemies and pray for those who persecute you." Jesus prayed for his enemies, "Father, forgive them, for they do not know what they are doing" (**Luke 23:34**). Muhammad taught, as we have seen, that aggression is permissible when it is justified. Christ says that it is at this very point that we are to love our enemies and pray for them. Then we are truly "sons of our Father" and show that God's life "remains" within us and that we are "born of God" (1 John 3:9).

b. Two kingdoms

■ **Did Jesus come to establish theocratic rule?**

Jesus said, "My kingdom is not of this world" (**John 18:36**). Christ's kingdom is established "through the word of Christ" (Rom. 10:17), which is that God "has rescued us from the dominion of darkness and brought us into the kingdom of the Son he loves" (Col. 1:13). Through the conviction of the law and the comfort of the gospel, the Holy Spirit brings people to faith in Christ as their Savior and King and hearts are changed. When hearts are changed, lives are changed.

Jesus also said, "Give to Caesar what is Caesar's" (Matt. 22:21). The "kingdom of Caesar"—that is, the state—is established by force and constitutions. It is ruled by civic laws. It motivates by tax incentive, penalty and prison, reward and recognition (Rom. 13:3–5).

c. Christians are not to retaliate

▨ **How are Christ's followers to respond to violence?**

In the Garden of Gethsemane, Peter felt justified in defending Jesus with the sword. But Jesus said, "Put your sword back in its place" (**Matt. 26:52**).

In **Romans 12:17** Paul instructs us, "Do not repay anyone evil for evil." Rather, believers in Christ are to "overcome evil with good." While early Islam was spread by the sword and the message of Islam, early Christianity was spread by the gospel and the blood of martyrs who refused to "repay anyone evil for evil." They were not to be "overcome by evil, but overcome evil with good" (**Rom. 12:21**).

Christians are in a spiritual "struggle" with their "old self" (see Eph. 4:22); and against "powers of this dark world and against the spiritual forces of evil in the heavenly realms" (see Eph. 6:12). They may be "considered as sheep to be slaughtered" (see Rom. 8:36), but if they suffer for doing good and endure it, "this is commendable before God. To this you were called, because Christ suffered for you, leaving you an example" (see 1 Pet. 2:20, 21). It is by such patient endurance, and by such sacrificial and unconditional love, that the grace of God is demonstrated and the heart of the "enemy" may be softened and led to repentance (see Rom. 12:20).

Like Muslims, Christians often feel threatened in their faith by the influences of the secular culture. The answer, however, is not to use the physical violence of "jihad" but to "put on the full armor of God," take the "sword of the Spirit, which is the word of God," and "pray in the Spirit on all occasions" (Eph. 6:13–18). They are to "commit themselves to their faithful Creator and continue to do good" (1 Pet. 4:19).

d. Example in the Acts of the Apostles

▨ **How did the early church respond to persecution?**

The early believers practiced forgiving, selfless love toward their enemies. Stephen, the first martyr, prayed for those who were stoning him: "Lord, do not hold this sin against them" (**Acts 7:59–60**). The Christians were persecuted, imprisoned, and executed, but they were exhorted by the apostle Peter to

The apostle Paul writes that "governing authorities" of the state are God's servants. They are "an agent of wrath to bring punishment on the wrongdoer." They do "not bear the sword for nothing" (Rom. 13:1, 4). Their judicious use of force against wrongdoers is justified.

"rejoice that you participate in the sufferings of Christ. . . . If you are insulted because of the name of Christ, you are blessed. . . . If you suffer as a Christian, do not be ashamed but praise God that you bear that name" (1 Pet. 4:13–16). When believers were threatened, they were to remember Christ's patient suffering: "when they hurled their insults at him, he did not retaliate; when he suffered, he made no threats" (1 Pet. 2:23). Stephen provided an example of this for all believers to follow.

3. Summary

The Qur'an speaks of a striving (jihad) against temptation, the Jinn, and Satan. In the Bible, the apostle Paul speaks of our struggle against our own sinful nature, the world, and the devil. But the Qur'an does not speak of "striving" against our sinful nature, since according to the Qur'an human nature is not sinful.

The Qur'an also calls for a striving or fighting (jihad) against those who appear to be opposed to the Islamic faith. This striving or fighting (jihad) is a "holy war." One will find ample justification for militant aggression in the Qur'an and in the life of Muhammad. Muhammad himself organized military campaigns and mobilized military power. Islam in its first hundred years spread throughout the region of the Middle East, northern Africa, and Spain by military power and the message of Islam.

In the Bible, Jesus teaches his disciples to love their enemies, to put up their swords, and to be willing to die for his name. The early Christians practiced this kind of love. They did not return evil for evil, even if it meant they would die as martyrs. Stephen forgave those who stoned him even as Jesus had forgiven those who were crucifying him. Christians are still to practice nonaggression and have a forgiving, caring attitude toward those who persecute them and are hostile toward them. The Christian is not to resort to hostile aggression in the defense or promotion of the faith; rather, he or she is to spread and defend the faith by the Word of Christ in the spirit of love. Christians are to be known for love shown to everyone, not just to fellow Christians.

For discussion questions, see study guide 20.

D. Godly Life

How do the teachings of the Qur'an and the Bible manifest themselves in the lives of the people? What is the motivation for a "godly" life from the Qur'an, from the Bible? Are their ethical standards the same or similar?

The Qur'an	The Bible

1. Godly life to earn recompense

Surah 2:83b. Worship none save Allah (only), and be good to parents and to kindred and to orphans and the needy, and speak kindly to mankind; and establish worship and pay the poor-due.

Surah 16:90. Lo! Allah enjoineth justice and kindness, and giving to kinsfolk, and forbiddeth lewdness and abomination and wickedness. He exhorteth you in order that ye may take heed.[24]

Surah 16:97. Whosoever doth right, whether male or female, and is a believer, him verily We shall quicken with good life, and We shall pay them a recompense in proportion to the best of what they used to do.

Surah 17:25. Your Lord is best aware of what is in your minds. If ye be righteous, then lo! He was ever Forgiving unto those who turn (unto Him).

26. Give the kinsman his due, and the needy, and the wayfarer, and squander not (thy wealth) in wantonness.

31. Slay not your children, fearing a fall to poverty. We shall provide for them and for you. Lo! the slaying of them is great sin.

32. And come not near unto adultery. Lo! it is an abomination and an evil way.

33a. And slay not the life which Allah hath forbidden save with right.

34a. Come not near the wealth of the orphan.

35a. Fill the measure when ye measure.

37a. And walk not in the earth exultant.

2a. Godly life, the fruit of faith in Jesus

John 15:5. [Jesus's words:] "I am the vine; you are the branches. If a man remains in me and I in him, he will bear much fruit; apart from me you can do nothing."

2b. Godly life, the fruit of the Spirit

Galatians 5:19–24. The acts of the sinful nature are obvious: sexual immorality, impurity and debauchery; idolatry and witchcraft; hatred, discord, jealousy, fits of rage, selfish ambition, dissensions, factions and envy; drunkenness, orgies, and the like. I warn you, as I did before, that those who live like this will not inherit the kingdom of God. But the fruit of the Spirit is love, joy, peace, patience, kindness, goodness, faithfulness, gentleness and self-control. Against such things there is no law. Those who belong to Christ Jesus have crucified the sinful nature with its passions and desires.

2c. A godly life of love

Romans 12:9–21. Love must be sincere. Hate what is evil; cling to what is good. Be devoted to one another in brotherly love. Honor one another above yourselves. Never be lacking in zeal, but keep your spiritual fervor, serving the Lord. Be joyful in hope, patient in affliction, faithful in prayer. Share with God's people who are in need. Practice hospitality. Bless those who persecute you; bless and do not curse. Rejoice with those who rejoice; mourn with those who mourn. Live in harmony with one another. Do not be proud, but be willing to associate with people of low position. Do not be conceited. Do not repay anyone evil for evil. Be careful to do what is right in the eyes of everybody. If it is possible, as far as it depends on you, live at peace with everyone. Do not take revenge, my friends, but leave room for God's wrath, for it is written: "It is mine to avenge; I will repay," says the Lord. On the contrary: "If your enemy is hungry, feed him; if he is thirsty, give him something to drink. In doing this, you will heap burning coals on his head." Do not be overcome by evil, but overcome evil with good.

2d. Christ's love compels us

2 Corinthians 5:14–15. For Christ's love compels us, because we are convinced that one died for all, and therefore all died. And he died for all, that those who live should no longer live for themselves but for him who died for them and was raised again.

The Qur'an	The Bible
Surah 17:23. Thy Lord hath decreed, that ye worship none save Him, and (that ye show) kindness to parents. If one of them or both of them attain to old age with thee, say not "Fie" [expression of disapproval] unto them nor repulse them, but speak unto them a gracious word.	

1. The Qur'an: Godly life to earn recompense

■ **What commandments for godly living are set forth in the Qur'an?**

In **Surah 2:83**, certain conduct is emphasized: "Worship none save Allah (only), and be good to parents and to kindred and to orphans and the needy, and speak kindly to mankind; and establish worship and pay the poor-due." Thus, we see conduct set forth similar to the first, fourth (fifth), fifth (sixth), and eighth (ninth) commandments in the Bible. In **Surah 16:90**, Allah enjoins justice and kindness, giving to kinsfolk, and forbids lewdness, abomination, and wickedness.

Surah 16:97 promises that "whosoever doth right" and is "a believer" will be paid "a recompense in proportion to the best" of what he or she has done.

Surah 17:25 is one of the few Qur'an texts that state that Allah is "aware of what is in your minds." Another is Surah 3:154: "Allah is aware of what is hidden in the breasts (of men)." The observer may wonder whether this evokes fear or love of Allah. According to the Qur'an, Allah judges human motives: "If ye are righteous, then lo! He was ever Forgiving unto those who turn (unto Him)" (**Surah 17:25**). The forgiveness is conditional—"if ye are righteous."

The Muslim, says **Surah 17:26**, is to be concerned for his or her kinsman, the needy, and the wayfarer. Almsgiving (zakat) is one of the Five Pillars of Islam.

The follower of Islam is not to "slay" his children. It is a "great sin" (**Surah 17:31**). He is not to come "near unto adultery" (**Surah 17:32**). He is not to kill except for just cause (**Surah 17:33**). He is not to take wealth left to an orphan (**Surah 17:34**). He is not to steal but to give full measure (**Surah 17:35**). And he is not to walk proudly "in the earth" (**Surah 17:37**).

A Muslim is not to covet material wealth when he has been blessed over others (Surah 4:32). He is to worship Allah and be kind to his parents into their old age (**Surah 17:23**).

The Qur'an forbids the drinking of alcohol and gambling (Surah 2:219); it also forbids the eating of pork and blood (Surah 5:3).

Societal punishment for inflicted harm is prescribed in the Qur'an: "the life for the life, and the eye for the eye, and the nose for the nose, and the ear for the ear, and the tooth for the tooth, and for wounds retaliation" (Surah 5:45;

Clean versus Unclean Food

The Qur'an looks upon certain foods as forbidden and unclean, as in Leviticus 11. Jesus said, "Listen and understand. What goes into a man's mouth does not make him 'unclean,' but what comes out of his mouth, that is what makes him 'unclean'" (Matt. 15:10–11; see also Acts 10:9–16). On this basis, the New Testament states, "Everything God created is good, and nothing is to be rejected if it is received with thanksgiving, because it is consecrated by the word of God and prayer" (1 Tim. 4:4–5; see also Rom. 14:14–15).

---

see also Surah 2:178–79, 194). The Bedouin tribal code of blood vengeance is still strong in the minds of Middle Eastern Muslim people.

Chawkat Moucarry writes, "On the political level, Islam claims to govern interpersonal relationships. The law of retaliation given in the Torah (Lev. 24:17–21) remains in force: 'life for life, eye for eye, nose for nose, ear for ear, tooth for tooth.'"[25] In Islam, the ideal is for religion, politics, and culture to be integrated as one.

■ **Can a Muslim be a "grave sinner" and still enter Paradise?**

A question raised early on in Islam was whether a Muslim could be a "grave sinner" and still be a Muslim and enter Paradise. The extreme sect of the Khorijites ("Seceders") maintained that a grave sinner no longer remained a Muslim.[26]

According to W. Montgomery Watt, "Eventually the consensus moved toward the view that the only sin that excluded a man from the Islamic community and from Paradise was *shirk*, polytheism, the acknowledgment of deities other than God. . . . Other sins would be punished, but, since membership of the charismatic community was retained, the sinner would ultimately reach paradise."[27] Thus, the Muslim "grave sinner" attains Paradise by undergoing punishment for bad deeds. Such works of suffering eventually earn Paradise for those who believe in Allah.

2. The Bible

■ **How does the Bible present the godly life?**

In the Scriptures, the godly life is possible only for the person who is righteous before God by faith. "Without faith it is impossible to please God" (Heb. 11:6). By faith in Christ, the believer is able to offer "spiritual sacrifices acceptable to God through Jesus Christ" (1 Pet. 2:5).

a. Godly life, the fruit of faith in Jesus

■ **How does Jesus bring forth godliness in us?**

As Jesus teaches in **John 15:5**, the godly life is the result of remaining attached to him by faith. This union is like the union of a vine and its branches. Jesus is the Vine: "If a man remains in me and I in him, he will bear much fruit; apart from me you can do nothing." The person who "remains in" Christ and Christ in him brings forth much fruit in his or her life.

b. Godly life, the fruit of the Spirit

■ **How does the Holy Spirit nurture godly life in us?**

Galatians 5:19–24 contrasts the acts of the sinful nature and the fruit of the Spirit. The sinful human nature brings forth "sexual immorality, impurity and debauchery; idolatry and witchcraft; hatred, discord, jealousy, fits of rage, selfish ambition, dissensions, factions and envy; drunkenness, orgies, and the like." The reality is that a human being is sinful and naturally brings forth sinful acts. A person does not need to be taught such vices; they just naturally appear. They come from a person's fallen human nature.

It is the Holy Spirit in the heart of the believer who brings forth the fruit of "love, joy, peace, patience, kindness, goodness, faithfulness, gentleness and self-control" (**Gal. 5:22–23**). The Bible emphasizes that the godly life is rooted in the inner heart of faith. Such inner attributes are not possible for the sinful human nature; they come from the indwelling Holy Spirit.

c. A godly life of love

■ **What is the source of a godly life?**

As we see in **John 15:5**, the godly life comes from a heart of faith in the Messiah as Savior and Lord. This love is defined in Scripture; it is not just doing what we feel comfortable with, what feels good. Love is to be authentic: "Hate what is evil; cling to what is good" (**Rom. 12:9**). Genuine love distinguishes between good and evil. It is defined by God's holy commandments.

Jesus addresses the revenge tendency of human beings with the words, "You have heard that it was said, 'Eye for eye and tooth for tooth.' But I tell you, . . . If someone strikes you on the right check, turn to him the other also" (Matt. 5:38–39). His followers are to love and forgive their enemies and leave any vengeance to God, who says, "It is mine to avenge; I will repay" (**Rom. 12:19**).

Romans 12:9–21 describes a life of brotherly love, honor, service, prayer, charity, hospitality, blessing, rejoicing, sympathy, harmony, humility, peace, and compassion. In short, the godly life is not overcome by evil but overcomes evil with good. This beautiful and inspiring description of the godly life might well be read in every Christian worship service and be put to memory by every believer in Christ.

The person who "remains" in Christ, the vine, brings forth much fruit (**John 15:5**). Christ is not only our redemption and righteousness but also the source of our holiness of living (1 Cor. 1:30).

The believer in Christ will "look after the orphans and widows in their distress" and keep from "being polluted by the world" (James 1:27). A believer will "provide for his relatives, and especially for his immediate family" (1 Tim. 5:8).

d. Christ's love compels us

■ **What motivates Christian godliness?**

Second Corinthians 5:14–15 clearly sets forth the motive for the godly life. Believers in Jesus Christ no longer desire to live for themselves but "for him who died for them and was raised again." The moving force in the new life of the Christian is not fear, final judgment, or hope of reward but the undeserved and unconditional love of Christ: "Christ's love compels us."

3. Summary

The Qur'an calls for a godly life similar in many ways to that set forth in the Bible. On the question of human nature and the godly life, however, the Qur'an and the Bible differ radically. Since the Qur'an teaches the basic uprightness of human nature and the human heart, there is not the emphasis on inner transformation and renewal as necessary for godly living.

In the Qur'an, reverence for Allah, who is merciful, and mindfulness of the final judgment are frequently presented. The mercy of Allah, the fear of the coming judgment, and the promise of reward become the reasons for godly living.

The Bible summarizes the godly life in lists such as in the Ten Commandments (Exod. 20) and the Sermon on the Mount (Matt. 5–7) and in the epistles of Paul, Peter, and John. The New Testament emphasizes the love of the Father, the redeeming love of Christ, the indwelling of the Holy Spirit, the new life of faith in Christ, the inner motive of a grateful heart, and reliance on the Holy Spirit as the source for a godly life. The Bible presents the undeserved love and mercy of God in Christ and the death and resurrection of Christ as the "compelling" reason and source of power for godliness of life. The distinguishing factor in godliness of living for the Christian is the person and work of Christ. He is the Vine, the believer is the branch. Through him the believer is able to bear much fruit to the glory of the Father. The believer has the joy of knowing that his or her life is acceptable to God through Jesus Christ.

For discussion questions, see study guide 21. Read also "D. What meaning does my life have with God?" in chapter 14.

10

The End Times

A. Resurrection

What do the Qur'an and the Bible teach about the resurrection of the body?

The Qur'an	The Bible
1. Rising from death	**2. Rising from death**
Surah 36:51. And the trumpet is blown and lo! from the graves they hie unto their Lord.	**1 Thessalonians 4:16.** For the Lord himself will come down from heaven, with a loud command, with the voice of the archangel and with the trumpet call of God, and the dead in Christ will rise first.
Surah 17:13. And every man's augury have We fastened to his own neck, and We shall bring forth for him on the Day of Resurrection a book which he will find wide open.	**John 11:25–26.** Jesus said to her, "I am the resurrection and the life. He who believes in me will live, even though he dies; and whoever lives and believes in me will never die. Do you believe this?"
14. (And it will be said unto him): Read thy book. Thy soul sufficeth as reckoner against thee this day.	**John 5:28–29.** All who are in their graves will hear his voice and come out—those who have done good will rise to live, and those who have done evil will rise to be condemned.
15. Whosoever goeth right, it is only for (the good of) his own soul that he goeth right, and whosoever erreth, erreth only to its hurt. No laden soul can bear another's load. We never punish until We have sent a messenger.	**John 6:40.** [Jesus's words:] "For my Father's will is that everyone who looks to the Son and believes in him shall have eternal life, and I will raise him at the last day."

1. The Qur'an: Rising from death

■ **Does the Qur'an teach a resurrection of the body?**

The Qur'an teaches the bodily resurrection on the final day. **Surah 36:51** pictures it thus: "And the trumpet is blown and lo! from the graves they hie [hasten] unto their Lord."

Surah 17:13–15 states that on the day of resurrection a book is opened, revealing each person's life. Each will be instructed to "read thy book." Each person is held accountable. No soul can save another, "can bear another's load." No one will be punished who has not been "sent a messenger." All people will have had a chance from a messenger to learn about Allah.

2. The Bible: Rising from death

■ **What does the Bible teach concerning the resurrection of the body?**

The Scriptures teach in **1 Thessalonians 4:16** that "the Lord himself will come down from heaven, with a loud command, with the voice of the archangel and with the trumpet call of God" and raise the dead.

Jesus himself says, "I am the resurrection and the life," and whoever believes in him "will live" and "never die" (**John 11:25**). It is Jesus who gives eternal life and raises the dead to life, even as he raised Lazarus bodily to life.

All will be raised, but only "those who have done good will rise to live, and those who have done evil will rise to be condemned" (**John 5:28–29**). The evil works of unbelievers will condemn them. The good works of the believers will be cited as evidence of their saving faith. Because of faith in the Lamb of God, their sins will not be held against them. Their names are written in the Lamb's book of life (Rev. 21:27). In contrast, unbelievers' sins will stand as accusation against them. The unbelievers will still be in the guilt of their sins, and therefore they will be condemned (Matt. 25:45–46).

As we see in **John 6:40**, the Father's will is clear that everyone should look "to the Son" in faith and have eternal life. All those who look "to the Son" will be raised by him on the final day.

The bodies of believers will be like Christ's glorious body (Phil. 3:21). The resurrection will usher in the promised new creation for humankind and for all of creation. This new creation will be the Lord God's final victory over sin and death (1 Cor. 15:54–55).

3. Summary

The resurrection of the body is taught in both the Qur'an and the Bible. The difference is that in the Qur'an the works of the Muslim will be a deciding factor along with his or her submission to Allah. In the Qur'an, creation is not affected by original sin, and there is no need for creation to be released from the frustration and futility of the curse of sin (Rom. 8:20). For the Muslim, the grave is a place of fear, foreboding, and purging from sin.

In the Bible, good works are important and necessary expressions of the believer's faith relationship with Christ, but they do not earn the believer life eternal. Eternal life is a "gift . . . in Christ Jesus our Lord" (Rom. 6:23). Jesus is "the resurrection and the life." Those who look to him have eternal life and will be raised on the final day. The believer in Christ looks forward to the new heaven and new earth, in which righteousness will make its dwelling (Isa. 65:17; 2 Pet. 3:13). Indeed, "creation itself will be liberated from its bondage to decay and brought into the glorious freedom of the children of God" (Rom. 8:21). The believer in Christ has a sense of victory over death and the grave (1 Cor. 15:55–58).

For discussion questions, see study guide 22.

B. Judgment

According to the Qur'an and the Bible, how will human beings be judged at the end of time?

The Qur'an	The Bible
1. Recompense and punishment **Surah 39:68.** And the Trumpet is blown, and all who are in the heavens and the earth swoon away, save him whom Allah willeth. Then it is blown a second time, and behold them standing waiting! **69.** And the earth shineth with the light of her Lord, and the book is set up, and the Prophets and the witnesses are brought, and it is judged between them with truth, and they are not wronged. **70.** And each soul is paid in full for what it did. And He is best Aware of what they do. **71a.** And those who disbelieve are driven unto hell in troops till, when they reach it and the gates thereof are opened, . . . **Surah 3:106.** On that day when (some) faces will be whitened and (some) faces will be blackened; and as for those whose faces have been blackened, it will be said unto them: Disbelieved ye after your (profession of) belief? Then taste the punishment for that ye disbelieved. **Surah 23:102.** Then those whose scales are heavy, they are the successful. **103.** And those whose scales are light are those who lose their souls, in hell abiding. **Surah 84:7.** Then whoso is given his account in his right hand	**2a. Judgment of words, actions, fruits** **Matthew 25:31–32.** [Jesus's words:] "When the Son of Man comes in his glory, and all the angels with him, he will sit on his throne in heavenly glory. All nations will be gathered before him, and he will separate the people one from another as a shepherd separates the sheep from the goats. **Daniel 7:10b.** The court was seated, and the books were opened.[1] **Matthew 12:35–37.** [Jesus's words:] "The good man brings good things out of the good stored up in him, and the evil man brings evil things out of the evil stored up in him. But I tell you that men will have to give account on the day of judgment for every careless word they have spoken. For by your words you will be acquitted, and by your words you will be condemned." **Matthew 7:17.** [Jesus's words:] "Likewise every good tree bears good fruit, but a bad tree bears bad fruit."

The Qur'an	The Bible
8. He truly will receive an easy reckoning 9. And will return unto his folk in joy. 10. But whoso is given his account behind his back, 11. He surely will invoke destruction 12. And be thrown to scorching fire.	2b. Faith in Jesus gives escape from condemnation John 3:36. [Jesus's words:] "Whoever believes in the Son has eternal life, but whoever rejects the Son will not see life, for God's wrath remains on him." John 5:24. [Jesus's words:] "Whoever hears my word and believes him who sent me has eternal life and will not be condemned; he has crossed over from death to life."

1. The Qur'an: Recompense and punishment

■ Does the Qur'an point to a final judgment day?

The Qur'an frequently and repeatedly reminds the reader of the coming resurrection and day of judgment. One cannot read the Qur'an without being confronted with the final resurrection and the judgment every few pages.

According to **Surah 39:68**, "the Trumpet is blown" on that day, and all "in the heavens and the earth swoon away" except those whom Allah wills to remain. The trumpet is blown a second time. "The book is set up," and a just judgment is rendered by "the Prophets and the witnesses" (**Surah 39:69**), who include Jesus. "Each soul is paid in full for what it did" (**Surah 39:70**). Those "who disbelieve are driven unto hell" (**Surah 39:71**).

"On that day," as **Surah 3:106** states, "faces will be whitened and (some) faces will be blackened," clearly indicating sentence to Paradise or hell.

Allah will weigh each person's deeds and reward them accordingly. **Surah 23:102** shows that those whose "scales are heavy" with good deeds will succeed in going to Paradise. Those "whose scales are light" (**Surah 23:103**), lacking in good deeds, will lose their souls in hell. Allah will give greater weight to good deeds over bad deeds, double or tenfold (Surah 4:40; Surah 6:160). Thus, the full requirements of justice will be compromised and reduced to meet human effort.

The Qur'an and the Islamic tradition emphasize good works, distinction between that which is clean and unclean, purification, prayer rituals, fasting, and pilgrimage so as to make a person acceptable to Allah and worthy of eternal reward. This approach is similar to that of the Pharisees of Jesus's day. By doing what is prescribed, a person tips the scales of justice in his or her favor.

The person, in **Surah 84:7–12**, who is "given his account in his right hand" will be united with his family with joy, while those whose account is given "behind his back" will go to "destruction" and "scorching fire."

The majority of Muslims believe that Jesus will appear before the final judgment. He will battle the antichrist, personally profess Islam, kill all pigs, break all crosses (since he was not crucified), and establish a reign of righteousness. People will convert to Islam, and Islamic law will be established among the nations. Jews will recognize that Jesus is a prophet, and Christians will realize that he is not the Son of God. Completing his mission, Jesus will then die and be buried next to Muhammad in Medina, where a vacant place is reserved for him. The death of Jesus will be the signal for the general resurrection.[2] The majority of Shi'ite Muslims identify the person of righteousness who brings in the resurrection not as Jesus but as Muhadi (divinely guided one). "According to Shi'ite tradition, *Muhadi* was the twelfth Imam (successor and descendant of Muhammad) who miraculously disappeared and will one day reappear to establish righteousness on the earth."[3]

2. The Bible

a. Judgment of words, actions, fruits

■ **What does the Bible teach concerning the final judgment?**

A final day of judgment is surely coming. As depicted in **Matthew 25:31–32**, at the end of time the Lord Jesus, as the Son of Man, will come in great glory and all the holy angels with him. The angels will gather all people of all time before him. As the Son of God, he will sit as judge alone on his throne (John 5:22). As righteous judge, he will separate the "sheep" from the "goats": the righteous from the unrighteous, the believer from the unbeliever.

The books are opened (Dan. 7:10; compare Rev. 20:12). Each person will be judged according to his or her works as evidence of faith in Christ. Each person "will have to give account" on the judgment day, even of "every careless word" (**Matt. 12:35–37**). The good person brings forth evidence of good in his or her life (**Matt. 12:35**) much as a good tree produces good fruit (**Matt. 7:17**). A good person is one rooted and grounded in the grace of the Lord Jesus Christ. Such an attachment by faith in the living Christ brings forth much fruit to the glory of the Father (John 15:7–8). Only those whose names are "written in the Lamb's book of life" through faith in Jesus will enter into the eternal city (Rev. 21:27).

b. Faith in Jesus gives escape from condemnation

The New Testament Scriptures clearly state many times that faith in Jesus as the Son of God and Savior is essential for obtaining eternal life and escaping the final condemnation. "Whoever believes in the Son has eternal life, but whoever rejects the Son will not see life, for God's wrath remains on him" (**John 3:36**). Escape from condemnation now and at the final judgment is promised by Jesus: "Whoever hears my word and believes him who sent me has eternal life and will not be condemned; he has crossed over from death to life" (**John 5:24**).

3. Summary

Both the Qur'an and the Bible teach a final judgment day when every person will have to give an account of his or her life. The Qur'an repeatedly sets forth the final judgment as a reminder, warning, and motivator in life. Since the scales' tipping in one's favor depends on one's effort, one's final destiny is always uncertain. The Muslim may always wonder, "Have I done enough to tip the scales of judgment in my favor?"

The Bible in the New Testament emphasizes the person and redeeming work of Christ as the means by which we can escape condemnation at the final judgment. It is because of the blood of the Lamb that believers will be able to stand before the throne of God clothed in white robes (Rev. 7:14–15). At the final judgment a person's good works will be cited as evidence of saving faith; however, it is by God's grace through faith in Christ alone that believers have eternal life and will not be condemned (John 5:24). Even now the believer in Christ has a peaceful certainty of eternal life (John 3:36).

For discussion questions, see study guide 22.

C. Paradise

What can the believer in Allah look forward to after death? According to the Bible, what can the believer in Christ look forward to in the life to come?

The Qur'an	The Bible

1a. The gardens of Paradise
    Surah 55:46. But for him who feareth the standing before his Lord there are two gardens.
    48. Of spreading branches.
    50. Wherein are two fountains flowing.
    52. Wherein is every kind of fruit in pairs.
    54. Reclining upon couches lined with silk brocade, the fruit of both gardens near to hand.
    56. Therein are those of modest gaze, whom neither man nor jinni will have touched before them.
    62. And beside them are two other gardens.
    Surah 78:32. Gardens enclosed and vineyards,
	2a. The beatific vision of paradise
	    Luke 23:43. Jesus answered him, "I tell you the truth, today you will be with me in paradise."
	    1 John 3:2b. But we know that when he appears, we shall be like him, for we shall see him as he is.
	    Revelation 22:1–5. Then the angel showed me the river of the water of life, as clear as crystal, flowing from the throne of God and of the Lamb down the middle of the great street of the city. On each side of the river stood the tree of life, bearing twelve crops of fruit, yielding its fruit every month. And the leaves of the tree are for the healing of the nations. No longer will there be any curse. The throne of God and of the Lamb will be in the city,

134&

 Comparing the Qur'an and the Bible

The Qur'an	The Bible
33. And maidens for companions [Dawood: high-bosomed maidens for companions], 34. And a full cup. **Surah 52:20.** Reclining on ranged couches. And We wed them unto fair ones with wide, lovely eyes.	and his servants will serve him. They will see his face, and his name will be on their foreheads. There will be no more night. They will not need the light of a lamp or the light of the sun, for the Lord God will give them light. And they will reign for ever and ever.
1b. Paradise for believers who do good **Surah 7:42.** But (as for) those who believe and do good works—We tax not any soul beyond its scope—Such are rightful owners of the Garden. They abide therein. **Surah 48:29b.** Allah hath promised, unto such of them as believe and do good works, forgiveness and immense reward.	**2b. Paradise, a gift of grace through faith** **Revelation. 7:14–15.** These are they who have come out of the great tribulation; they have washed their robes and made them white in the blood of the Lamb. Therefore, they are before the throne of God and serve him day and night in his temple. **Ephesians 2:8–10.** For it is by grace you have been saved, through faith—and this not from yourselves, it is the gift of God—not by works, so that no one can boast. For we are God's workmanship, created in Christ Jesus to do good works.

1. The Qur'an

a. The gardens of Paradise

■ **How does the Qur'an describe Paradise?**

Surah 55:46 describes Paradise as having two gardens (or four, Surah 55:62) with spreading branches (Surah 55:48), flowing fountains (Surah 55:50), every kind of fruit (Surah 55:52), silk brocade couches (Surah 55:54), and pure virgins (Surah 55:56). These maidens, to which men are wed, are beautiful with "wide, lovely eyes" (Surah 52:20; see also 78:33). Note that the men are "wed" to virgins. Apparently these were not their wives in this life. No mention is made in the Qur'an of the actual number of virgins. The number of 70 virgins comes from the Qur'anic scholar, Ibn Kathir. The number of 72 virgins comes from a hadith related by Abu Sa'id al-Khudhri, narrated in Sunan al-Tirmidhi.

As to what Paradise is like specifically for women, the Qur'an is silent. Women do share with "believers" in the promise of the "Gardens of Eden" (Surah 9:72). However, three times in the Hadith "Mohammad said, 'I was shown the Hellfire and that the majority of its dwellers are women.'"[4]

b. Paradise for believers who do good

■ **According to the Qur'an, how does one attain Paradise?**

In the Qur'an, Paradise is attained by those "who believe and do good works" (Surah 7:42; see also Surah 2:277; 3:57). In Islam, it is by submission to Allah and good works that a person gains Paradise. No soul is asked to do anything "beyond its scope" (**Surah 7:42**); the demands are not too hard (see Surah 2:286). The commandments and Allah's justice do not demand perfection. Allah is "Forgiving [Rodwell: Indulgent], Merciful" (Surah 4:110). The good must outweigh the bad. A good deed has much more weight than a bad deed (Surah 4:40; 6:160).

Those who win Paradise will receive "forgiveness and immense reward" (**Surah 48:29**). Forgiveness is given not as a gift but as a reward, again, to those who "believe and do good works" (Surah 47:12; see also 3:136). "Allah hath pleasure in them and they have pleasure in Him" (Surah 98:8).

It is commonly believed among orthodox Muslims (except Shi'ites) that almost all Muslims, except prophets and martyrs, may have to endure some suffering in the grave for purification before they enter permanently into Paradise. "According to a hadith related by Aisha, the prophet claimed that 'the torment of the grave is a fact.'"[5] All believers in Allah go to hell and will pass through, or by, or over the fire, but are hastened by their good works to Paradise: "The bridge over Hell is like the sharp edge of a sword. . . . Allah will save the believers and the righteous people from it because of their deeds. Therefore their passing over the bridge and their speed will be based upon their deeds that they did in this life."[6] Muhammad ibn Ismail al-Bukhari records: "So the hooks over the bridge will be like thorns of As-Sadan except that their greatness in size is only known to Allah. These hooks will snatch the people according to their deeds. Some people will be ruined because of their evil deeds, and some will be cut into pieces and fall down in Hell, but will be saved afterwards, when Allah has finished the judgments among His slaves [Muslims], and intends to take out of the Fire whoever He wishes."[7] (See the discussion of the "grave sinner" under "D. Godly Life" in chapter 9.) Finally, one's destiny is determined by the will of Allah (see Surah 14:4; 16:93).

2. The Bible

a. The beatific vision of paradise

■ **What does the Bible teach concerning paradise?**

In the Scriptures, Christ assures believers that when they die they will be "with me in paradise" that very day (**Luke 23:43**). They will be in the Father's house (John 14:2) and feast in fellowship with Abraham, Isaac, and Jacob in the kingdom of God (Matt. 8:11).

The great blessing of paradise will be the "beatific vision" of seeing God and the Lamb (**1 John 3:2; Rev. 22:3b–4a; Ps. 17:15; Job 19:26–27**). Seeing the Lord with our eyes will be our great joy (Ps. 16:11), and we will be changed "like him"—we will "share in his glory" (Rom 8:17; cf. John 17:22; Phil. 3:21; 2 Thess. 2:14; 1 Pet. 5:10); reflect his love, righteousness, and holiness; and live in perfect harmony with him. Eternal life is described in **Revelation 22:1–5** as

the heavenly Jerusalem with the "river of the water of life," the "tree of life
. . . yielding its fruit every month" and the leaves "for the healing of the nations." The throne of God and the Lamb is in the city and "his servants will
serve him." "They will see his face" and "they will reign for ever and ever."
God personally "will wipe every tear from their eyes." Indeed "there will be no
more death, or mourning, or crying, or pain" (Rev. 21:4). The New Testament
emphasis is on an intimate relationship with God and the Lamb.

Jesus taught that in paradise believers "will neither marry nor be given in
marriage" (Matt. 22:30). They will not be angels, but they will be "like the
angels" in that they will not be married.

b. Paradise, a gift of grace through faith

■ How is entrance into paradise attained?

Who are those who stand before God in white robes? In **Revelation 7:14** the
answer is given: "they have washed their robes and made them white in the
blood of the Lamb." Only the blood of the Lamb (Jesus) makes it possible to
stand clothed in white robes of purity before the throne of God.

The Scriptures teach that God is holy and his "eyes are too pure to look
on evil." He "cannot tolerate wrong" (Hab. 1:13). The law of God is holy
and demands perfection. Therefore, because all of us have sinned, we "fall
short of the glory of God" (Rom. 3:23). Human beings cannot achieve God's
holiness and perfection, and thus paradise is not attainable by good works.

The only hope for sinful human beings is that they are saved, as **Ephesians
2:8–9** states, "by grace . . . through faith," and "this . . . is the gift of God—
not by works, so that no one can boast." We are "justified freely by his grace
through the redemption that came by Christ Jesus. God presented him as a
sacrifice of atonement, through faith in his blood" (Rom. 3:24–25). Now the
Lord God pleads with every sinner to be reconciled to him through the blood
of the Lamb of God (2 Cor. 5:20).

3. Summary

Paradise in the Qur'an is filled with many pleasures that delight the senses.
Paradise is a beautiful garden, like an oasis in the desert, with flowing streams
and every kind of fruit. Paradise is promised to men and women who "believe
and do good works." Allah promises the men who come to Paradise that they
will wed beautiful virgins. For men, then, the emphasis is on the sensual pleasure of sexual relations with virgins.

Sunnis hold that one must pass over the bridge of hell and may have to be
purged of misdeeds before entering Paradise. Allah will "take out of the Fire
whoever He wishes."

According to the Bible, a person is able to stand before the throne of the
Lord God only because he or she is clothed in robes washed white in the blood

of the Lamb. Paradise is a gift by God's grace through faith in the cleansing blood of Jesus. Eternal life is depicted as the heavenly city of Jerusalem, where the river of life flows from the throne of God bringing life, health, and wholeness to the people. God and the Lamb are the focus of worship and life. The believers' great joy will be that they have a beatific vision of beholding God and the Lamb with their own eyes and that "they are before the throne of God and serve him day and night in his temple" (Rev. 7:15). Those who have been given eternal life are likewise depicted as dwelling securely and intimately in the "Father's house," where there are many rooms (John 14:2). The child of God will "dwell in the house of the Lord forever" (Ps. 23:6).

For discussion questions, see study guide 23.

11

Sacred Writings

A. Primary Sources: The Qur'an and the Bible

A religious faith is only as trustworthy as the primary source from which it derives its teaching. How are the Qur'an and the Bible presented as the "primary sources" for Islam and Christianity?

The Qur'an	The Bible

1. Copy of the eternal book
    Surah 43:2–4. [Dawood: We have revealed the Koran in the Arabic tongue that you may understand its meaning. It is a transcript of the eternal book in Our keeping, sublime, and full of wisdom.]
    Surah 4:82. Will they not then ponder on the Qur'an? If it had been from other than Allah they would have found therein much incongruity [Dawood: many contradictions].
    Surah 85:21–22. [Dawood: God surrounds them all. Surely this is a glorious Koran, inscribed on an imperishable tablet.]
    Surah 10:37. [Dawood: This Koran could not have been devised by any but God. It confirms what was revealed before it and fully explains the Scriptures. It is beyond doubt from the Lord of the Universe.]
	2. Inspired by God
	    2 Timothy 3:16–17. All Scripture is God-breathed and is useful for teaching, rebuking, correcting and training in righteousness, so that the man of God may be thoroughly equipped for every good work.
	    1 Corinthians 2:13. This is what we speak, not in words taught us by human wisdom but in words taught by the Spirit, expressing spiritual truths in spiritual words.
	    2 Peter 1:16. We did not follow cleverly invented stories when we told you about the power and coming of our Lord Jesus Christ, but we were eyewitnesses of his majesty.

1. The Qur'an: Copy of the eternal book

■ **How do Muslims look upon the Qur'an?**

The Qur'an is the highest authority in the Islamic faith. "It is a transcript of the eternal book" in heaven; it is "sublime, and full of wisdom" (**Surah 43:3–4**). For Muslims it is without error; otherwise, there would have been "found therein much incongruity [that is, contradiction]" (**Surah 4:82**).

It is "glorious" and "inscribed on an imperishable tablet" (**Surah 85:21–22**). Only Allah could have devised it. It "confirms" and "explains" the Scriptures (Bible) and is "beyond doubt from the Lord of the Universe" (**Surah 10:37**).

■ **How does the Qur'an account for its inconsistencies in relation to the Bible?**

The people of the Book (the Jews and Christians) "knowingly" changed it, "after they had understood it" (Surah 2:75), and used to "[hide] a testimony" (Surah 2:140), "conceal the truth" (Surah 2:146), "distort the Scripture" (Surah 3:78), and "hide much [thereof]" (Surah 6:91). The belief of Islam is that Jewish scholars and Christian authors such as Paul, Peter, and John have changed, concealed, corrupted, and distorted the original Scriptures. Thus, the present Jewish and Christian Scriptures have been perverted, contaminated, and falsified.

2. The Bible: Inspired by God

■ **What do Christians believe concerning the Scriptures?**

Referring to the Scriptures of his day, the apostle Paul asserts, "All Scripture is God-breathed" (**2 Tim. 3:16**).

The prophets of the Old Testament Hebrew Scriptures attest again and again that their testimony comes from Lord God (Isa. 1:1; Jer. 1:1; Ezra 1:3; Hosea 1:1; Joel 1:1; Amos 1:1; Obad. 1:1; Jonah 1:1; Micah 1:1; Nahum 1:1; Hab. 1:1; Zeph. 1:1; Hag. 1:1; Zech. 1:1; Mal. 1:1).

Similarly, the New Testament writers say that their writings are validated by God's Spirit and by eyewitnesses. The apostle Paul speaks "not in words taught us by human wisdom but in words taught by the Spirit" (**1 Cor. 2:13**). Peter, in **2 Peter 1:16**, states, "We did not follow cleverly invented stories when we told you about the power and the coming of our Lord Jesus Christ, but we were eyewitnesses of his majesty." John asserts, "That which was from the beginning, which we have heard, which we have seen with our eyes, which we have looked at and our hands have touched—this we proclaim" (1 John 1:1).

3. Summary

The primary source for Islam is the Qur'an. The Qur'an affirms that it accepts the Scriptures, especially the Injil ("Gospel," according to the Qur'an). However, is also affirms that the Scriptures—including the annunciation, the

The Holy Scriptures were inspired by God, are eyewitness accounts of what actually took place, and thus are a true and trustworthy testimony to Jesus as the Messiah and Son of God.

Some have conjectured that the belief in Jesus as Savior and Son of God was a notion that evolved gradually over time and was finally affirmed by the Council of Nicaea. However, during the lifetime of Jesus, Peter confessed, "You are the Christ, the Son of the living God" (Matt. 16:16). The religious leaders of that time understood well the claim of Jesus and asserted, "He must die, because he claimed to be the Son of God" (John 19:7).

Nor is the substitutionary death of Jesus a later development. Jesus gives his mission statement in the Gospel of Matthew: "The Son of Man did not come to be served, but to serve, and to give his life as a ransom for many" (Matt. 20:28; Mark 10:45). When Jesus instituted the Lord's Supper, he announced that his blood was "poured out for many for the forgiveness of sins" (Matt. 26:28).

Saul of Tarsus (before his conversion, when he became Paul) was a contemporary of Jesus, perhaps in his early twenties, when Jesus was crucified. With the phenomenal growth in belief in Jesus after his death and resurrection, Saul set out swiftly to uproot any belief in Jesus as the Messiah and the Son of God. He considered belief in Jesus as the Son of God to be blasphemy (just as a Muslim would). Yet upon his conversion, "at once he began to preach in the synagogues [pl.] that Jesus is the Son of God . . . proving that Jesus is the Christ" (Acts 9:20, 22). In his writings Paul quotes from the earliest hymns and faith declarations of believers (1 Cor. 15:3–8; Phil. 2:6–11; 1 Tim. 3:16), all of which joyfully proclaim the deity, the incarnation, the sacrifice, the resurrection, and the exaltation of Jesus the Christ, the Son of God.

As to the assertion by some that the Gospel of John is far advanced in its theology and must have developed much later, the theology of Paul in Romans, Philippians, and Colossians is as clear and substantive as that of John in declaring that Jesus is the Messiah, the eternal Son of God, and the Savior of the world. Paul in his teaching (e.g., Romans 1–6; Eph. 1:3–10; Col. 1:15–20) is as profound as are the eyewitness accounts of the apostle John in his Gospel. The New Testament proclaims Jesus as the Son of God (or Son of Man) approximately two hundred times. If one rejects Jesus as the Savior and Son of God, one must abandon or rewrite the entire New Testament.

life of Jesus, the crucifixion, and so on—are filled with contradictions, distortions, and changes. There are large portions of the Bible that are not referred to in, or are omitted from, the Qur'an. It includes only one clear quote from the Bible (compare Surah 21:105 and Ps. 37:29). (See also "F. What about the differences between the Qur'an and the Bible?" in chapter 14, and section C.1, "The Reliability of the Bible," in chapter 15.)

In the Qur'an there is no mention of sacrifice (other than Abraham's willingness to sacrifice his son and Allah's ransom of Ishmael). The Qur'an disregards the prophecy of the suffering servant of God (Isa. 53). It denies the crucifixion of Jesus. The Islamic faith takes strong exception to Paul's writings, yet Paul, a young adult at the time of Jesus's public ministry, was opposed to Christ and persecuted Christ's followers for blasphemy, but was changed completely immediately after Christ appeared and spoke to him: he then began to proclaim in the synagogues of Damascus that Jesus was the Messiah and the Son of God.

In reading the Bible, one cannot escape the towering person of Christ. The testimony of eyewitnesses and the early believers is strong. The believer in Jesus affirms that the Bible truly is the inspired Word of God and confesses with Jesus, "Your word is truth" (John 17:17).

For discussion questions, see study guide 24.

B. Conflicting Statements: The Qur'an versus the Bible

What are some of the discrepancies between the Bible and the Qur'an in assertions of fact?

The Qur'an manifests a number of contradictions and anachronisms in relation to the Bible.

1. Cain, Abel—and a Raven?

The Qur'an	The Bible
Surah 5:31. Then Allah sent a raven scratching up the ground, to show him [Cain] how to hide his brother's naked corpse.	Genesis 4:8. And while they were in the field, Cain attacked his brother Abel and killed him.

Surah 5:31 recounts how Cain learns to bury Abel from the example of a raven. Anis Shorrosh states that Surah 5:27–32 echoes "an ancient Jewish tradition (c. AD 150–200), preserved by Pirke Rabbi Eleazer," according to which Adam and Eve, sitting by the corpse of Abel, learned how to bury him from the example of a raven that "took the dead body of its fellow (mate), and having scratched up the earth, buried it thus before their eyes."[1] Shorrosh also cites further examples of Muhammad appropriating material from apocryphal and fable traditions.[2]

2. Saul or Gideon?

The Qur'an	The Bible
Surah 2:249. And when Saul set out with the army, he said: Lo! Allah will try you by (the ordeal of) a river.	Judges 7:5–7. So Gideon took the men down to the water. There the LORD told him, "Separate those who lap the water with their tongues like a dog from those who kneel down to drink." Three hundred men lapped

The Qur'an	The Bible
Whosoever therefore drinketh thereof he is not of me, and whosoever tasteth it not he is of me, save him who ta-keth (thereof) in the hollow of his hand. But they drank thereof, all save a few of them. . . . they said: We have no power this day against Goliath and his hosts. . . .	with their hands to their mouths. All the rest got down on their knees to drink. The LORD said to Gideon, "With the three hundred men that lapped I will save you and give the Midianites into your hands." **1 Samuel 17:4.** A champion named Goliath, who was from Gath, came out of the Philistine camp. He was over nine feet tall. **1 Samuel 17:50.** So David triumphed over the Philistine with a sling and a stone; without a sword in his hand he struck down the Philistine and killed him.

Surah 2:249 tells of Saul drinking water "in the hollow of his hand" and going with his men to fight against Goliath and the Philistines. Thus, the story of Gideon choosing three hundred men (**Judg. 7:5–7**), who did not take time to kneel to drink but, eager to fight the Midianites, lapped water like a dog with their hands to their mouths, is conflated and confused with the biblical account of David, many years later, killing the giant Goliath with a sling and stone and thus leading the defeat of the Philistines (**1 Sam. 17:4, 50**).

3. One of Noah's sons drowned, or all of them saved?

The Qur'an	The Bible
Surah 11:42. Noah cried unto his son—and he was standing aloof—O my son! Come ride with us, and be not with the disbelievers. **43.** He said: I shall betake me to some mountain that will save me from the water. . . . And the wave came in between them, so he was among the drowned.	**Genesis 7:13.** On that very day Noah and his sons, Shem, Ham and Japheth, together with his wife and the wives of his three sons, entered the ark.

In **Surah 11:42–43**, one of the sons of Noah is drowned, whereas in **Genesis 7:13**, Noah and his wife and all his sons and their wives enter the ark.

4. How many years does Jacob work for Rachel?

The Qur'an	The Bible
Surah 28:27. He said: Lo! I fain would marry thee to one of these two daughters of mine on condition that thou hirest thyself to me for (the term of) eight pilgrimages.	**Genesis 29:20.** So Jacob served seven years to get Rachel.

In **Surah 28:27**, Jacob works eight years for Rachel, whereas in **Genesis 29:20**, he serves Laban seven years for her.

5. How long was Zechariah struck dumb?

The Qur'an	The Bible
Surah 3:40a. He said: My Lord! How can I have a son when age hath overtaken me already and my wife is barren? 41a. He said: My Lord! Appoint a token for me. (The angel) said: The token unto thee (shall be) that thou shalt not speak unto mankind three days except by signs.	Luke 1:20. [The angel Gabriel said,] "And now you will be silent and not able to speak until the day this happens [the day John, the Baptizer, is born]."

In **Surah 3:40–41**, Zechariah is dumb and unable to speak for three days, whereas in **Luke 1:20**, he is "not able to speak" for nine months, until John the Baptizer is born.

6. Did Pharaoh threaten crucifixion?

The Qur'an	The Bible
Surah 7:123a. Pharaoh said: Ye believe in Him before I give you leave! 124. Surely I shall have your hands and feet cut off upon alternate sides. Then I shall crucify you every one.	The Bible makes no mention of crucifixion in relation to the pharaoh of Egypt, nor indeed in the whole Old Testament.

In **Surah 7:123–24**, Pharaoh threatens to "crucify you every one," whereas according to historical record crucifixion was not practiced until centuries later by the Medes and Persians. The *Zondervan Pictorial Encyclopedia of the Bible* specifies that crucifixion was "a method of execution which arose in the E[ast] . . . practiced by the Medes and Persians and passed on to the W[est] among the Greeks and Romans."[3]

7. How many plagues did God send on the Egyptians?

The Qur'an	The Bible
Surah 27:12a. And put thy hand into the bosom of thy robe, it will come forth white but unhurt. (This will be one) among nine tokens unto Pharaoh and his people.	Exodus 7–11 records ten plagues, the tenth being the killing of firstborn sons by the angel of death.

Surah 27:12 mentions "nine tokens" or signs spoken against Pharaoh, whereas Exodus 7–11 records ten plagues, with the tenth being the all-important slaying of firstborn sons, which occasions the Passover among the Hebrews and their deliverance through the blood of the Passover lamb. The omission of the tenth plague is significant because of its foreshadowing of Christ as the sacrificial paschal lamb.

8. Why did Haman build a tower?

The Qur'an	The Bible
Surah 28:38. And Pharaoh said: O chiefs! I know not that ye have a god other than me, so kindle for me (a fire), O Haman, to bake the mud; and set up for me a lofty tower in order that I may survey the god of Moses; and lo! I deem him of the liars. Surah 40:36. And Pharaoh said: O Haman! Build for me a tower that haply I may reach the roads,— 37a. The roads of the heavens, and may look upon the God of Moses, though verily I think him a liar.	In Esther 5, which records events that occurred long after the days of Pharaoh, Haman builds his own gallows, intended for Mordecai. It was to be "seventy-five feet high." Genesis 11 speaks of the building of the Tower of Babel in the early history of humankind, long before the days of Pharaoh and Moses.

In **Surah 28:38** and **Surah 40:36**, Pharaoh has Haman building "a lofty tower." The Qur'an seems to conflate Esther 5, where Haman (who is in Persia) builds his own gallows, with Genesis 11, where the tower of Babel is built long before the days of Pharaoh and Moses.

9. Was it Pharaoh's wife or daughter who adopted Moses?

The Qur'an	The Bible
Surah 28:9a. And the wife of Pharaoh said: (He will be) a consolation for me and for thee. Kill him not . . . we may choose him for a son.	Exodus 2:10. When the child [Moses] grew older, she took him to Pharaoh's daughter and he became her son.

In **Surah 28:9**, the wife of Pharaoh chooses Moses as her son, whereas in **Exodus 2:10**, the woman who adopts Moses is the daughter of Pharaoh.

10. How many days did Allah / Lord God take to create the earth?

The Qur'an	The Bible
Surah 41:9–12. Who created the earth in two Days, . . . He placed therein firm hills. . . . in four Days, . . . He ordained them seven heavens in two Days.	Exodus 20:11. For in six days the LORD made the heavens and the earth.

In **Surah 41:9–12**, the time of creation adds up to eight days. In Surah 57:4, on the other hand, Allah "created the heavens and the earth in six Days." In **Exodus 20:11**, the Bible speaks of a six-day creation.

11. Summary

More examples of discrepancies could be listed.

Those who hold that the Bible is inspired by the Lord God believe that its accounts are trustworthy and true. Jesus himself affirmed that the words of the Hebrew Scriptures were true (Matt. 5:17–18; John 5:39). Further, he promised his disciples that the Holy Spirit would guide them "into all truth" (John 16:13). The Bible presents the Lord God dealing with real people in real places. In its final book, Revelation, a warning is given not to add or detract from the words of "this book," in which Jesus is exalted as the Son of God and the "King of kings and Lord of lords" (Rev. 22:18; 19:16). (Also see section C.1, "The Reliability of the Bible," in chapter 15.)

How is it possible that the Qur'an contains so many factual inconsistencies with the Bible? Islam would answer that the mistakes are in the Bible, which has been corrupted. The Qur'an holds that the Qur'an is a "confirmation" of the Bible, which was revealed before the Qur'an (Surah 10:37). But how is it that the Lord God would allow the Bible to be corrupted? Why and how were some facts in historical accounts changed in the Qur'an? Would not the original account of prophets and other servants of God recorded in the Bible take precedence over a revelation received approximately 1500 to 550 years later?

For discussion questions, see study guide 24. Also see "F. What about the differences between the Qur'an and the Bible?" in chapter 14.

12

Practices of Faith

The teaching of Islam is summarized in the Five Articles of Faith: belief in Allah, his Angels, his Books, his Apostles, and the Day of Judgment. Primary among the works of faith are the "Pillars of Islam":

    I. The Creed (Shahada)
    II. Prayer (Salat)
    III. Almsgiving (Zakat)
    IV. Ramadan: Fast (Sawm), Honoring the First Giving of the Qu'ran
    V. Pilgrimage (Hajj)

Here each pillar will be compared with corresponding elements of Christian faith and practice.

A. The Creed

How does Islam's creed (the Shahada) compare with the most widely used Christian creed?

Islam	Christianity

1. First Pillar: The creed (Shahada)
    There is no god but Allah. Muhammad is the messenger of Allah.
	2. The Apostles' Creed
	I believe in God, the Father Almighty,
	    Maker of heaven and earth.
	    and in Jesus Christ, his only Son, our Lord:
	Who was conceived by the Holy Spirit,

146

Islam	Christianity
	born of the Virgin Mary,
	suffered under Pontius Pilate,
	was crucified, died, and was buried.
	He descended into hell.
	The third day he rose again from the dead.
	He ascended into heaven
	and sits at the right hand of God the Father Almighty.
	From thence he will come to judge the living and the dead.
	I believe in the Holy Spirit,
	the holy Christian Church,
	the communion of saints,
	the forgiveness of sins,
	the resurrection of the body,
	and the life everlasting. Amen.

1. Islam: First Pillar: The creed (Shahada)

▣ What is Islam's creed?

The creed (Shahada) is the First Pillar of Islam: "There is no god but Allah. Muhammad is the messenger of Allah." Allah is one. There is no other god, and there is no partner to him or like him. Allah is transcendent. Human beings are not created in the "image of God" (in the sense of possessing attributes of the invisible God himself). That is unthinkable. What Allah wills is, and what Allah does not will does not happen. Muhammad is the messenger of Allah. He is the final and authoritative prophet of Allah.

Allah is not Father. Allah does not become man; that would be beneath him. He has no son, because he has no wife. Allah is approached directly without a mediator by those who acknowledge him. This is possible because Allah is merciful and forgiving and does not demand more than we can achieve. Since in Islam humankind is not inherently sinful, a Muslim who believes in Allah is able with Allah's help, prayer, and the Qur'an to overcome temptations and triumph through trials. He or she can meet the requirements of Allah and secure his or her own salvation. (See "A. The Nature of Allah / Lord God" in chapter 4.)

2. Christianity: The Apostles' Creed

▣ What are the core elements of Christian belief?

The baptismal creed from the earliest centuries of Christianity is the Apostles' Creed.

"I believe in God"

Like Islam, Christianity is a monotheistic religion. God alone is the living Lord, the great I AM. There is no other God beside him. He is almighty, all knowing, all-present, just, holy, righteous, merciful, gracious, and loving.

"The Father Almighty, Maker of heaven and earth"

The Father is the almighty Creator of the universe and the earth, the source and sustainer of all things. God is revealed by Jesus as Father. The Creator of the cosmos has in the center of his being a Father's heart that beats in love for his wayward children. He longs for human beings to know him personally through his Son. He demonstrates his unexpected and undeserved love in sending his Son as our Savior. His desire is to call people into friendship and fellowship with him through his Son and through the Holy Spirit.

"And in Jesus Christ, his only Son, our Lord . . ."

The Apostles' Creed professes that Jesus, the Christ (Messiah), Son of the Father, is "our Lord." He is *our* Lord because he was conceived in human life by the Holy Spirit, born of the Virgin Mary (Luke 1:35), suffered under Pontius Pilate (Matt. 27), was crucified, died, and was buried (Matt. 27–28). He offered himself as the Lamb of God, an atoning sacrifice (1 John 4:10) and a ransom for all (Mark 10:45). He rose from the dead and was victorious over sin and death for us (1 Cor. 15:20–22). Having come from the Father, he returned to the Father and ascended into heaven (John 16:28). God has exalted him to his right hand as Lord of all (Phil. 2:10, 11). He will return to judge the living and the dead (Acts 1:11). Jesus, the Son of the Father, is our Savior and "our Lord."

Strong statements of faith in the Son of God appear in Matthew 16:16; Mark 1:11; Luke 1:32–33; John 1:1–4; 1 Corinthians 15:3–8; Philippians 2:6–11; Colossians 1:15–20; 1 Timothy 3:16; 1 Peter 1:3–9; 1 John 1:1–4, and many other biblical passages.

The historic Nicene Creed of the Christian church professes what the Scriptures proclaim that Jesus is: "God of God, Light of Light, very God of very God."

"I believe in the Holy Spirit . . ."

Jesus promised that after his ascension he would send the Counselor, the Holy Spirit, "whom the Father will send in my Name." He would "teach you all things" (John 14:26), being the "Spirit of truth" (John 15:26). He would convict the world "in regard to sin and righteousness and judgment" (John 16:8). And indeed, soon after Jesus ascended his followers "were all filled with the Holy Spirit and spoke the word of God boldly" (Acts 4:31). By the Holy Spirit the believers were strengthened and encouraged and grew in numbers (Acts 9:31). The Holy Spirit is the believer's "seal" for the final day of redemption (Eph. 4:30).

Thus God has revealed himself as the Holy Spirit, who calls people out of the world into a new family of the "holy Christian church." In this holy church are proclaimed the Word and Sacraments, and with them is conveyed "the forgiveness of sins." Believers in Christ are given the assurance of "the resurrection of the body and the life everlasting."

3. Summary

The Qur'an sets forth the basic creed that "there is no god but Allah and Muhammad is his messenger." Allah is mighty, merciful, forgiving, knowing, wise, and far transcendent over his creation. He is like the sun and the moon, which remain far removed but send their rays to humankind. He has made himself known through a series of messengers, chief of whom is Muhammad.

In the Bible, the living Lord (Yahweh / I AM) is a very personal God to Adam, Abraham, Moses, David, and the prophets. The words of Jesus and the eyewitness accounts of his disciples in the New Testament convey clearly that this living Lord God has revealed himself in three divine persons: the Father, the Son, and the Holy Spirit (Matt. 28:19). God is a personal, loving, and relational God. There is an intimate, loving unity between the Father and the Son and the Holy Spirit in the Godhead.

This loving, relational God longs for reconciliation and direct relationship with his creatures. He created them to live in intimacy with him. It is to achieve this that he is "conceived by the Holy Spirit and born of the Virgin Mary," becoming a human being in the person of Jesus, the Son of God. This "friend of sinners" lives our life, bears our guilt, and endures our death. By his precious blood, he pays the price for our sins that we could not pay. By his resurrection from the dead, he conquers death and gives us life eternal. By the power of his life-giving Word, his Holy Spirit calls us to faith so that we might be members of his holy family, the church.

As children of the Father, we know Jesus as our Savior and Lord and live in security in his kingdom. We desire to honor the Lord God in our lives. We find joy and purpose in serving him now and forever.

For discussion questions, see study guide 25.

B. Prayer

Prayer is an important element in the Qur'an and the Bible. How do the two differ on this important aspect of the godly life?

The Qur'an	The Bible
1. Second Pillar: Five times of prayer 1. The Sunset Prayer (magrib) **Surah 11:114.** "two ends of the day"	2. How and when to pray Matthew 6:7–13. [Jesus's words:] "And when you pray, do not keep on babbling like pagans, for they think they will be heard because of their many words. Do not be like them, for your Father knows what you need before you ask him.

The Qur'an	The Bible
2. The Night Prayer ('isha) **Surah 24:58.** "after the late-night prayer" 3. The Dawn Prayer (subh) **Surah 24:58.** "before the morning prayer" 4. The Noon Prayer (zuhr) **Surah 17:78.** "the middle of the day" 5. The Midafternoon Prayer ('asr) **Surah 2:238.** "the midmost prayer"	This, then, is how you should pray: 'Our Father in heaven, hallowed be your name, your kingdom come, your will be done on earth as it is in heaven. Give us today our daily bread. Forgive us our debts, as we also have forgiven our debtors. And lead us not into temptation, but deliver us from the evil one.'" **1 Thessalonians 5:16–18.** Be joyful always; pray continually; give thanks in all circumstances, for this is God's will for you in Christ Jesus. **Acts 2:42.** They devoted themselves to the apostles' teaching and to the fellowship, to the breaking of bread and to prayer.

1. The Qur'an: Second Pillar: Five times of prayer

■ **How were Islamic prayer times established, according to tradition?**

According to Islam, Muhammad rode Buraq, a horselike animal with a human face, from Mecca to the al-Aqsa Mosque in Jerusalem and ascended to the seventh heaven. Adam was in the first heaven, Jesus and John the Baptizer in the second, Joseph in the third, Enoch in the fourth, Aaron in the fifth, Moses in the sixth, and Abraham in the seventh. When he got to the seventh heaven, he was told to prescribe prayer fifty times a day. When Muhammad came to Moses in the sixth heaven, Moses told Muhammad to go back and ask for a lower number. Muhammad returned three times and succeeded in having the prayer requirement reduced to five times a day.

■ **What are the five times of prayer?**

(1) The Sunset Prayer time "begins when the sun has completely set." (2) The Night Prayer time "begins when the red of sunset leaves the sky." (3) The Dawn Prayer time "begins at true dawn and ends at sunrise." (4) The Noon Prayer time "begins after the sun reaches the zenith for the day." (5) The Midafternoon Prayer "begins at the end of the noon prayer's time and ends at sunset."[1] Shi'ites, however, may double up on two prayer times and pray on three occasions a day.

■ **What are the ablutions in preparation for prayer?**

All prayer must be preceded by ablution or purification. In the absence of water, clean dry soil or sand may be used. These are the instructions Muslims follow for purification:

• Wash hands three times up to the wrists.
• Rinse the mouth three times.

- Cleanse nostrils by sniffing three times.
- Wash from forehead to chin, from ear to ear.
- Wash forearms up to the elbow three times.
- Pass wet hand over the whole of the head.
- Wash feet up to the ankles, right ankle first then left.[2]

Passing digestive excretions through the intestines, including gas, solids, or urine, nullifies the ablution. The same is true for falling asleep. In all cases, the purification must be repeated.

What is the content of the prayers?

Prayer involves a series of movements and recitations:

- The Muslim faces Mecca, stating his intention, and using various gestures with his hands, and saying, "Allahu Akbar" (Allah is the Greatest [literally, "Greater"]).
- Standing in a prescribed way, the Muslim recites "the Key" to prayer, Surah 1, in Arabic.
- Bowing, the Muslim says, "Allah is Great. Allah Akbar. Glory be to Allah, the Great."
- Standing, "Allah responds to those who praise him. Allahu Akbar."
- Prostrating, "Glory be to Allah, the Most high."
- Sitting position, "Allahu Akbar."
- Going down in prostration, "Allahu Akbar."
- In prostration, "Glory be to Allah, the Most High."
- Standing, "Allahu Akbar."

Other prayers are said with slight variations. The Dawn Prayer includes the added sentences "I bear witness that there is no god beside Allah. He alone is God; He has no partners."

The Friday Congregational Prayer replaces the Noon Prayer every Friday. The Friday Prayer consists of listening to two sermons delivered by an imam (spiritual leader) and two units of prayer.[3] Friday is the day on which Allah finished creation and Muhammad entered into Yathrib (Medina).

2. The Bible: How and when to pray

What is prayer for the Christian?

Prayer for a believer in the Christ is an intimate communion with the heavenly Father through faith in his Son, Jesus.

Jesus revealed to his disciples (**Matt. 6:7–13**) that God is our Father and that we are his dear children. Prayer is not empty repetition to gain the favor of God (Matt. 6:5). It is rather a heartfelt response to the kindness of a loving Father. Jesus, who came from the Father, teaches that the Lord God is a loving, waiting Father who yearns for the return of his children (Luke 15:11–32). He gladly hears their prayers offered in Jesus's name (John 16:23).

God himself has "sent the Spirit of his Son into our hearts, the Spirit who calls out, 'Abba, Father'" (Gal. 4:6). This intimate indwelling of the Spirit is unique. It is not to be found in the teaching of the Qur'an.

First Thessalonians 5:16–18 tells us to "be joyful always; pray continually; give thanks in all circumstances." As a little child is continually aware of the presence of his mother, calls on her whenever he needs help and comfort, and joyfully shares with her whatever delights him, so the child of God is in tune with the heavenly Father, prays "continually," and gives thanks "in all circumstances." The believer in Christ will have special times of meditation and communion with the heavenly Father. He or she will also have shared prayer with brothers and sisters in God's family.

> Nowhere in the Qur'an is Allah described as a Father. Nowhere are believers described as children of the heavenly Father. While in his knowledge of the human being Allah is characterized as "nearer to him than his jugular vein," this fact is not necessarily comforting, since Allah knows what each person's "soul whispereth to him" (Surah 50:16). Allah is not Father, and he is not an indwelling presence. In Islam, this would contradict his transcendence.

The early believers in Christ "devoted themselves to the apostles' teaching and to the fellowship, to the breaking of bread and to prayer" (**Acts 2:42**). The follower of Christ, a child of the Father, cherishes prayer in his or her private room, with family members, and in the church, the "house of prayer," with other believers.

3. Summary

Prayer is an important element in the Islam faith. The devout Muslim will pray five times a day. The ablutions and prayers are prescribed in the Qur'an. The very specific obligation of ablution and repeated prayer recitations are reminiscent of the practice of the Pharisees in Jesus's day.

Prayer for the Muslim is an act of submission and reverence to Allah. It acknowledges Allah as the One God and declares that there is no other. It is a powerful means of uniting Muslims in a common faith.

Jesus took exception to the prescribed, repetitious prayers practiced by the Pharisees in his day. He himself had a disciplined and intimate prayer life. Jesus would spontaneously look to heaven and give thanks to the Father. He would rise early and spend time in private prayer. He longed for prayer with his disciples and in the "house of prayer," the synagogue or the temple.

Following the example of the Lord and of the early believers, believers in Christ today will be people of prayer. Prayer in the Bible is always "through Jesus Christ" or "in my [Jesus's] name" (John 16:23). It is a privilege granted by the Father in grace through his Son, who is our mediator and intercessor. Jesus said, "No one comes to the Father except through me" (John 14:6). The kindly invitation of Jesus is "Come to me . . . and I will give you rest" (Matt. 11:28).

He promises, "Whoever comes to me I will never drive away" (John 6:37). In his name, "Ask and you will receive, and your joy will be complete" (John 16:24).

For discussion questions, see study guide 26.

C. Almsgiving

What do the Qur'an and the Bible teach about giving to the poor?

The Qur'an	The Bible
1. Third Pillar: Almsgiving (zakat) Surah 2:271a. If ye publish your almsgiving, it is well, but if ye hide it and give it to the poor, it will be better for you, and will atone for some of your ill-deeds. Surah 2:277. Lo! those who believe and do good works and establish worship and pay the poor-due, their reward is with their Lord and there shall no fear come upon them neither shall they grieve.	**2. Meeting needs of the poor** 1 John 3:17. If anyone has material possessions and sees his brother in need but has no pity on him, how can the love of God be in him? Matthew 25:37–40. Then the righteous will answer him, "Lord, when did we see you hungry and feed you, or thirsty and give you something to drink? When did we see you a stranger and invite you in, or needing clothes and clothe you? When did we see you sick or in prison and go to visit you?" The King will reply, "I tell you the truth, whatever you did for one of the least of these brothers of mine, you did for me." Acts 20:35. In everything I did, I showed you that by this kind of hard work we must help the weak, remembering the words the Lord Jesus himself said: "It is more blessed to give than to receive." 2 Corinthians 9:7. Each man should give what he has decided in his heart to give, not reluctantly or under compulsion, for God loves a cheerful giver. 2 Corinthians 8:9. For you know the grace of our Lord Jesus Christ, that though he was rich, yet for your sakes he became poor, so that you through his poverty might become rich.

1. The Qur'an: Third Pillar: Almsgiving (zakat)

■ **What should Muslims give to the poor, and why?**

Almsgiving (literally, purification) "cleanses the Muslim of greed and self-ishness while exacting the equitable distribution of goods to the entire community. It is intended to bring unity and betterment to the society as a whole."[4] Almsgiving has great value: "If ye publish your almsgiving, it is well, but if ye hide it and give it to the poor, it will be better for you, and will atone for some of your ill-deeds" (**Surah 2:271**). Besides helping to alleviate fear of judgment, giving alms assures the Muslim of eternal reward: "Lo! those who believe and do good works and establish worship and pay the poor-due, their reward is with their Lord and there shall no fear come upon them neither shall they grieve" (**Surah 2:277**).

Muslims are obligated to give 2.5 percent of their net income after paying personal expenses, family expenses, due credits, taxes, and the like. At the end of the year, anything over approximately $1,400 in cash or articles of trade must be given at the minimum rate of 2.5 percent.[5]

2. The Bible: Meeting needs of the poor

■ **What is the biblical motivation for generosity toward the poor?**

The Bible exhorts us to be generous to the poor and the needy: "If anyone has material possessions and sees his brother in need but has no pity on him, how can the love of God be in him?" (**1 John 3:17**). Jesus personalizes our compassion by saying, "I tell you the truth, whatever you did for one of the least of these brothers of mine, you did for me" (**Matt. 25:40**). The very first believers were taught that "it is more blessed to give than to receive" (**Acts 20:35**) and "to remember the poor" (Gal. 2:10). Many Christians give a tithe (a tenth) or more of their income to the Lord. The Lord desires "a cheerful giver" (**2 Cor. 9:7**). Believers give because they know "the grace of our Lord Jesus Christ, that though he was rich, yet for your sakes he became poor" (**2 Cor. 8:9**).

3. Summary

The Qur'an frequently reminds Muslims to have a compassionate heart for the poor and needy. From the earliest of days, the Qur'an required people to give "the poor tax." This is still mandatory for Muslims.

According to the Bible, Jesus and his apostles taught disciples to care for the poor and needy. In the New Testament no prescribed amount is designated. The money given is a thank-offering and not a "tax" or "dues." The Christian is moved by the goodness of the Lord God and the grace of the Lord Jesus Christ to share with others to the measure of his or her faith and love for Jesus Christ. Thus, he or she becomes a "cheerful giver."

For discussion questions, see study guide 25.

D. Fasting

What place does fasting have in the lives of the faithful according to the Qur'an and the Bible?

The Qur'an	The Bible

1. Fourth Pillar: Fasting (sawm) in Ramadan
 	
    Surah 2:183. O ye who believe! Fasting is prescribed for you, even as it was prescribed for those before you, that ye may ward off (evil);
    184. (Fast) a certain number of days; and (for) him who is sick among you, or on a journey, (the same) number of other days; and for those who can afford it there is a ransom: the feeding of a man in need—But whoso doth good of his own accord, it is better for him: and that ye fast is better for you if ye did but know—
    185. The month of Ramadan in which was revealed the Qur'an, a guidance for mankind, and clear proofs of the guidance, and the Criterion (of right and wrong). And whosoever of you is present, let him fast the month, and whosoever of you is sick or on a journey, (let him fast the same) number of other days. Allah desireth for you ease; He desireth not hardship for you; and (He desireth) that ye should complete the period, and that ye should magnify Allah for having guided you, and that peradventure ye may be thankful.
	2. Fasting
	
	    Mark 2:19–20. Jesus answered, "How can the guests of the bridegroom fast while he is with them? They cannot, so long as they have him with them. But the time will come when the bridegroom will be taken from them, and on that day they will fast.
	    Matthew 6:16–18. When you fast, do not look somber as the hypocrites do, for they disfigure their faces to show men they are fasting. I tell you the truth, they have received their reward in full. But when you fast, put oil on your head and wash your face, so that it will not be obvious to men that you are fasting, but only to your Father, who is unseen; and your Father, who sees what is done in secret, will reward you.

1. The Qur'an: Fourth Pillar: Fasting (sawm) in Ramadan

■ **What place does fasting have in Islam?**

Muslims believe Muhammad received the call to be Allah's messenger, and also the first revelation for the Qur'an, during the month of Ramadan. Fasting is prescribed in the month of Ramadan that "ye may ward off (evil)" (**Surah 2:183**). Ramadan is the ninth lunar month in the Islamic calendar.

During Ramadan "the Muslim, from sunrise to sunset, is required to abstain from sexual intercourse, eating, drinking, and smoking. In [their] place, he is to read the Qur'an introspectively, performing an act of worship in his or her self-restraint."[6] The sick, prepubescent youths, and women who are menstruating or pregnant are exempt from the fast.

2. The Bible: Fasting

■ **What does the Bible say about fasting?**

The Bible speaks of fasting. Jesus assumed that his disciples would fast once he was no longer with them (**Mark 2:20**). But they were not to fast as the

Pharisees did, for show and merit. They were to fast "in secret." Such fasting would have a reward (**Matt. 6:16–18**).

It is recorded that Jesus fasted before he began his public ministry (Matt. 4:2). When Paul and Barnabas were commissioned for missionary work, the people fasted and prayed beforehand, and then Paul and Barnabas were sent forth to share the good news of Jesus (Acts 13:3).

Biblical fasting is not merely displacing eating and other pleasurable activities from daytime to nighttime. Nor is it abstaining from food for its own sake. Rather, its purpose is to focus the heart on the Lord God in meditation on God's Word and prayer. The act of fasting in itself has no merit or benefit. It is not to be done for show or to gain favor with God (Isa. 58:3; **Matt. 6:16**). It is not to be a substitute for true repentance (Luke 18:12). When God's people are undertaking a specific mission for the Lord, fasting is appropriate (Ezra 8:23; Acts 13:3). Its blessing is obtained when we focus elsewhere than the hunger of the body and satisfy the inner spirit's hunger for communion with the Lord God through prayer and receiving the Word of God.

3. Summary

For the Muslim, the month of Ramadan is the time to fast and to focus in thanksgiving to Allah for the calling of Muhammad and the revelation given to him. It is a time to be generous toward the poor and needy. It is a monthlong observance that unites Muslims in their faith.

While Christians are not required to fast, they benefit from it when it is done alongside prayer and immersion in the Word of God. Historically, fasting was a common practice before partaking of Holy Communion and during the season of Lent. Believers who voluntarily practice fasting today consider it a great blessing to themselves spiritually.

For discussion questions, see study guide 25.

E. Pilgrimage

What is the hajj? Does the Bible require a practice of pilgrimage?

The Qur'an	The Bible

1. Fifth Pillar: Pilgrimage (hajj)
    Surah 2:196. Perform the pilgrimage and the visit (to Mecca) for Allah. And if ye are prevented, then send such gifts as can be obtained with ease. . . . And whoever among you is sick or hath an ailment of the head must pay a ransom of fasting or almsgiving or offering. . . . Observe your duty to Allah, and know that Allah is severe in punishment.
	2. Pilgrimage not required
	    The Bible does not instruct Christians to make a pilgrimage.

The Qur'an	The Bible
197b. There is (to be) no lewdness nor abuse nor angry conversation on the pilgrimage. And whatsoever good ye do Allah knoweth it. **199.** Then hasten onward from the place whence the multitude hasteneth onward, and ask forgiveness of Allah. Lo! Allah is Forgiving, Merciful. **200a.** And when ye have completed your devotions, then remember Allah as ye remember your fathers.	

1. The Qur'an: Fifth Pillar: Pilgrimage (hajj)

Surah 2:196–200 describes the pilgrimage to Mecca and provisions for those who are unable to make the journey. (For more on the hajj, see section D.1, "Abraham Builds the Ka'aba in Mecca," in chapter 1.)

2. The Bible: Pilgrimage not required

The Bible does not instruct Christians to make a pilgrimage.

Before Christ, the Israelites were to observe three pilgrimages to Jerusalem: (1) Passover and Unleavened Bread; (2) the Feast of Weeks and First Fruits; and (3) the Feast of Pentecost and the Feast of Tabernacles or Ingathering (Leviticus 23). Since Jesus the Messiah has come, these feasts and pilgrimages need no longer be observed. Jesus is the Passover Lamb sacrificed for us (1 Cor. 5:7). The Feast of Pentecost reached a culmination when all peoples were united by the coming of the Holy Spirit (Acts 2:1–11). But feasts of thanksgiving can be observed by Christians at appropriate times.

It is no longer necessary to come to the temple for sacrifice since Christ "entered the Most Holy Place once for all by his own blood, having obtained eternal redemption" (Heb. 9:12b). To those who looked for a central outward temple and nation, Jesus said, "A time is coming when you will worship the Father neither on this mountain [in Samaria] nor in Jerusalem. . . . Yet a time is coming and has now come when the true worshipers will worship the Father in spirit and truth, for they are the kind of worshipers the Father seeks" (John 4:21, 23; see also Luke 17:21b; John 3:5–6).

3. Summary

Muslims throughout the world are united by the prescribed pilgrimage (hajj) to Mecca at least once in their lifetime. It is a time of unity that strengthens the Muslims' identity and encourages them to have a global view of their religion. The observance combines elements of humility and thanksgiving.

While pilgrimage has been practiced by Christians in some periods and places, it is not prescribed in the New Testament. However, various days of celebration, such as the festivals of Christmas and the Feast of the Resurrection

(Easter), are celebrated almost universally in the church. Many Christians down through the ages have preceded the celebrations of Christmas and Easter with special services during the seasons of Advent and Lent. These observances of meditation and prayer are spiritually beneficial to the individual and unite Christians in a spirit of joy and devotion.

Here is how Ergun Mehmet Caner and Fetthi Emir Caner contrast the meanings of holy days in Christianity and Islam:

> Christians must understand that Islamic holidays differ in both essence and meaning from the holy days that Christians observe. First, and of most importance, Christian holidays remember divine interventions, while Islamic celebrations are based upon human accomplishments. In Christianity, we celebrate Easter as the resurrection of our Lord Jesus and His completion of the sacrifice for our sins. In Islam, 'Eid-ul-Adha celebrates Abraham's willingness to sacrifice Ishmael, not Allah's substitution of the ram in the thicket. In Christianity we celebrate the birth of the Savior, Jesus Christ, for our redemption. Islam celebrates Mawlid al-Nabi, the birth date of Muhammad. . . . Christianity and Judaism recognize Passover as the work of God sparing the firstborn children of the Israelites. Muslims mark the end of their own personal sacrifice in Ramadan with 'Eid-ul-Fitr. The complete inversion of the purpose of holy days cannot be overstated.[7]

For discussion questions, see study guide 25.

13

Brief Summation

1. **Qur'an:** Allah is transcendent and merciful and responds to those who surrender to him.
   Bible: God is transcendent, merciful, and personal, and demonstrates his love for the ungodly and his enemies by sending his Son.

2. **Qur'an:** Allah adjusts his justice to meet human ability.
   Bible: God is holy and just and meets his own just requirements in his Son, the Messiah.

3. **Qur'an:** The crucifixion of Jesus did not take place. It only "appeared so" (Surah 4:157).
   Bible: The crucifixion is a biblical and historical fact. The cross is a sign of the love of God. On it the Lamb of God willingly offered himself for the sins of the world.

4. **Qur'an:** Jesus is the son of Mary.
   Bible: Jesus is the human son of Mary and the eternal Son of God.

5. **Qur'an:** Jesus is a great prophet.
   Bible: Jesus is more than a prophet. He is the Savior and Redeemer of the world.

6. **Qur'an:** Salvation is by Allah's decree, his mercy, and forgiveness without atonement, plus human works, which one hopes will tip the scales of justice in one's favor.
   Bible: Salvation is by God's grace through faith in Jesus, the Savior, who by his atoning sacrifice tipped the scales completely in our favor.

7. **Qur'an:** An optimistic view of human nature as having no inborn sin.
   Bible: A realistic view of human nature as being sinful.

8. **Qur'an:** A life under the burden of requirements, sin, guilt, and uncertainty.
   Bible: A life under the grace of God, lived by faith in Jesus, the Son of God.

9. **Qur'an:** A life that is lived under the shadow of the final judgment: Have I done enough? Must I suffer on the "bridge of hell"? What has Allah decreed for me?
   Bible: A life under the grace of God, lived by faith in the Savior, free from condemnation, in the certainty of eternal life.

10. **Qur'an:** A life lived as a slave complying with and conforming to the "straight path" (Surah 1:6) of submission to Allah with prescribed ablutions, prayers, fasting, pilgrimage, poor dues, foods, and dress.
    Bible: A life lived as a child of the Father "by faith in the Son of God" (Gal. 2:20), delighting in the godly life as a child of light.

11. **Qur'an:** A life in awe of Allah's greatness in hope of personal reward.
    Bible: A life in awe of God's grace in Jesus Christ lived in thanksgiving.

12. **Qur'an:** A righteousness through submission to Allah and by acts of piety and charity.
    Bible: A righteousness that comes from God and is by faith in Jesus, the Messiah, the Son of God, evidencing the fruit of the Spirit to the glory of God the Father.

Part II

14

The Ultimate Questions of Life

A. How can I have the certainty of eternal life?

■ Is this life all there is? Is it possible to know for sure that I need not fear the final judgment? Can I have certainty of eternal life?

1. The Qur'an

The Qur'an answers that to gain Paradise you are to believe in the God of Abraham, who is Allah; be a Muslim, "one who submits" to Allah; and acknowledge that Allah is the living God and that Muhammad is his prophet. This, however, is not all that is required for certainty. According to the Qur'an, you must live the life of a Muslim. That is, you must pray, observing the ablutions and prescribed prayers; you must pay the poor-dues; you must observe Ramadan; and you must participate in the hajj once in your lifetime, if possible. While there is forgiveness with repentance and Muhammad's intercession, your good works must outweigh your bad deeds on the scales of justice at the final judgment (Surah 23:102). Those who give up their life in jihad will enter Paradise immediately, unless they have "some debts to pay" or "a major problem." Many hold that all believers in Allah, except some prophets and martyrs, must still pass over the "bridge of hell" and may have to suffer for sins in order to be assured of Paradise. The when and if of entering Paradise is always a question. When can I be sure that the scales of justice will tip in my favor? A Muslim submits to the will of Allah, but what has Allah willed? Has Allah willed that I should be in Paradise or in hell? These questions arise in view of what the Qur'an states: "Allah sendeth astray whom He will, and whom He will He guideth" (Surah 74:31), and "if We [Allah] had so willed, We could have given every soul its guidance, but . . . I will fill hell with the jinn and mankind together" (Surah 32:13). One's final destiny always remains doubtful.

2. The Bible

In the Bible there is no uncertainty concerning the heart and will of God. The Lord God "wants all men to be saved and to come to a knowledge of the truth" (1 Tim. 2:4). The Bible states that we may have certainty of eternal life through Jesus, the Lamb of God, who is the atoning sacrifice for our sins. The question is asked in the book of Revelation, "These in white robes (before the throne of God)—who are they, and where did they come from?" The answer is given, "They have washed their robes and made them white in the blood of the Lamb" (Rev. 7:13–14).

Jesus's perfect life and sacrificial death are sufficient atonement to pay for all the sins of the world. On the cross Christ accomplished the "great exchange." He took my sins and in exchange gave me forgiveness. He took my condemnation and in exchange gave me his righteousness. He took my death and in exchange gave me life eternal. Through faith in him the "great exchange" becomes mine. This eternal life in Christ is a present reality that continues on into eternity. Through daily repentance and faith, "the blood of Jesus . . . purifies us from all sin" (1 John 1:7). We can be certain that by God's grace through faith in Jesus as Savior, we shall indeed enter paradise. There is no need to suffer for sins on the bridge of hell before we enter God's presence. Jesus assured the criminal on the cross, "Today you will be with me in paradise" (Luke 23:43). This assurance gives us great "comfort and joy" in the present and until our dying day.

B. What is the nature of humankind?

1. The Qur'an

The Qur'an presents human beings as basically upright, as Adam was when he was created. Human beings are "weak," however, and may sin in time of testing and temptation. Allah does not demand more than human beings are able to accomplish. He is merciful and forgiving, diminishing his justice for the sake of mercy. However, human beings will be judged. They must surrender to Allah, must observe the Five Pillars of a godly life, and must ask for forgiveness before they die.

2. The Bible

The Bible presents human beings as created in the image of God. They fell from that perfect state in which they reflected the glory of God, however, in response to the temptation of Satan. They fell into a state of sin, and thenceforth all humankind has been born sinful (Ps. 51:5). This explains why "every inclination of his heart is evil from childhood" (Gen. 8:21). It explains why it is "human nature" to be rebellious and indifferent toward God and selfish and neglectful of our fellow human beings. It is not hard to sin. It is not just a weakness; there is an *inclination* to do so. One does not have to think, "Now I will think or do something that is wrong." It comes naturally. Since "out of the heart proceed evil thoughts" quite naturally, human beings are sinful and unable to rescue themselves from their predicament.

In view of this, how does God save humankind? Does he diminish his justice and accommodate himself to human weakness, or does he deny his love and condemn all sinners to eternal death? How does God satisfy both his love and his justice? The Bible reveals that God in mercy, out of pure undeserved love, came in the person of his Son. The Lord God became a human being, lived our life, died our death, and paid the price we could not pay. He atoned for our sins, thus fully satisfying both his love and his justice.

This "amazing grace" of God in Jesus, his Son, has freed us from the curse of God's holy law and has given us forgiveness of our sins and eternal life. God's love has met his justice in the life, death, and resurrection of his Son. God remains God. God remains merciful and righteous. Neither God's love nor his justice are compromised, nor is humankind abandoned. God in his "amazing grace" has found a way for humankind to have friendship and intimate fellowship with him. It is by God's grace through faith in his Son.

C. How does God connect with me personally?

1. The Qur'an

The Qur'an reveals that Allah has chosen some for life and some for death. However, a person is held accountable. Surah 3:31 exhorts humankind to love Allah: "If ye love Allah, follow me [Muhammad]; Allah will love you and forgive you your sins." By loving Allah, a person gains His love and forgiveness. People must surrender to and obey Him. Paradise is not a free gift but is given to those who love Allah and "believe and do good works" (Surah 47:12; 85:11). Allah "connects" with people through the Qur'an. In the Qur'an, Allah is merciful but transcendent. He is not in close fellowship or relationship with his people. He is not father or friend to his people. One surrenders to him as his slave. One is required to believe in the Five Articles of Faith (belief in Allah, his Angels, his Books, his Apostles, and the Day of Judgment) and to observe the Five Pillars of Islam: The Shahada (Creed), Salat (Prayer), Zakat (Almsgiving), Sawm (Ramadan), and the Hajj (Pilgrimage). One's final destiny is dependent on the determinate will of Allah: He "sendeth whom He will astray, and guideth whom He will" (Surah 14:4; 16:93).

2. The Bible

The Bible reveals that the Lord God of Abraham connected with me by becoming a human being himself. He passionately pursued me while I was still far from him. The great wonder is that God's heart is filled with such intense love for me that he gives his one and only Son so that "whoever believes in him shall not perish but have eternal life" (John 3:16). Jesus, as the good Shepherd, came seeking, saving, calling, and beckoning me as his sheep to come back to him. This he did long before I came to faith or did acts of obedience, piety, or charity. As the Lord God says, "I was found by those who did not seek me. I revealed myself to those who did not ask for me" (Rom. 10:20).

This great love for me, expressed in the Shepherd's becoming the sacrificial Lamb, is so powerful on the cross that as a magnet it draws me to him in faith (John 12:32). In the Gospels, in the acts of those who betray Jesus, deny him, condemn him, abuse him, speak ill of him, and fail to defend him, I see the greatness of my own sin. Nevertheless, in the person of Christ, in his resolute love, his patient suffering, his strong determination, his offering himself as the atoning sacrifice, his words "Father forgive them," I see that "where sin increased, grace abounded all the more" (Rom. 5:20 RSV). Drawn to that cross, I am moved to repent of my sins and trust in Jesus as my Savior. I personally know the love of Christ, and in knowing it, I know the love of God my Father.

Through faith in Christ I am welcomed into a personal, intimate relationship with God as my Father, and I become "a temple of the Holy Spirit" (1 Cor. 6:19). God is my Father, and I am his child and heir of eternal life. In the person of his Son my restless heart finds rest, pardon, peace, purpose, wholeness, and hope. Nothing in this life or the next can separate me from the love of God in Christ Jesus my Lord and Savior.

Because of Christ, I now look upon myself and all other human beings differently. Now we are not only precious because we are special creatures of the Lord God, but we are doubly precious because we are redeemed with the priceless blood of the Lamb of God.

D. What meaning does my life have with God?

1. The Qur'an

The relationship of a Muslim to Allah is one of submission as a slave. Muhammad spoke of himself as a slave of Allah. The devout Muslim likewise delights in being Allah's slave. Muslims live under the compassionate Allah, subject to the determinate will of Allah. There are daily prescribed ablutions and prayers that must be done. There is the repeated reminder in the Qur'an that one must face the final judgment, where the scales of justice must be tipped in one's favor. The relationship with Allah is not the intimate relationship of a child to a Father, since Allah is far above and transcendent of his creation.

Meaning in life for the Muslim is found in being a slave of Allah, living by the Five Pillars of Islam, and belonging to Umma, or the Islamic community.

2. The Bible

By God's grace through faith in Jesus, I become a child of God and intimately know God as Father. (To say that God is Father does not imply that God has a wife. Mary was the wife of Joseph, and Jesus was conceived by the Holy Spirit [see Matt. 1:20].) I belong to the Father's family. I am no longer alone; I belong. I pray with other members of the family, "Our Father . . ." In Jesus, the Messiah, God has revealed his heart of love. As a child of God I need not fear, for by knowing Jesus I know the Father's heart. In this is eternal certainty and eternal comfort in the midst of trial and temptation, trouble and tragedy, crisis and distress.

Because of Christ, my life is not without meaning or significance. God, my Father, has a purpose for me. My life is not empty. I am created for God. I am redeemed from the past "futile ways" of this world by the precious blood of the Lamb (1 Pet. 1:18 RSV). I find meaning in my life by living for the One who for my sake died and rose again (2 Cor. 5:15). Even the smallest act of love, such as giving a cup of cold water to someone, has significance and is recognized by the Lord as an act of worth (Matt. 10:42). My life of love and service is not coerced, or forced. It is freely offered in thanksgiving as a "living sacrifice" acceptable to God through Jesus Christ (Rom. 12:1; cf. 1 Pet. 2:5).

Now I walk through this life not in fear or uncertainty, not in apprehension of the final judgment, not in passive surrender, but in a living, dynamic faith. "The life I live in the body, I live by faith in the Son of God, who loved me and gave himself for me" (Gal. 2:20).

E. How can I face adversity?

1. The Qur'an

The Muslim faces adversity with an attitude of submission and surrender: "It is the will of Allah." In the will of Allah is peace. With the strength of Allah, one can endure the testings of life. The Muslim may say, "I am Allah's slave; whatever he wills I will accept. Allah is merciful and compassionate."

2. The Bible

As a Christian, I submit and surrender to the will of the Father. I do so not as a slave but as a child, one who knows the heart of the Father. I am comforted by the providence of God and the fact that God is in control. However, we have all wondered, if God is in control, why does he allow such disasters in the world and in my personal life? My ultimate comfort is in the loving heart of the Father, revealed in the life of Jesus and especially in his suffering, death, and resurrection.

As a Christian in the midst of adversity, I stand with the risen Christ and look back through the empty tomb and the blood-stained cross to my Father's heart, who in love gave his only Son. Through the suffering, death, and resurrection of Jesus, I see the heart of the loving Father and know that "God is for" me (Rom. 8:31) and nothing can separate me from his love in Christ (Rom. 8:35). In fact, I am more than a conqueror through him who loved me (Rom. 8:37). As a child of God, I know and believe that in all things my Father is even now working for my good (Rom. 8:28). As a father weeps for his suffering child, so the Father weeps with me, cares for me, and comforts me. I know this because Christ "was deeply moved in spirit and troubled" at the loss of his friend Lazarus and "wept" (John 11:33, 35). I am therefore drawn to him to receive comfort, hope, and strength. No matter what the struggle or suffering, because of Christ my life will not end in defeat but in triumph over sin, death, and Satan (John 16:33).

F. What about the differences between the Qur'an and the Bible?

As one reads the Qur'an and in it the criticism of the Bible, one cannot help but wonder, why would so much of the Bible be considered to be corrupted unless one has a problem with some of the Bible's teaching? Further, why would the Qur'an, which was recorded six hundred years after Christ, be more accurate than the eyewitness accounts recorded in the Bible—accounts that were written twenty to sixty years after Christ's resurrection?

There are serious doctrinal differences between the Qur'an and the Bible, such as the Qur'an's many denials that Jesus is the Son of God, denial of the crucifixion and Christ's atoning sacrifice for sin, omission of the Passover at the culmination of the plagues in Egypt, and affirmation that eternal life is obtained by submission to Allah plus good works. Could it be that these doctrinal differences with the Bible contribute to the view that the Bible has been corrupted?

The Bible presents Jesus as the Son of God and Savior of the world; therefore Jesus cannot be merely a prophet or messenger. If Jesus is only a prophet, he is a deceiver. He cannot be merely a prophet on the second rung of the ladder to heaven, under Joseph, Enoch, Aaron, Moses, and Abraham. Either Jesus is Lord or he is a liar. Either he was a deranged deceiver or he is the Son of God come to this earth as Savior for all people.

The Bible's eyewitness accounts of Jesus's miracles, his casting out demons, his raising the dead, his sacrifice on the cross, his glorious resurrection, and his triumphant ascension all proclaim that he came to this earth with a plan and a purpose. He was filled with a burning desire to rescue human beings and bring them back into a relationship of friendship and fellowship with the Father.

G. How should the faith be propagated?

1. The Qur'an

The Qur'an projects a vision of the world being united under submission to Allah through the message of the Prophet Muhammad in the Qur'an. This submission involves all of a person's life, all of government, and all of society. Ideally, it takes the form of an Islamic theocratic state such as Muhammad established in Medina.

According to the Qur'an, there is to be no "compulsion" in religion; however, there is justifiable jihad. When there is any form of resistance to, rejection of, or threat to the message given to Muhammad, one may take extreme forms of aggressive or "defensive" measures.

2. The Bible

The New Testament calls for the teaching of Jesus to be heralded to all people. The Lord God has a vision of uniting humankind with himself through the death of his Son and of uniting human beings with one another through the body of Christ on the cross. Christ's followers are to be witnesses of this good news.

Jesus predicted that his followers would be rejected, persecuted, put in prison, and falsely charged, but they were to count it joy to suffer for the name of Christ. His followers are not to retaliate or return evil for evil. Rather, since the Father has shown them undeserved kindness, they are to love their enemies and pray for those who despitefully use them. They are to return good for evil and so show themselves to be children of the heavenly Father. They are to remember that the kingdom of God is not outward but "within you" (Luke 17:21). Thus they are to live lives of love and godliness.

The believers in Christ are lights and leaven in society. They change people's lives with the Word of Christ. They transform society by transforming the human heart with the gospel. They are "in the world" but "not of the world." They are "living letters" and "ambassadors" of peace and reconciliation, bringing faith, hope, and love to all people.

H. Who is the God of Abraham?

■ As never before, we are aware of many religions and many views of God. How can I be certain who the true God is?

You may recall that this book began with Abraham. Both the Islamic faith and the Christian faith profess belief in the God of Abraham. The question then is, Who is the God of Abraham?

1. Is the God of Abraham Our Father?

Muslims look for the answer to the question, Who is the God of Abraham? in the revelation given to Muhammad. As the Qur'an states, "We believe in Allah and that which is revealed unto us and that which was revealed unto Abraham" (Surah 2:136). Again, "(We follow) the religion of Abraham" (Surah 2:135). Allah, the God of Abraham, is the "Lord of the Worlds: The Beneficent, the Merciful" (Surah 1:2–3). However, the Qur'an never speaks of Allah as Father, nor says that Jesus is his Son.

Jesus in the Gospels reveals that the God of Abraham is his and our Father. Jesus has a unique, divine, eternal, and personal relationship with his Father: "I came from the Father and . . . now I am leaving this world and going back to the Father" (John 16:28). Jesus is declared by the Father to be "my Son, whom I love; with him I am well pleased" (Matt. 3:17). Jesus taught his disciples to pray, "Our Father . . ." (Matt. 6:9). On the cross he prayed, "Father, forgive them" (Luke 23:34), and "Father, into your hands I commit my spirit" (Luke 23:46). The God of Abraham is Father, the Father of the Son of God, our Lord Jesus Christ. Through Christ, the God of Abraham is our Father and we are his children.

2. Is the God of Abraham a God of Love?

The Qur'an reveals that Allah responds in love to his followers when they ward off evil (Surah 3:76), are "steadfast" (Surah 3:146), "put their trust (in Him)" (Surah 3:159), and are "equitable" (Dawood: deal justly; Surah 5:42). Allah's love is conditional upon a person's uprightness of life and a person's first loving Allah: "If ye love Allah, follow me [Muhammad]; Allah will love you and forgive you your sins" (Surah 3:31).

In the Bible Jesus reveals that the God of Abraham is a God of love. The Lord God of Abraham is a God of undeserved and unconditional love through Jesus his Son. The loving heart of God finds Abram in Ur of the Chaldeans while his family is involved in worship of the moon god and belief in the zodiac. He shows Abram his unexpected love and rescues him from a life of idolatry and superstition. The Lord God calls him to a new land with a promise that in his offspring all the nations of the earth will be blessed. Jesus, in the fullest sense, was that "offspring." Jesus was the very personification of God's promise of love and grace given to Abram/Abraham. The Bible says, "God is love. . . . This is love: not that we loved God, but that he loved us and sent his Son as an atoning sacrifice for our sins" (1 John 4:8, 10). The God of Abraham is the God of love revealed in his Son.

3. The God of Abraham Is the Great I AM

Genesis 15:1 states, "The word of the LORD [Hebrew: Yahweh] came to Abram in a vision." The covenant God, Yahweh, is the great I AM revealed to Moses (Exod. 3:14). Centuries after Abraham and Moses, in a dialogue with some Jewish leaders, Jesus said: "Your father Abraham rejoiced at the thought of seeing my day; he saw it and was glad." The Jews sneered, "You are not yet fifty years old, . . . and you have seen Abraham!" Jesus responded, "Before Abraham was born, I am!" Considering these words blasphemous, "they picked up stones to stone him" (John 8:56–59). Here Jesus clearly identifies himself as the great I AM; thus *he identifies himself as the God of Abraham.*

Philip expressed to Jesus the yearning that is in every person's heart: "Show us the Father and that will be enough for us." Jesus gave him a straightforward answer: "Don't you know me, Philip, even after I have been among you such a long time? Anyone who has seen me has seen the Father" (John 14:8–9). In other words, when I want to see the God of Abraham, I can look at Jesus. As a believer in Jesus, I rejoice with Abraham to see Jesus as the God of Abraham, the great I AM, the Savior of the world. (See also section A.2.b, "The deity of Jesus," in chapter 4.)

15

Sharing the Good News with Muslims

A. Become Loving and Respectful

1. Be Loving

Now that you have considered this comparison between the Qur'an and the Bible, my prayer is that you have a burning desire to share the living Christ with a Muslim. With the world Muslim population having grown to 1.6 billion in 2009, and with the growth of Muslims in North America, our contact with Muslims, and our children's contact with them, will become more and more frequent. There are exciting opportunities coming our way to give a "reason for the hope" we have in Christ. When these opportunities come, may we give our witness with "gentleness and respect" (1 Pet. 3:15).

God's great love is passionate, persistent, and pursuing in a very personal way in his Son Jesus, the Messiah. His great love yearns to reach the heart of the person who is Muslim. Jesus came as the seeking Shepherd (John 10). Jesus is in earnest to rescue every person. He eagerly longs "to save what was lost" (Luke 19:10). As followers of Jesus, the Messiah, we earnestly and eagerly desire to demonstrate that same passion for reaching out to our Muslim acquaintances. Pastor Peter Reid, missionary to Muslims in Indonesia, suggests this acrostic:

I   I
S   SINCERELY
L   LOVE
A   ALL
M MUSLIMS

2. Be Convinced of the Need to Witness

As Christians we are to be convinced of the need and importance of witnessing to Muslims. We are compelled by the love of God in Christ for us and for all people to share Jesus as Son of God and Savior with Muslims. Jesus died on the cross for people who are Muslim. He is the "way and the truth and the life" (John 14:6) for all people, including Muslims. He is the Lamb of God who takes away the sin of the world and of each and every person. Muslims are beloved to him and to us. Do not cease to pray that they may come to faith in Jesus as their Lord and Savior.

3. Be a Friend to the Muslim

Dudley Woodberry, professor of Islamic studies at the School of World Missions at Fuller Theological Seminary, says that after 9/11 "it is a very open situation for us to befriend Muslims [in the United States] and accompany them shopping, do things with them, try in various ways to support them and do things that will help them feel more like they belong. In building friendships in this way, often it becomes very natural to share our own motivations and concerns." Avery Willis, senior vice president of the Southern Baptist Convention International Mission Board, states: "All we want to do is give them an opportunity to know the truth in Jesus Christ. . . . The biggest difficulty is just getting an opportunity for them to be exposed to the truth."[1] To do so we must first win their trust and be a friend to them.

B. Become Aware and Informed

Before we can effectively witness, it is imperative that we become aware and informed of the cultural and religious differences between Christians and Muslims. Alert to these differences, as representatives of Christ, we want to demonstrate understanding and unconditional love to the Muslim. As Christians we will want to build a relationship with our Muslim acquaintance. The believer in Christ will attempt to show goodwill and the authentic love of Christ. The Christian can expect the Holy Spirit to open doors (Acts 14:27) and present opportunities to witness to the good news of Jesus Christ. As believers, we will want to be alert to these "door openers."

When the opportunity presents itself, you and I as believers in Christ, will want to be fortified and equipped to share in a personal and winsome way what Jesus means to us. And we want to be sufficiently informed so that we are able to share the gospel in a way that is meaningful and relevant to our Muslim acquaintance. Therefore, consider the following.

1. Important Customs to Keep in Mind

Because of differences in what is considered proper, it is important that you and I are aware of the customs that are generally considered acceptable or unacceptable.

The Caner brothers (former Muslims) list some customs important to remember:

1. Upon entering a Muslim home, you may ask, "Shall I leave my shoes here?"
2. When a guest at mealtime, eat everything that is offered to you.
3. Never greet Muslims by shaking their left hand.
4. When extending hospitality in your home, do not offer alcoholic beverages.
5. Do not serve pork, lard-based food, or shellfish.
6. Do not have your dog in the house. Dogs are considered unclean, except by those of the Maliki school.
7. Most Islamic cultures, although not all, forbid casual conversation with members of the opposite sex. For a woman to speak forcefully to a man shows disrespect. A Christian man who speaks to a Muslim woman without her husband present insults her husband.
8. Do not call a Muslim your "brother." This has theological implications that will bother him.[2]

To their list can be added:

9. Don't attack and ridicule aspects of the Islam faith, especially Muhammad and the Qur'an.
10. Open your home to your new friend.

Roland Cap Ehlke in *Speaking the Truth in Love to Muslims* adds some additional dos and don'ts:[3]

Do	Don't
Know what the Bible teaches.	*Don't treat the Qur'an disrespectfully.* It is one thing to disagree with the teachings of Islam, another to ridicule them.
Respect Muslims. Remember that Jesus died for them.	*Don't treat the Bible disrespectfully.* For example, don't place it on the floor.
Show sincere respect and friendship to Muslims.	*Don't get into the battle of the books—the Qur'an versus the Bible.* Let the Bible speak for itself. The straightforward assertions of the Bible are powerful, and the Holy Spirit works through them.

Do	Don't
Listen to Muslims' needs. Ask questions.	*Don't make assumptions about what the Muslims believe.* Ask him or her. Muslims often are not that well informed about their own faith.
Become well informed about Islam.	*Don't attack the name of Allah.* This is a touchy issue, since Arabic-speaking Christians use the name Allah to refer to the God of the Bible.
Be available. We may not appreciate what a tremendous step it is for Muslims to convert.	*Don't be insulting.* Never hold the Qur'an below one's waist, because it would be insulting to do that.
Pray for Muslims. Ask that Muslim hearts may be softened to the gospel by the Holy Spirit.	*Don't be afraid.* Paul writes, "For God did not give us a spirit of timidity, but a spirit of power, of love and of self-discipline" (2 Tim. 1:7).

2. Background Information

a. Muslim Views on "Western Christianity"

Muslims in general do not distinguish between Christianity and America. In our conversations with Muslims, we need to be mindful to distinguish between our Christian faith and values and the secular influence in North American culture.

It is good to know and recognize that there are moral values that we as Christians have in common with Muslims, such as honoring the sanctity of life and the importance of respect in relationships, decent speech, and behavior. We need to share that we are concerned about the materialism and decadence of the secular culture. We do well to make it clear that as believers in Christ we stand for sexual purity, convey that we are honest in our dealings with others, and share how important it is for us to show love and respect between husband and wife and children in our family, and our desire to support and help one another, including our elderly parents. *This is important to the Muslim.*

In your association with a beloved Muslim, share how you value the fellowship you have with believers in Jesus. While you are "in the world," you do not want to be "of the world." Note that a person's wearing a cross does not necessarily mean that the person is a Christian. Explain that the immoral behavior of any person wearing a cross is very painful for you to see. Also, avoid making political statements and defending America's foreign policy.

b. Muslim Assumptions concerning the Christian Faith

■ **Assumption: The true Christian gospel was changed by Peter, Paul, and John.**

The Gospels and Epistles were written twenty-five to sixty years after Jesus's resurrection, when eyewitnesses were still living. The Qur'an was given to

Muhammad approximately six hundred years later. The Qur'an itself extols the Christian Scriptures (although it states that they are inaccurate).

The truthfulness of the New Testament Scriptures is demonstrated by: (a) the great change from Saturday to Sunday as a day of worship; (b) the discontinuation of temple sacrifices; (c) believers' willingness to die for the living Christ; (d) the worship of Jesus; (e) the growth of the church. These all testify to the truth of Jesus's crucifixion, death, and resurrection and the great social change brought about because of the person of Jesus, the Messiah.

■ **Assumption: Christians are divided and weak.**

Muslims also are divided into various groups, such as Sunnis and Shi'ites; the Sufis; the Druze and the Ahmadiyya. Muslims are divided on such basic doctrines as free will and who is a true Muslim. Various Islamic groups have fought against one another going back to the days of Ali, the fourth caliph, who was assassinated in AD 661.

■ **Assumption: Western "Christian" civilization is decadent.**

"As governments have strayed from Christian principles, immorality has increased. Europe is not Christian, and no society is any more diverse in religion than that in North America."[4] So while the Western nations may have had Christian roots, it is questionable whether they can be considered Christian nations today. The love of Jesus for us, however, is strong, and many Christians are living a sincere, godly life.

3. Be Aware of Similarities and Differences

To witness effectively as Christians, we must first be clear with regard to the similarities and the differences between the Christian and the Islamic faiths.

a. Similarity in Belief

1. Muslims believe that Jesus was born of the Virgin Mary and is the Messiah.
2. Muslims believe that Jesus was a great prophet.
3. Muslims believe that Jesus will return.
4. Muslims believe in the sanctity of life; however, the soul [Arabic: ruh] is given in the fourth month.

b. Differences of Belief

1. Muslims do not believe that Jesus is the eternal Son of God. He is only a great "messenger."
2. Muslims do not believe that Jesus is the Savior, the Mediator, and the Reconciler to God. Human beings do not need a Mediator, Reconciler, or Savior; they are born "upright."

3. Muslims do not believe that Jesus was actually crucified. It only "appeared" so.

4. Muslims do not believe that Jesus died on the cross and rose on the third day. He did not die but was taken up to Allah.

5. Muslims believe that Jesus will return and destroy all crosses because he was not crucified. They believe that he will compel all people to become Muslim.

6. Muslims do not believe that human beings are born sinful. They are born "upright" and sinless as Adam. Christians believe we are born sinful and in need of rebirth (Ps. 51:5; John 3:5–7).

7. Muslims do not believe that we are saved by grace through faith alone in Jesus Christ. A person is saved at the final judgment by surrendering to Allah, asking for forgiveness, living a life of good works, and, many believe, suffering on the "bridge of hell." Christians believe that they are saved now from sin and eternal death by God's grace through faith in Jesus, "the Lamb of God who takes away the sin of the world" (John 1:29), that "whoever believes in the Son has eternal life" (John 3:36), and that they "will not be condemned" (John 5:24).

4. The Challenge of Secular Relativism

Relativism in the culture in which we live holds that in a pluralistic society there are numerous ethnic and religious views of equal worth. All beliefs and principles are not only to be respected but accepted as of equal value. No judgments are to be made. All truth is relative depending on one's viewpoint or perspective. Therefore, there is no absolute foundation of truth.

The principles of relativism and toleration would maintain that both the Qur'an and the Bible are equal sources of divine revelation. The Caner brothers, Mehmet Ergun and Fethi Emir, both former Muslims, state: "The tolerant postmodernist asserts that both books are divine because both contain some truth. [But] unless God lies, changes his mind, or makes mistakes—in which cases He is less than God—it cannot be that both books are divine. . . . The Bible is either absolute or it is obsolete."[5]

The Muslim believes that the Qur'an is the true revelation of Allah. The Bible, in particular the Injil ("Gospel," according to the Qur'an), is to be treated with respect but also caution. The Muslim believes that various persons changed the Bible that has come down to us. They are those who hide (Surah 2:140), "knowingly conceal the truth" (Surah 2:146), "distort," and "speak a lie concerning Allah" (Surah 3:78). It is on this basis that Muslims can reject the clear words of Scripture pointing to Jesus as the Son of God and Savior of the world and tell of his being crucified and raised from the dead.

C. Be Fortified with Biblical Truth

1. *The Reliability of the Bible*

It is wise not to get into a "battle of the books" with a Muslim. The Muslim must first come to know Jesus for who he really is. Then he or she will also believe the word of Jesus. However, it is good for us to be informed as to the different understandings of the Qur'an and the Bible.

To the Muslim, the Qur'an is a direct copy of the original "Mother Book" written by Allah in heaven and transmitted to Muhammad. Thus, the Qur'an is not words of Muhammad but direct words of Allah. The Muslim may question whether the Bible is the Word of God, asking, "Why are not the Gospels all the same? Why does the Bible include the writings of men such as Peter, John, and Paul?" We might answer that the biblical books are written from the different perspectives of eyewitnesses, just as witnesses of an auto accident might give different perspectives on the same event.

For our part, we ought to speak of the Bible as the inspired Word of God and emphasize that it is the eyewitness account of people who saw Jesus. Do not be alarmed at the questions raised by a Muslim. Be quietly assured and resolved in your heart as to the Bible's truthfulness. You may point out that even the Qur'an states that the gospel contains God's guidance and light: "We [Allah] bestowed on him [Jesus] the Gospel wherein is guidance and a light, confirming that which was (revealed) before it in the Torah" (Surah 5:46).

It is imperative that as Christians we are certain concerning the inspiration, inerrancy, reliability, and authenticity of the Bible so that we may speak with quiet confidence. The testimony of the Scriptures is consistent and powerful.

1. Jesus in his day believed that the very words of the Old Testament were inspired and were not corrupted: "Do not think that I have come to abolish the Law or the Prophets; I have not come to abolish them but to fulfill them. I tell you the truth, until heaven and earth disappear, not the smallest letter, nor the least stroke of a pen, will by any means disappear from the Law until everything is accomplished" (Matt. 5:17–18). Note how the prophets received messages "from God." It was not their thoughts but God's Word that they received. (For examples, see Ezekiel 2:1; 6:1; 7:1; 12:1; 13:1; 15:1; 16:1; 17:1; 18:1; 21:1; 22:1; 23:1; 25:1; 26:1; 27:1; 29:1, and so on.)
2. St. Peter refutes the idea that in his writing he is presenting stories similar to the Greek and Roman myths: "We did not follow cleverly invented stories when we told you about the power and coming of our Lord Jesus Christ, but we were eyewitness of his majesty" (2 Pet. 1:16).
3. St. John likewise cites his personal eyewitness testimony: "That which was from the beginning, which we have heard, which we have seen with our eyes, which we have looked at and our hands have touched—this

The Text of the Qur'an

The Qur'an in the first generation was memorized and recorded on bone, camel hide, palm leaves, stones, and the like. Abu Bakr (632–34), the first caliph, collected the first fragments and copies of the Qur'an. During the rule of the third caliph, Uthman (644–56), the second stage of the compilation of the Qur'an took place.

> Apart from the compilation of the Qur'an that Hafsa [wife of Muhammad] had in Medina, there were four other collections in circulation: in Kufa (Iraq), Bassora (Basra; Iraq), Damascus (Syria) and Homs (Syria). A commission was therefore made responsible for establishing the definitive text of the Qur'an. It was based on Hafsa's compilation, and because discrepancies were found between the versions of the Qur'an the commission had to decide which one was authentic and conformed to the Prophet's own version. 'Uthman then ordered that all other versions of the text be destroyed. . . .
>
> 'Uthman's decision did not please all Muslims. The Shi'i Muslims in particular believed that their teachings were more clearly supported by the Kufa collection attributed to Ibn Mas'ud (one of the Prophet's companions) than by the official compilation of 'Uthman. This played an important part in his ['Uthman's] assassination by Shi'i Muslims.
>
> The original text of the official compilation has not survived and our earliest fragments of the Qur'an date from the second century of the Islamic era.[a]

In *An Introduction to Shi'i Islam* Moojan Momen states, "With regard to the question of the text of the Qur'an, it has already been noted that the early Shi'is believed that the Qur'an had been altered and parts of it had been suppressed."[b] Later Momen states: "The text of the Qur'an in the recension compiled under the direction of the third Caliph, 'Uthman, is accepted by both Sunnis and Shi'is."[c]

Some questions arise: "1. Why did he ['Uthman] have to standardize a common text if a standard text was already in existence? 2. Why did he try to destroy all the other manuscripts if there were no other conflicting manuscripts? 3. Why did he have to use the threat of death to force people to accept his text if everyone had the same text? 4. Why did many people reject his text in favor of their own text?"[d]

[a] Chawkat Moucarry, *The Prophet & the Messiah* (Downers Grove, IL: InterVarsity, 2001), 38–39.
[b] Moojan Momen, *An Introduction to Shi'i Islam: The History and Doctrine of Twelver Shi'ism* (New Haven: Yale University Press, 1985), 81.
[c] Ibid., 173.
[d] Riccoldo da Montrecroce and Martin Luther, *Islam in the Crucible: Can It Pass the Test?*, trans. Thomas C. Pfotenhauer (Kearney, NE: Morris Publishing, 2002). Quoting Robert Morey, *The Islamic Invasion* (Eugene, OR: Harvest House, 1992), 97.

we proclaim concerning the Word of life. The life appeared; we have seen it and testify to it, and we proclaim to you the eternal life, which was with the Father and has appeared to us" (1 John 1:1–2).

4. St. Paul, who was a contemporary of Jesus, likewise states that he is "passing on" that which was believed from the very beginning, following

Jesus's resurrection: "Now brothers, I want to remind you of the gospel I preached to you, which you received and on which you have taken your stand. By this gospel you are saved, if you hold firmly to the word I preached to you. Otherwise, you have believed in vain. For what I received I passed on to you as of first importance: that Christ died for our sins according to the Scriptures, that he was buried, that he was raised on the third day according to the Scriptures, and that he appeared to Peter, and then to the Twelve" (1 Cor. 15:1–5). Paul clearly states: "This is what we speak, not in words taught us by human wisdom but in words taught by the Spirit" (1 Cor. 2:13).

5. The Evangelist St. Luke, an educated medical doctor, a companion of St. Paul, and a careful historian, takes care to present only what is trustworthy and verifiable: "Many have undertaken to draw up an account of the things that have been fulfilled among us, just as they were handed down to us by those who from the first were eyewitnesses and servants of the word. Therefore, since I myself have carefully investigated everything from the beginning, it seemed good also to me to write an orderly account to you, most excellent Theophilus, so that you may know the certainty of the things you have been taught" (Luke 1:1–4).

Your Muslim conversation partner may ask how the books of the Bible became the canon or "standard" of the Word of God. The explanation is that the books endorsed in the canon had established themselves and authenticated themselves as the Word of God. Subsequently, they were recognized by the believing community as being authoritative and the inspired Word of God. The above witnesses state emphatically that their testimony is not distorted, corrupted, or changed. Their testimony, under the Holy Spirit, from the days of Jesus, and recorded when other eyewitnesses were still living, is to be believed rather than the testimony of Muhammad approximately 550 years later. (A helpful resource for such discussions is *The Case for Christ* by Lee Strobel [Zondervan, 1998].)

If your Muslim acquaintance should question the authenticity of the Bible, then, you might reply that you understand that early on there were various versions of the Qur'an and all of them were burned except one, and the early Shi'ites believed some facts were omitted from it. *However, it is wise not to become involved in the ancient controversy between Sunni and Shi'ites. Rather, confidently proceed with your witness.*

Should the Muslim cite liberal critics of the Bible who question the supernatural, one might point out that the same methodology applied to the Bible could be applied to undermine the credibility of the Qur'an as well. In love, do not argue but continue to uphold and quote from the Bible as the Word of God.

2. What the Bible Teaches about Jesus

Before discussing Jesus with a Muslim, the Christian should be aware of what the Bible teaches about Jesus.

a. Jesus Is the Son of God

Muslims, following the Qur'an, are under the impression that Christians believe in three gods. When discussing this with a Muslim, make it clear that we believe only in one God. We do not believe that Jesus is a second god produced by God and his wife, Mary. As we confess in the Nicene Creed, "Jesus is of one 'being' or 'substance' with the Father." We believe in one God with three divine persons. We baptize "in the name [singular] of the Father, and of the Son, and of the Holy Spirit." Jesus is "begotten of the Father from eternity"; that is, he is God's Son from eternity who "was made man." This is a mystery that we accept. We rejoice in the truth that God became man so that we might become children of the heavenly Father.

Here is a list of biblical evidence that Jesus is the Son of God. (The passages marked with asterisks [*] are helpful to cite when a Muslim asks, "When did Jesus ever say he was the Son of God or God?")

1. The Father testified that Jesus is his Son: "This is my Son, whom I love" (Matt. 3:17; Mark 1:11).
2. The angel Gabriel (Gabriel is prominent in the Qur'an) testified that Jesus is the Son of God: "He will be great and will be called the Son of the Most High" (Luke 1:32).
3. The devils testified that Jesus is the Son of God: "Whenever the evil spirits saw him, they fell down before him and cried out, 'You are the Son of God'" (Mark 3:11).
4. Jesus's enemies recognized that he claimed to be the Son of God: "He must die, because he claimed to be the Son of God" (John 19:7).
5. Peter, in answer to Jesus's question "Who do you say I am?" proclaimed on behalf of the apostles that Jesus was the Son of God: "You are the Christ, the Son of the Living God" (Matt. 16:16). To this Jesus gave his approval: "Blessed are you, Simon son of Jonah, for this was not revealed to you by man, but by my Father in heaven" (v. 17).*
6. Jesus himself testified to his being the Son of God: "Father, the time has come. Glorify your Son, that your Son may glorify you. . . . Father, glorify me in your presence with the glory I had with you before the world began" (John 17:1, 5).* "Whatever the Father does the Son also does. . . . Moreover, the Father judges no one, but has entrusted all judgment to the Son, that all may honor the Son just as they honor the Father. He who does not honor the Son does not honor the Father, who sent him" (John 5:19, 22–23).* "Anyone who has seen me has seen the

Father. . . . Believe me when I say that I am in the Father and the Father
is in me" (John 14:9, 11).*

7. Thomas, encountering the risen Lord, exclaimed, "My [the] Lord and
my [the] God." (Thomas's profession is very powerful with the definite
articles in Greek.) Jesus approves of his profession by saying, "Because
you have seen me, you have believed; blessed are those who have not
seen and yet have believed" (John 20:28–29).*

8. Paul (a contemporary of Jesus), persecuted and imprisoned Jesus's
followers. He considered belief in Jesus as the Son of God to be blasphemous (just as a Muslim would). When Jesus appeared to him and
he was converted, however, Paul immediately "began to preach in the
synagogues that Jesus is the Son of God" (Acts 9:20).

9. Jesus was "declared with power to be the Son of God by his resurrection from the dead" (Rom. 1:4). The New Testament records eleven
appearances of the risen Christ.

10. The New Testament refers to Jesus as the "Son of God" 121 times.

b. Jesus Is the Savior

The Bible also teaches that Jesus is the Savior. Jesus proclaimed his mission
to save the lost. His role as Savior was foretold by the angel Gabriel and is
emphasized by the apostles throughout the New Testament.

Here is a list of biblical evidence that Jesus is the Savior. (The Scriptures
marked with an asterisk [*] are helpful to cite when a Muslim asks, "When
did Jesus ever say that he would suffer and die for the sins of the world?")

1. Jesus proclaimed his mission to save.

Luke 19:10: "For the Son of Man came to seek and to save what was
lost."

Mark 10:45: "For even the Son of Man did not come to be served, but
to serve, and to give his life as a ransom for many" (see also Matt.
20:28).*

John 3:14–15: "Just as Moses lifted up the snake in the desert, so
the Son of Man must be lifted up [on the cross], that everyone who
believes in him may have eternal life" (see also John 12:32–33).*

John 10:11: "I am the good shepherd. The good shepherd lays down
his life for the sheep."* Verse 28: "I give them eternal life, and they
shall never perish: no one can snatch them out of my hand." (See
also Luke 15: the search for the lost sheep and the lost coin, and the
longing for the lost son.)

Luke 24:46–47: "This is what is written: The Christ will suffer and
rise from the dead on the third day, and repentance and forgiveness
of sins will be preached in his name."*

Matthew 26:26, 28: "This is my body. . . . This is my blood of the covenant, which is poured out for many for the forgiveness of sins."*

2. The angel Gabriel (who is prominent in the Qur'an) proclaimed Jesus's mission to save from sin: "She [Mary] will give birth to a son, and you [Joseph] are to give him the name Jesus, because he will save his people from their sins" (Matt. 1:21).

3. The apostle Peter (an eyewitness—Muslims may not know that Peter and John were disciples of Jesus and thus knew him personally) proclaimed Jesus's mission to save: "For you know that it was not with perishable things such as silver or gold that you were redeemed from the empty way of life handed down to you from your forefathers, but with the precious blood of Christ, a lamb without blemish or defect" (1 Peter 1:18–19).

4. The apostle John (an eyewitness) proclaimed Jesus's mission to save: "This is love: not that we loved God, but that he loved us and sent his Son as an atoning sacrifice for our sins" (1 John 4:10).

5. The apostle Paul (to whom Jesus appeared) proclaimed Jesus's mission to save: "God was reconciling the world to himself in Christ, not counting men's sins against them. . . . We implore you on Christ's behalf: Be reconciled to God. God made him who had no sin to be sin for us, so that in him we might become the righteousness of God" (2 Cor. 5:19–21).

3. What the Bible Teaches about Human Sinfulness

The Qur'an teaches that every human being at birth is like Adam in his creation and that people are not sinful in their nature. Further, Muslims do not believe that human beings need a Savior, since people are born without sin and can gain eternal life by surrendering to Allah, asking for forgiveness, and living a good life based on the Pillars of Islam.

Jesus, however, was clear about the sinful heart of each person: "Out of the heart come evil thoughts, murder, adultery, sexual immorality, theft, false testimony, slander. These are what make a man 'unclean'" (Matt. 15:19–20).

It is a common belief in America that people are "basically good." Now it is true that the way we are created as creatures of God is good and wonderful. And it is good to accept and love people: we are to look upon all people as precious creatures of the Lord God and doubly precious because they are redeemed by the blood of Jesus. We are to be filled with compassion toward them, for the sad fact is that human beings are sinful, enslaved to sin, and born with an inclination to sin. That is, we do not need to teach a child to be sinful. The little child demonstrates his selfish will by stomping his little foot demanding that we do his bidding. We do not even need to say to ourselves, "I will think a selfish, hurtful thought"; such thoughts just come into our mind unexpectedly on their own. We are doing just "what comes naturally."

And when we see a sinful attitude or action expressed in others we say, "Well, that's human nature."

The basic problem of sin originates neither in society nor in one's upbringing (although these may contribute to one's attitude); the basic problem is within each person. That is why Jesus said, "No one can see the kingdom of God unless he is born again" (John 3:3). One needs to be reconciled and reunited with God by his grace through faith in Jesus, the Messiah, and Savior and to be born "of the Spirit."

D. How to Share the Good News with a Muslim

Having been fortified and informed, we are now ready to consider an approach to sharing the good news with a Muslim. The following approach is intended to assist you in developing your own way of witnessing to Muslims. It is not intended as a rigid methodology. You might begin with any of the following suggestions, whichever seems appropriate.

1. Use the Psalms (Arabic: Zabur), David's Songs of Praise (Surah 34:10).

After establishing a relationship with your Muslim acquaintance, you might give him or her a Bible as a gift (but give it in an inconspicuous gift bag). You might mark Psalm 23 with a book marker. Muslims may well learn to love the Psalms.

Later you can ask: "Have you had an opportunity to read Psalm 23, the Good Shepherd Psalm?" Ask permission to read Psalm 23 aloud: "The LORD [YAHWEH / I AM] is my shepherd . . ." Share what Psalm 23 means to you personally. Be open to questions.

Point out how Jesus spoke of himself with this same imagery: "I am the good shepherd" (John 10:11).

Continue to read from John chapter 10. Have your Muslim acquaintance follow. Repeat certain verses and pause (vv. 11, 14–18, 27–30). "Isn't it remarkable what Jesus says about himself as the good shepherd?" As you read, ask, "What do you think Jesus is saying here?" Let your friend discover for himself or herself. Let the words of Jesus speak for themselves. Share your joy: "To me this is remarkable. I have the *certainty* that Jesus laid down his life for me and gave me eternal life. I will never perish. I need not fear the final judgment. No one can snatch me out of his hand."

Your Muslim friend may object, "Anyone can say, 'I am the good shepherd.'" You can answer, "But not anyone can say, 'I lay down my life for the sheep. . . . I give them eternal life, and they shall never perish'" (John 10:15, 28). Jesus is identifying himself with the Lord and Shepherd of the psalm. Only the great I AM is able to give eternal life.

You might suggest that your friend read Psalm 22, the Passion Psalm. When you return at a future meeting, inquire if he or she had opportunity to read it. Ask if you might read Psalm 22:1–18 with him or her. As you read, compare with relevant passages from the Gospels:

Psalm 22:1 with Matthew 27:45 and Galatians 3:13
Psalm 22:7–8 with Matthew 27:39–44
Psalm 22:16 with Matthew 27:31
Psalm 22:17–18 with John 19:23–24

Reflect, "Isn't it remarkable how Psalm 22 was fulfilled in the life of Jesus?"

If your acquaintance is open to your sharing the Psalms, you might suggest looking at Psalm 27, especially verse 1, "The LORD [Yahweh, I AM] is my light and my salvation." Now look at the eyewitness account of John 8:12. Then ask, "What does Jesus say about his being the 'light of the world' in verse 12?"

Say, "Isn't it remarkable how Jesus applies Psalm 27 to himself?" Share what it means to you personally that Jesus is your light and your personal salvation, dispelling sin, giving the light of eternal life, showing the way.

As you go through Psalms 23 and 27, note the first verse of each:

The LORD [Hebrew: YAHWEH / I AM] is my shepherd. (Ps. 23:1)

The LORD [YAHWEH / I AM] is my light and my salvation. (Ps. 27:1)

It was the LORD (I AM) who appeared to Abraham in Genesis 12 and Genesis 15. This is important, since Allah appeared to Abraham, and for Muslims Abraham was the first Muslim.

Taking these very clear statements in Psalms 23:1 and 27:1, Jesus clearly applies "I AM" to himself: "*I am* the good shepherd" and "*I am* the light of the world." That is, Jesus attributes to himself the titles that only the Lord God Yahweh has. Jesus ascribes divinity to himself. He is the divine Good Shepherd and God's very Life and Light come to this earth.

If you sense a resistance to consulting Psalms, you might skip to point 2, "Quote Gabriel," or any of the steps below. But if your Muslim acquaintance is open, you may proceed with the following.

This time or next, share how John, who was the disciple closest to Jesus, also spoke of Jesus being the Light for every person. "Please permit me to read John 1:1–18." Invite the person to follow in his or her Bible. As you read John 1:1, "In the beginning was the Word," you might pause for emphasis. (The Qur'an in Surah 4:171 states that Jesus is Allah's "word which He conveyed unto Mary." One cannot say that the Word is not God and that the Word is not eternal.)

Then continue to read slowly the next four verses, which go on to reveal Jesus as God's Life and Light. Explain how we were spiritually dead and in darkness, but Jesus, who is God's Life and Light, came to enlighten each of us and give us forgiveness and eternal life. Explain that through Jesus your friend can have the assurance of forgiveness of all sins. With this forgiveness, she or he will have the certainty of eternal life now and forever. Because Christ connects us to the God of life, eternal life begins now. When we are connected to the God of Life, we are "alive in Christ." Because of Jesus's sacrifice for sin, we need not fear the final judgment.

Reflect: "To me this is wonderful. I have the certainty of God's eternal life and light through Jesus now and forever."

Be prepared to be accused of "blasphemy." Point out that this is not new, since Jesus in speaking of himself as the good shepherd was accused of blasphemy (John 10:33). Jesus stated, "I and the Father are one" (John 10:30). Does not Allah in the Qur'an speak of himself as "We"? It is not blasphemous for Jesus to speak of himself as one with the Father. What could be more loving and logical, if the Lord God, the great I AM, wanted to save us from our sins, than that he himself would come and lay down his life to give us eternal life? For another example of Jesus's assertions of divinity and being accused of blasphemy, see John 8:58–59.

If appropriate, you may once again go over the psalms discussed above, asking: "What is Psalm 23 saying?" (compare John 10); "Psalm 22?" (compare Matt. 27–28); "Psalm 27?" (compare John 8:12). "Isn't it a wonder how God speaks to us? Isn't it remarkable that Jesus is the Good Shepherd? How he gave his life for us all? How he is God's Light?"

Do not be surprised if your Muslim acquaintance tells you that Jesus appeared to him or her in a dream. Muslims have been made open to Christ by the Lord appearing to them in a dream.

2. Quote Gabriel (Arabic: Jibra'il)

There is a strong belief in angels in Islam. Gabriel transmitted the message of the Qur'an to Muhammad, and the angel spoke to Mary in the annunciation. You may find it helpful to quote Gabriel again and again regarding the person and mission of Jesus (Luke 1:26–38; Matt. 1:18–21). Speak highly of Gabriel. Tell of his special mission to Mary (which the Qur'an relates in a different manner).

Read from Luke 1:26–38 and invite him or her to follow. Then invite your friend to consider: "What do you think Gabriel is saying about Jesus? Who is he? What is Gabriel saying about the kingdom of Jesus?"

Read from Matthew 1:18–21. What special name does Gabriel give to the child to be born? How does Gabriel explain to Joseph the reason for giving the child the name Jesus?" (Jesus is the same as Hebrew Joshua, meaning "Yahweh saves.")

Even Muhammad needed to ask for forgiveness: the Qur'an in Surah 40:55 exhorts him to be patient and to "ask forgiveness of thy sin." Jesus, even according to the Qur'an, is conceived without sin: he is "faultless" (Surah 19:19). Nowhere in the Qur'an is Jesus spoken of as in need of forgiveness. In the Bible, the angel Gabriel proclaims Jesus to be the "Son of the Most High" (Luke 1:32), "Son of God" (Luke 1:35), and the one who will "save his people from their sins" (Matt. 1:21).

3. Read in the Gospels How Jesus Performed Miracles and Cast Out Demons

Those who have been converted from Islam relate that they were very impressed by the miracles of Jesus and his power over demons. Suggest reading the Gospels. You might begin with the Gospel of Mark, which is dramatic and carries you along with its fast-moving account of Jesus's ministry. Note the powerful healings and the statements of the demons:

Mark 1:24: "I know who you are—the Holy One of God!"

Mark 3:11: "Whenever the evil spirits saw him, they fell down before him and cried out, 'You are the Son of God.'"

Read the Gospel of St. Luke for the same kind of dramatic account of the ministry of Jesus. Such events show us that Jesus is more than a prophet; he is the Son of God come to this earth.

Since Muslims fear Satan and the evil Jinn, assure your acquaintance that Jesus came to "destroy the devil's works" (1 John 3:8). When we are tempted, we can say, "In the name of Jesus, 'Get behind me, Satan!'" (Matt. 16:23), and he must flee. The believer in Christ can put on "the full armor of God" so as to take a stand "against the devil's schemes," and he or she can "take the helmet of salvation and the sword of the Spirit, which is the word of God" (Eph. 6:11, 17). Since the believer is righteous in Christ, the devil cannot accuse and lead him or her to despair.

4. Cite the Crucifixion

You might give your Muslim acquaintance the video *Jesus of Nazareth*. The film wonderfully weaves the teachings of Jesus into realistic settings. The scene where Jesus tells the story of the faithful father and the prodigal son and the subsequent depiction of reconciliation between Matthew and Peter is very powerful.

You might ask whether your Muslim acquaintance has seen the film *The Passion of the Christ*. If not, you might watch it together. (It has been popular in the Arab world.) Does your friend have any questions? What made an impression on him or her? Share what you found especially compelling in the movie. Were you moved by Jesus's great love and resolve to go to the cross? Did your friend also see it? Were you touched by Jesus's words "Father, forgive them, for they do not know what they are doing" (Luke 23:34)? Isn't the love of Jesus remarkable?

Open your Bible to Isaiah 53 to read the words that appear on the opening screen of *The Passion of the Christ*: "He was wounded for our transgressions, crushed for our iniquities; by his wounds we are healed" (see Isa. 53:3–5).

After viewing the film, ask questions such as, "What are the words of Isaiah describing?" Read the Passion account from Matthew 27 or Luke 23. Take your time to let the words sink in. Pause for questions and reflections.

Your Muslim acquaintance may ask, "Where does it say in Isaiah 53 that this prophecy is foretelling the suffering of the Messiah?" He may say it refers to Israel. However, it cannot refer to Israel as the Suffering Servant, since "for the transgression of my people *he* was stricken" (v. 8), "the Lord makes *his* life a guilt offering" (v. 10), and "*he* will bear their iniquities" (v. 11). Rather than referring to Israel, it was Jesus who was "led like a lamb to the slaughter, and as a sheep before her shearers is silent, so he did not open his mouth" (v. 7). When one reads the account of the Gospels and sees the Lord's patient suffering and death, one recognizes clearly how this prophecy was fulfilled by the Lamb of God, who "was numbered with the transgressors, . . . bore the sin of many, and made intercession for the transgressors" (v. 12). Read Acts 8:26–34 to answer the question, "About whom is Isaiah 53 talking?"

Further, an informed Muslim might ask you, as I have been asked, "When did Jesus ever say that he died for our sins?" You might reply, "Jesus said in Matthew 20:28 that he 'did not come to be served, but to serve, and to give his life as a ransom for many.' Jesus also said, 'This is my body given for you' and 'my blood . . . poured out for many for the forgiveness of sins' [Luke 22:19; Matt. 26:28]." If your friend replies, "It is only bread and wine," you might reply, "But Jesus clearly said that his body was 'given for you' and his blood was 'poured out for many *for the forgiveness of sins.*' Thus Christ stated that his upcoming death would be a *sacrifice.*"

An informed Muslim may cite the expert in the law coming to Jesus and asking, "What must I do to inherit eternal life?" Jesus replied, "What is written in the Law?" He answered, "'Love the Lord your God with all your heart and with all your soul and with all your strength and with all your mind'; and 'Love your neighbor as yourself.'" Jesus replied, "Do this and you will live" (see Luke 10:25–28). The Muslim might say that this is how we gain eternal life. However, the law expert recognized his inability to keep the law and sought to "justify himself," asking, "Who is my neighbor?" Raise the question "Do we love God with all our heart, soul, strength, and mind, with every fiber of our being, all the time? Do we love our neighbors as ourselves all the time?" Many Muslims are struck with Jesus's words "Love your enemies" (Luke 6:27). You can ask, "Do we love our enemies?" It is for this very reason that we need a Savior. As Jesus said to the sinful woman, "Your sins are forgiven. . . . Your faith has saved you; go in peace" (Luke 7:48, 50).

Since Muslims recognize John the Baptist as a great prophet sharing the second rung of the ladder leading to Paradise with Jesus, at some point it is well to say, "Jesus, in great love for us, was crucified as the Lamb of God, just as the prophet John the Baptist *twice* pointed to Jesus and said, 'Look, the Lamb of God, who takes away the sin of the world'" (John 1:29, 36). Cross-reference Isaiah 53:7: "He was led like a lamb to the slaughter."

> Even in the story of Abraham and Ishmael, Surah 37:107 states, "Then We [Allah] ransomed him [Ishmael] with a tremendous victim [Dawood: a noble sacrifice]." According to the Qur'an, Allah saw the need for a ransom sacrifice on behalf of Abraham's son Ishmael. According to the Bible, the Lord God saw the need and saved the whole world by the ransom sacrifice of his Son.

Show how the cross is necessary because of our sin. The Lord God in his holy law requires that we love him with all our heart, soul, and mind and that we love our neighbor as ourselves (Matt. 22:37, 39). The law of the Lord God requires that we love him and others with all of our being, every moment of the day, every day of our lives. Thus it is impossible to gain eternal life by our works (see Luke 10:25–28). Because we "fall short of the glory of God" (Rom. 3:23), we are under the curse of the law. Our sins made the cross necessary. Our sins in a sense nailed Jesus to the cross, but his great love kept him there. The Bible assures us: "Christ redeemed us from the curse of the law by becoming a curse for us, for it is written: 'Cursed is everyone who is hung on a tree'" (Gal. 3:13).

Thus, the cross has become the great "Plus Sign" of the Lord God. On the cross "God was reconciling the world to himself in Christ, not counting men's sins against them" (2 Cor. 5:19). Explain the "great exchange" and how "God made him [Christ] to be sin for us, so that in him we might become the righteousness of God" (v. 21). The great exchange is further explained in Romans 5:15–21: Jesus took our sin and gave us forgiveness, took our condemnation and gave us justification (we are declared just), took our death and gave us life eternal. What a great exchange! By it we are given *certainty* that the scales of judgment will not be tipped against us and that we are "saved from God's wrath through him [Christ]" (v. 9).

Now God is "imploring [your friend] on Christ's behalf: Be reconciled to God" (2 Cor. 5:20).

Personal Example: The Plus Sign of the Cross

I was having a body scan before an operation. The attendant seemed to be from the Middle East. I asked him what his name was.

"Anwar," he said.

I asked, "Oh, like Anwar Sadat?"

He answered, "Yes."

I asked him where he came from. He said, "Pakistan."

I inquired, "What does the name Pakistan stand for?"

He said, "Clean place."

I politely asked, "Are you Muslim?"

He said, "Yes."

I told him, "Oh, I have been reading the Qur'an."

He asked, "What did you learn?"

I replied, "I learned that Muslims believe that Jesus was born of the Virgin Mary and that he is a great prophet."

He said, "That is right."

I continued, "But one thing that puzzled me is that the Qur'an says that he was not actually crucified, it only 'appeared so.'"

Anwar said, "That's right."

I proceeded, "For me the cross is a 'plus sign' of God's great love. Just as John the Baptist said, Jesus is 'the Lamb of God, who takes away the sin of the world' [John 1:29]."

With that, I was passing through the body scan, and our conversation needed to end. But in our brief conversation, I managed to do several important things:

1. I established communication.
2. I used my knowledge of the Qur'an as a door opener.
3. I turned the cross into a "plus sign." Anwar will always remember this, since among Muslims the cross is despised. They believe that when Jesus returns he will destroy all crosses.
4. Finally, because the Qur'an has a high regard for John the Baptist (Yahya) as "a Prophet of the righteous" (Surah 3:39), in the ascent of Muhammad to the seventh heaven, John the Baptist is said to share the second heaven with Jesus. I hope that my Muslim acquaintance will always remember that John the Baptist declared that Jesus is "the Lamb of God who takes away the sin of the world" (John 1:29).

Let us take every opportunity to share the cross of Christ as God's great "plus sign."

Reflect: "Isn't it remarkable that God loved us before we ever loved him? Do you see how much God loves you in sending Jesus to be your Savior? Isn't the exchange comforting?"

The crucifixion is recorded in all the Gospels. Jesus predicted his death by crucifixion. Secular historians Tacitus, Josephus, and others corroborate the fact that Jesus was crucified. (See also "D. The Crucifixion" in chapter 5.)

5. Share What the Grace of God Means to You

Muslims are unsure of their salvation, how they will stand on the final judgment day. They fear the scales of judgment, and many of them fear suffering on the "bridge of hell."

a. "Amazing Grace"

Explain to your Muslim friend that grace means the unconditional, undeserved, unexpected, and unimaginable love of God in sending Jesus as the Savior of the world. Share how Jesus showed "amazing grace" to the criminal on the cross: "Today you will be with me in paradise" (Luke 23:43).

"Do you see how Jesus assured the robber on the cross of paradise?"

"Do you hear Jesus speaking to you, telling you that you may have that same assurance?"

"Forgiveness and life eternal are God's sure gift to you in Christ."

Romans 6:23: "The wages of sin is death, but the gift of God is eternal life in Christ Jesus our Lord." "What does this say to you?"

"Do you see how Jesus died as payment for your sins to give you the gift of eternal life?"

"That gift of eternal life is yours now through Christ. Christ died for your sins that you need not fear the judgment of God."

The Qur'an continually reminds the Muslim that they must face the judgment. Be kind and respectful. Remind yourself that you are not trying to "defend" Christianity but to share the love of God in his Son, Jesus. Listen patiently. Muslims may have to hear the gospel many times before they come to faith in Jesus as their Savior and Lord.

When you feel that it is appropriate, read the story of the sinful woman from Luke's Gospel (Luke 7:36–50) and Christ's grace shown to her. Pause to reflect. "What is remarkable about this account?"

Consider how deeply the woman appreciated Christ's forgiveness and acceptance—how she was compelled to come and show her love even though it would mean ridicule and disapproval.

Note that Jesus says in verse 50: "Your faith [not your works] has saved you; go in peace." It is not good works but faith in Jesus that saved her. Her actions were a response to her debt's being paid. Her acts of love were a demonstration of her faith in the forgiveness of Jesus.

Share what this forgiveness means to you from day to day, and the certainty it will give you on your dying day, that you are sure of being in paradise.

Tell the story of a Muslim, Gulshan Esther (Fatima), who had been crippled for nineteen years. She prayed to Jesus for healing. He appeared as a bright light and said, "I am Jesus. I am Immanuel. I am the Way, the Truth and the Life. I am alive, and I am soon coming."[a] She was healed and became a follower of Christ.

[a] Gulshan Esther, *The Torn Veil* (Fort Washington, PA: CLC Publications, 1984), 61.

The amazing truth is that the Lord God loved us long before we believe in him or love him. In the Qur'an, Allah loves those who first love him, submit to him, and obey him. (Read about the conditionality of Allah's love in chapter 4.) In contrast, the Lord God of Abraham loved Abraham, chose him, and called him long before he was circumcised. The Lord God loved each of us when we were powerless, ungodly, sinners, and enemies (Rom. 5:6–11). His love was shown to us before we ever came to him in that "while we were still sinners, Christ died for us" (Rom. 5:8).

Share with your beloved Muslim John 3:16–18. Note that John was the disciple especially close to Jesus. "What is this text saying? What good news is it announcing? Who is Jesus? What did he do? How does God give eternal life to us personally?"

b. Can a person have certainty of eternal life? Yes!

Ask: "Can a person have certainty that at death he or she will go immediately to paradise? Do you have that certainty? If you were to die today, are you certain that you would go to paradise?

Explain that you have the certainty of eternal life. The Bible says, "He who has the Son *has* life; he who does not have the Son of God does not have life. I write these things to you who believe in the name of the Son of God so that *you may know* that you have eternal life" (1 John 5:12–13).

State that you understand that some Muslims believe they must first pass over the "bridge of hell" and may suffer for their sins before they can enter Paradise. "Is this true?" Express your certainty of entering God's presence immediately when you die. Jesus said to the criminal on the cross, "Today you will be with me in paradise" (Luke 23:43). It is possible for your friend also to have that certainty.

Read again John 3:16. "What is it saying to you?" For added comfort, read Romans 5:1: "Since we are justified through faith, we have peace with God through our Lord Jesus Christ."

Speak of the *certainty* and the *joy* that you have in Jesus Christ as your personal Savior. Assure your acquaintance that Jesus unconditionally loves him or her as well—dying, paying for his or her sin, and offering eternal life as a gift. They need not fear the final judgment or the bridge of hell.

When it appears that the Holy Spirit has called your Muslim acquaintance to faith in Jesus through the gospel, you may want to ask him or her, "Do you believe that Jesus, the Messiah, is the Son of God and your Savior from sin?" (If not, listen to his or her questions. Review the above as often as necessary. Then repeat the question.) "Would you like to go in prayer to the Father through Jesus and ask for forgiveness on the basis of what Jesus has done for you, and thank God for the certainty of forgiveness and the assurance that when you die you will be in paradise?" If he or she says yes, then offer to lead him or her in prayer, inviting him or her to repeat after you:

> Lord God, heavenly Father, I come to you in the name of your beloved Son, Jesus. I thank you that you sent Jesus to be my Savior. I ask you to forgive me all my sins for the sake of his suffering and death, and to remember them no more. I thank you that through Jesus I have the certainty of eternal life and that when I die, just like the robber on the cross, I will be in paradise. Thank you, Father, that I am your child and that you are my loving heavenly Father through Jesus Christ. In Jesus's name I pray. Amen.

> When former US president Reagan was asked whether he was ready to meet God when he was shot and his life was ebbing from him, he said, "Yes. . . . I'm ready to meet God because I have a Savior." Even as he was lying on the operating table, he remembered Jesus's parable of the lost sheep and forgave his would-be assassin.[a]
>
> [a] Paul Kengor, *God and Ronald Reagan: A Spiritual Life* (New York: Regan, 2004), 184–85.

Then assure the new believer in Christ that the heavenly Father has heard his or her prayer and he or she has forgiveness and eternal life. Thank and praise God the Father with him or her.

Continue further instruction. Explain baptism and arrange for his or her baptism as soon as possible.

E. How to Disciple the New Believer

1. Living the Godly Life

With a new believer, you will want to emphasize the importance of continuing in the Word, daily repenting of sin and trusting Jesus as our Savior and Lord, and living a godly life as a Christian, since the ungodly lives of "Christians" are often criticized in the Muslim world. Point out that as Christians we *want* to live a godly life in Christ. However, Christians do not live a godly life to gain the favor of the Lord God, nor out of fear of eternal judgment, but in *thanksgiving* for the ransom and sacrifice provided by Jesus, the Son of God. The sacrificial love of Jesus and his glorious resurrection are the reason and the power for living the godly life.

Recall that Muslims observe the Feast of Sacrifice in remembrance of Abraham's willingness to sacrifice his son. Christians offer their whole selves as a "sacrifice of thanksgiving" for the substitutionary ransom and sacrifice provided by Jesus as the Lamb of God. Peter writes that we are a holy priesthood "offering spiritual sacrifices acceptable to God through Jesus Christ" (1 Pet. 2:5). Such a life of thanksgiving brings great joy.

2. Continuing in the Faith

Once you have shared key Scriptures and your personal witness, encourage your friend through continued sharing of the Gospel of St. Luke, Acts of the Apostles, and the Gospel of St. John.

Share your delight with your friend as together you learn more about Jesus. Your commitment in love to your beloved new brother or sister is a lifelong commitment to stand by him or her. Continue to share the love of Jesus with him or her. Invite your friend to your small group, a Bible class, and worship services. There may also be a Christian fellowship of former Muslims in your community. Family life has always been very important to Muslims. Treat your friend as a part of your family.

3. Open Doors

It may well be that God will open doors to lead others to Jesus. Pray for faithfulness. Believe that the Holy Spirit is using your witness to call your believing friend to a stronger faith in Jesus. Take him or her to worship, to Bible class, to your small group, and to fellowship gatherings. Assure your friend that God's love in Jesus is steadfast and unchanging. Together seek to share the love of Jesus with other Muslims.

Never forget that the Savior who died for you, who offered himself for you and your believing friend, is the Savior who continues to seek the lost that they might have eternal life. God grant it. To him be all the glory. Amen.

Background Information on the Life of Muhammad

We cannot understand Islamic belief, life, and practice unless we become familiar with the life of Muhammad. In the Islamic religion, Muhammad is the last and greatest of all prophets. According to Islam, not only was he given the revelation of the Qur'an from Allah, but his life is a model for every Muslim and the guidance of all Islamic practice.

Early Childhood

Muhammad was born in the year AD 570 in the region of Mecca, in what today is Saudi Arabia. His father, Abdullah, died shortly before his birth, and his mother died when he was six years old. At age eight he lost his influential grandfather, Abd al-Muttalib. He then came under the care of a loving uncle, Abu Talib. He worked as a shepherd boy, and at the age of twelve he traveled with his uncle on a merchant caravan to Syria.

Early Adulthood and First Marriage

In early adulthood Muhammad came under the employ of a wealthy widow, Khadijah. He was recognized as an able, honest, dependable person and conducted a successful caravan trade with Syria. At the age of twenty-five he was married to Khadijah, who was fifteen years his senior. They had six children, of whom four girls survived.

Mecca

Mecca was a thriving center of commerce. Two annual caravans of twenty-five hundred camels traveled from Mecca to Yemen, Palestine, Syria, and Iraq. The people of Mecca could invest in the enterprises through a system of banking, bookkeeping, and credit that fostered capital investments and new ventures. The Meccans claimed descent from Abraham through Ishmael, and their tradition stated that the Ka'aba had been built by Abraham.

The Ka'aba was surrounded by 360 idols. People from the region would come on pilgrimages to worship these idols. In the Meccan community there was a small group of Hunafa (the Trustworthy), who were disillusioned with idolatry. Muhammad belonged to this group of skeptics who questioned the validity of idolatry.

The Call

Muhammad made it his practice to take a monthlong retreat in a cave in the desert with his family during the month of Ramadan. They would go to Hira, a desert hill, about two miles north of Mecca. When he was forty years of age, in the year 610, according to the Islamic faith, Muhammad had a vision of the angel Gabriel coming to him and saying, "Read!" Being illiterate, Muhammad was unable to read.

Some say the angel actually said "Recite" or "Proclaim." "The injunction to 'recite' meant 'make vocal what is already written,' says Islamicist Kenneth Cragg, which means it was the 'sending down' of a pre-existent book (Qur'an is Arabic for 'recitation')."[1]

Dawood renders the command thus:

> Recite in the name of your Lord who created, created man from clots of blood.
> Recite! Your Lord is the Most Bountiful One, who by the pen taught man what he did not know. (Surah 96:1–5)

In the introduction to the explanatory translation of the Qur'an by Mohammad M. Pickthall, in response to the command "Read!" Muhammad said, "I cannot read." The voice repeated, "Read!" He said, "I cannot read." The voice said a third time, "Read!" He said, "What shall I read?"

The voice said,

> Read: In the name of thy Lord who created,
> Created man from a clot.
> Read: And thy Lord is the Most Bounteous,
> Who taught by the pen,
> Taught man that which he knew not. (Surah 96:1–5)

He went out of the cave, and Gabriel again spoke: "O Muhammad! Thou art Allah's Messenger, and I am Gabriel."[2]

After this vision Muhammad was filled with great fear and wondered whether he had been possessed by a demon. His wife assured him that Allah would not allow such a good man as he to be demon possessed. A very old cousin, Waraqa ibn Naufal, was consulted. He knew both the Jewish and the Christian Scriptures. He said that the voice was like that which had spoken to Moses and that indeed Muhammad had been called to be prophet.

After the first revelation, there was a period of silence that lasted about three years. During this time Muhammad sank into a deep depression, feeling suicidal and forsaken by God.

Early Years of Ministry

Muhammad began his ministry by preaching only to relatives and to the poor. He then began to preach against idols, telling the Meccans that their relatives were in hell and warning them of the judgment of God. He also preached the resurrection of the body. All this challenged the beliefs of the people of Mecca, who revered nature deities and assumed that their destiny was determined by time and fate. They believed in the power of their idols. Also, pilgrimages to the Ka'aba were very profitable to them. In order to win the support of his opponents, Muhammad proclaimed that their favorite deities, Al-Lat (Sun), Al-Uzza (Venus), and Manat (Fate), could be considered divine beings whose intercession was effective with God. This proclamation is known as the "Satanic Verses." Muhammad soon retracted this concession and substituted other verses in the revelation in Surah 53:19–23.

Muhammad's wife, Khadijah, and his unbelieving protector and uncle, Abu Talib, both died in 619. With his uncle's demise, his safety was no longer secure. According to Islamic tradition, it was during this time that Muhammad was transported to Jerusalem and thence to the seventh heaven by Buraq (a horse-like creature with a human face) and negotiated with Allah from fifty down to five times of daily prayer. This vision increased the hostility of the Meccans.

Because of his preaching, the Meccans ostracized Muhammad's entire clan, and for three years his family took refuge in their family stronghold in one of the gorges leading to Mecca. Some of his followers fled to Christian Abyssinia (Ethiopia).

In the summer of 621, a dozen men from the city of Yathrib (later named Al-Madinah, or Medina) came to Mecca on pilgrimage and secretly professed Islam. At the pilgrimage in the succeeding year, seventy-three people came from Yathrib and professed Islam. They invited Muhammad to come to their city and pledged to defend him as they would their own families. The Meccans feared his going to Yathrib and were furious over his influence there.

They decided to assassinate him, but to prevent blood vengeance, one person would be chosen from each tribe and they would assassinate him together. Some authorities hold that it was during this time that Muhammad received his first revelation of jihad, giving him permission to wage war against his persecutors (Surah 22:39–40). An early revelation at Medina commands, "Fight in the way of Allah, and know that Allah is Hearer, Knower" (Surah 2:244).

The Migration/Flight (Hijra)

The migration (Hijra) to Yathrib took place on September 24, 622, and this date ultimately became the beginning of the Islamic lunar calendar. Muhammad was asked to be a mediator between the various tribes of Yathrib, including three Jewish tribes. He succeeded in settling the dispute and was made ruler of the city-state. The three Jewish tribes were assured religious liberty and equal rights as citizens. The worship of idols and the killing of unwanted newborn girls were forbidden. The followers of Muhammad prayed toward Jerusalem and kept the Jewish Day of Atonement as a day of fasting.

The Jewish people soon questioned Muhammad's teaching, however, and rejected his claim to be a prophet. He then changed the time of fasting to the month of Ramadan and instructed his followers no longer to face Jerusalem but Mecca in prayer. Muhammad's revelations thenceforth took on a more aggressive tone.

A few of his followers found employment in Yathrib, but the majority joined Muhammad in raiding the commercial caravans to Mecca. John L. Esposito states, "Muhammad initiated a series of raids against Meccan caravans, threatening both the political authority and the economic power of the Quraysh."[3] (The Quraysh were the keepers of the Ka'aba and one of the wealthiest and most powerful tribes of Arabia.) In the fighting against the Quraysh tribe in January 624, a person was killed, and two were taken captive and brought back to Medina. The pagan Arabs of Medina were shocked that this had taken place during what was a sacred month for them. However, Muhammad received a revelation that defended the right to fight and divide up the booty: "They question thee (O Muhammad) with regard to warfare in the sacred month. Say: Warfare therein is a great (transgression), but to turn (men) from the Way of Allah, and to disbelieve in Him and in the Inviolable Place of Worship, and to expel its people thence, is a greater (transgression) with Allah" (Surah 2:217). In other words, the defense of Islam was the lesser evil.

Battle of Badr

The battle of Badr took place in March 624. With three hundred men, Muhammad attacked a large caravan of great wealth (50,000 dinars' worth) returning from Syria. The caravan learned of Muhammad's plan and sent word for help from Mecca. Mecca responded with 950 men. The battle at first went against the Muslims but ended in victory for them. Forty-five of the Meccans, some of them leading men in the city, were killed. Seventy-five Meccan prisoners were taken. The Muslims lost only fourteen people. Surah 8:17 states, "Ye (Muslims) slew them not, but Allah slew them."

Muhammad, having gained new popularity and power, killed some of the poets who had maligned him and expelled one of the three Jewish tribes from Medina.

Muhammad also began a series of new marriages, some of which strengthened his position as leader. In all, Muhammad eventually had eleven wives and took two more women as concubines. One of his marriages was to Aishah, who was six years old when she was betrothed to him and nine years old when their marriage was consummated. Another wife was Zaynab, the former wife of his adopted son Zaid. Muhammad received special revelations allowing him to marry more than four wives (Surah 33:50) and also permission to marry Zaynab (Surah 33:37).

Battle of Uhud

In 625, Mecca sent three thousand soldiers to destroy Medina. Muhammad faced them with a thousand. The battle cry was "Allah Akbar"—Allah is great! In the battle Muhammad was wounded and the Muslims took heavy casualties. The Meccans rejoiced in their "victory" and decided to return to Mecca. Muhammad then led attacks on neighboring tribes, extended his alliances, and prevented them from joining in alliance with the Meccans.

Less than a year after the defeat at Uhud, Muhammad expelled the second Jewish tribe from Medina and confiscated their property. This resulted in much wealth being given to his followers.

War of the Trench

In the spring of 627 (fifth year of Hijra), the Meccans led an Arab confederacy of ten thousand men against the Muslims of Medina, who had three thousand men. Muhammad used the defense of trenches, which he had learned from the Persians. The trenches were a bewilderment and a great obstacle to the Meccans. Also, a severe wind arose from the sea, destroying the tents of the Meccans and making it very difficult to fight. After a time, the Meccans lost their determination and began to withdraw back to Mecca. The standing of Muhammad was greatly strengthened after this "silent victory." Esposito observes, "The failure of the Quraysh enhanced Muhammad's prestige and leadership among the tribes of Arabia, placing him in the ascendant position."[4]

Muhammad turned on the one remaining Jewish tribe in Medina, whose members had plotted with the Meccans when it seemed that Muhammad faced insurmountable odds. Eight hundred Jewish men were beheaded on the edge of the trench, and the women and children were sold into slavery.

Muhammad's strength in numbers and wealth increased over the next two years. He led more successful campaigns, acquiring more plunder. "Muhammad established his authority over much of Arabia. The Bedouins who resisted were defeated militarily."[5] More and more people joined the ranks of Islam. At the same time, the military and economic strength of Mecca declined.

In 628 (fifth year of Hijra), 1,400 Muslims went to Mecca for the annual pilgrimage.

Mecca resisted the pilgrimage, but agreed that the following year they might have a pilgrimage to the Ka'aba. They made the Hudaybiah peace treaty with Muhammad, both sides agreeing not to war against one another for ten years. The signing of this treaty was a clear indication that Muhammad was now recognized as an opponent of equal rank.

In 629, Muhammad waged war against the Jewish forts of Kheybar. The Jews became "tenants" of the Muslims. One by one, the strongholds of Jewish tribes in northern Arabia were overcome. (All Jews were expelled from Arabia under Umar, the second caliph of Islam, in 634–44.)

Mecca Is Subdued

Some of the allies of Mecca attacked the allies of Muhammad and broke the treaty of Hudaybiah. Muhammad, in January 630, confronted Mecca with ten thousand men. Abu Sufyan, leader of the Meccans, was constrained to recognize Muhammad as the apostle of Allah and to acknowledge that there is no god but Allah. Muhammad entered the city with virtually no resistance.

Ten people were executed, and a general amnesty was declared. Generous gifts were given to the leaders for their surrender, winning their appreciation and allegiance. Muhammad cleansed the Ka'aba of idols.

After Mecca's surrender, a large number of tribes professed allegiance to Muhammad. Others were defeated and brought into submission. In general, the heathen tribes had to renounce paganism and profess Islam. Christians and Jews could practice their own religion but could not propagate their faith. They had to pay tribute and taxes.

"The Prophet made Medina his permanent seat from which in 9/630 [yr. 9 Muslim calendar, yr. 630 Christian calendar] he also conducted a campaign against the northern Christian Arabs of Transjordania."[6] That is, the Muslims with 3,000 men went to fight against the Christian Byzantian army of 100,000 in Syria. This was the first battle against Christians. The Muslims lost but fought ferociously.

Pickthall summarizes the military campaigns of Muhammad thus: "The number of the campaigns which he [Muhammad] led in person during the last years of his life is twenty-seven, in nine of which there was hard fighting. The number of the expeditions which he planned and sent out under other leaders is thirty-eight. He personally controlled every detail of organisation."[7]

In March 632, Muhammad personally led the Islamic pilgrimage to Mecca and delivered his farewell address before a vast multitude. Three months later, on June 8, 632, at the age of sixty-three (lunar calendar), he died. Some say he had tasted poisoned meat some time before, or perhaps he contracted pneumonia, which weakened his health, while others hold that the cause is unknown. His tomb is located in the Prophet's Mosque in Medina.

Modern radical fundamentalist Muslims follow the example and methodology of Muhammad in their militant campaign to spread the message of Islam and to "out-endure" their enemies in the promotion of an Islamic society and state.

Background Information on Shi'ites and Sunnis

Following Muhammad, the first three caliphs (successors) were chosen by consensus and were not blood relatives of Muhammad. The fourth caliph was Ali Abu Taleb. He was the cousin of Muhammad and married to Fatima, the only daughter of Muhammad who remained living after his death. Ali had been a faithful "companion" of Muhammad. Many Muslims recognized Ali as caliph, except Muawiyah, governor of Syria and nephew of Uthman, the third caliph. Ali led a battle against Muawiyah. The Muawiyah army was being defeated. Its soldiers put the Qur'an on their spear tips, shouted, "Let God decide," and appealed for arbitration.

Ali agreed to arbitration, but the attempts were inconclusive. The Kharijites (seceders) objected to Ali arbitrating with Muawiyah and not establishing a more strict Islamic rule. A Kharijite assassinated Ali in 661. Ali is buried in Najaf, Iraq. Muawiyah, with tribal roots in Mecca, declared himself caliph. Muawiyah extended Muslim rule over North Africa, Spain, Portugal, France, and Afghanistan. The Kharijites, however, waged jihad against the "ungodly" Muawiyah and considered themselves instruments of God's justice. Some believe the roots of present-day extremism and terrorism reach back to the Kharijites.[1]

Husayn, younger son of Ali and grandson of Muhammad, led a small band of followers in rebellion against Yazid I, son of Muawiyah, in 680 and lost. This is considered a decisive rupture between the Sunnis and Shi'ites. A massacre took place at Karbala, where Husayn was buried. His death came to be seen as martyrdom, a sacred event. His burial place is one of the holiest shrines for Shi'ites. Annually, Shi'ites engage in self-flagellation in the Festival of Ashura to share in the sufferings of Husayn and to pray to him.

The Shi'ites (faction of Ali) believe the caliph should be a direct descendant from Muhammad. They believe that the "hidden" twelfth (some say the seventh) imam will return as the Mahdi (rightly guided one) to establish justice and a pure Islamic state. The president of Iran, Mahmoud Ahmadinejad, has been proclaiming that the coming of the twelfth imam is at hand. During the absence of the Mahdi, Shi'ites are led by ayatollahs (signs of Allah), who are learned and trusted teachers. Ayatollah al-Sistani of Iraq knew the Qur'an from memory by age five. The imams are also looked to for definitive guidance. The Shi'ites have shrines, or holy places, which the Sunnis consider idolatrous. Shi'ites believe in free will more than the Sunnis do, and in the necessity of good works to be a "true Muslim." Sixty percent of the people in Iraq and 90 percent of the people in Iran are Shi'ites.

The Sunnis (sunna: trodden path or tradition) believe in rule by "consensus" of the community. They look to learned scholars to interpret the Qur'an and the Hadith. They in general historically do not believe in free will but in the determinant will of Allah. Eighty-five percent of Muslims worldwide are Sunni.

Mary Habeck notes that scholars trace the evolution of present-day extreme Islamic fundamentalist jihadist beliefs from Ahmad ibn 'Abd al-Halim ibn Taymiyya (1263–1328) through Muhammad ibn 'Abd al-Wahhab (1703/4–92), Muhammad Rashid Rida (1865–1935), and Hassan al-Banna (1906–49), to Sayyid Abul A'la Maududi (1903–79) and Sayyid Qutb (1903–66).[2] As we can see, the present-day Islamic fundamentalism has been brewing for a long time. It calls for the return of all Muslims to the fundamentals, to become "true Muslims," and to fight all forms of idolatry and secularism, which exalt humankind over Allah and the Qur'an. Osama Bin Laden was Sunni, and Abu Musab al-Zarqawi was Sunni. Muqtada al-Sadr is a Shi'ite. Al-Qaida is Sunni, and Hezbollah is Shi'ite. Both Shi'ite and Sunni extremists want to destroy Israel.

The goal of Islamists is to establish a true Islamic Umma (community) under a caliph, with the Qur'an as its constitution and Sharia as its law. According to Habeck, jihadists consider themselves "honored participants in a cosmic drama, one that will decide the fate of the world and that will ultimately end with victory of the good, the virtuous, and the true believers. . . . This is a war that could last two hundred years."[3]

Testimony of a Former Muslim

Rev. Hicham Chehab[1]

Yes, in Christ there is no east and west. I come from the East, thousands of miles away from North America. I was born in Lebanon in 1960 into a conservative Muslim family. I belonged to an extremist Muslim group. I started like the right hand of Bin Laden at the age of thirteen. But God, Christ, has died for us when we were still sinners. Christ died for the ungodly. He died for you. He died for me. He died for Bin Laden. He died for Zarqawi. And he is able to reach into the darkness and save even someone like Bin Laden. He can save anyone who will bend the knee. He saved me while I was still ungodly. While I belonged to an extremist Muslim group, he saved me.

I came from a family that claimed descent from the tribe of Muhammad, the prophet of Islam. I grew up in Beirut, where my extended family numbers five thousand. I have more than a hundred first cousins. We were very proud Muslims and we had a lot of tension with the Christians who formed about 50 percent of the population in Lebanon. There was considerable tension since many Palestinians came out of Israel when the nation of Israel was established, and they settled in Lebanon and swelled the ranks of Muslims. There was a lot of strife and competition between the Muslims and the Christians for political power in Lebanon.

This tension was evident everywhere, even in the field where I played marbles. Any tension over marbles between Muslim boys and Christian boys would turn bloody. When I was seven years old, I had a firsthand experience with a Christian boy. I was playing marbles when the boy, also seven years old, appeared from nowhere holding a stick with a nail in it and banged me on the head. He missed my eye by an inch, and blood splattered my face. I was dragged home crying. This shows how difficult it is in such a situation to even think about hearing the gospel or reading the Bible. The Christian was the enemy for me and for my community.

I went to a conservative Muslim school, together with my brother, my only sibling. When we turned twelve, it was a must to go to noon prayer. Next to the school was a mosque, where I discovered a young Muslim preacher. He was very active and very intelligent. He was relating political issues to Islam and to the Qur'an, the holy book of Muslims. I was second best in my class at the Qur'an and first best at Arabic. I wanted to be a better Muslim and memorize more of the Qur'an. After a few weeks, that teacher started giving us books about what we today call "political Islam." The books told us that the world is divided into two parts: the world of Islam and the world of infidels. They said that it is the duty of Muslims to convert the other part of the world or subdue it by force. The teacher taught that infidels—Christians, Jews, atheists, communists, and the like—are worse than animals. They are bad stewards of the earth. They are corrupt and they will corrupt the earth—he pointed to Hollywood as an example. I asked him, "What about Christians living among us? They are 50 percent of the population." He said, "We are part of a global Islam movement that extends from India to Morocco, and one day we will rise all together and join hands and establish a global Muslim state. It is our duty as Lebanese Muslims to give those Christians among us a beating. They are spies for the West. They are spies for Israel. They are just crusaders."

By now I was just thirteen years old, and my brother was almost fourteen and a half. At that time, in 1973, we were invited to our first military training camp in the distant mountains of north Lebanon. There we were taught how to shoot rifles, rocket-propelled grenades, and mortars. I remember the statement that put in a nutshell the hate that was rankling in our hearts toward Christians. The man who was shooting put the rifle in position on his shoulder and said, "If you want to shoot straight, imagine that there is a Christian in your sights. Then you shoot straight." That was the hate.

Most of the Christians were not doing any better. They were forming militias and preparing for a showdown. They really started the all-out civil war. In 1975 they took to the streets and gunned down a Palestinian soccer team and then killed hundreds of civilian Muslims. So in 1975, when the civil war broke out in Lebanon, at the age of fifteen I found myself in the street with my brother carrying guns, going to high-rise buildings, sniping at Christian neighborhoods, and shelling Christian neighborhoods with mortars.

At one point I was shelling the main Christian neighborhood in Beirut. After the third mortar, I felt uneasy. I felt that this was not really a "holy war," that I should look into it more.

I went to the head of the Muslim group and told him, "Listen, I don't feel well about shelling civilian neighborhoods; those shells will land and injure innocent people—women and children."

He asked me a question: "Who is your example in life as a Muslim?"
I said, "Prophet Muhammad."
He said, "This is the right answer, because he is our example, our model in life, and when he had the problem with the Jews in Medina, he shelled their neighborhoods with catapults. Catapults were medieval instruments that hurled fire and stone. It is like this to weaken the enemy. We have to break their morale, because a dead civilian is better than a dead fighter."

I wanted to learn more to be in leadership, to be involved in decision making, and I thought I should sign up for a crash course in Islamic law and the sayings of Muhammad. The instructors saw that I was good at memorizing the Qur'an and excellent in Arabic, so after six months I was ready to give my first Friday service. (Muslims worship on Friday, not Saturday or Sunday.) Before that I did many things, such as door-to-door evangelism and Sunday school (in Christian terms). I was ready to give my first Friday sermon from the pulpit of Muhammad. I wrote out the sermon, and I was ready to go after rehearsing in front of fifty people. It was postponed a week, though, and I thought in the interim I would go visit my aunt in the mountains. As I rode with my cousin in a Volkswagen van, we suffered a head-on collision. Both of my legs were broken, and instead of giving that Friday service, I was bedridden for a year.

A year in bed without crutches was too much for a sixteen-year-old kid. To pass the time, I started reading things in English, and then I discovered comics—easier, more interesting, and more amusing. I discovered Charlie Brown, Snoopy and Lucy, Tarzan, Superman, and so on. (No Star Wars in those days.) I discovered a novel written by a Western author. I liked cowboys and Indians then. His name was Louis L'Amour. I discovered he had written over a hundred novels. After a year I had read them all. My English got better, and I went back to school and forgot about becoming a preacher. Then in 1979–80 I qualified to enter the American University in Beirut, the Harvard of the Middle East. I signed up to study biology and chemistry, intending to study medicine in the future. It was like a dream come true. I wanted to focus on my studies, but again something happened that changed the course of my life.

My only brother had been the shoulder I cried on. We learned how to bike together, to swim together, to shoot together. He was a captain in the Muslim militia. In November 1980, he was killed by a Christian militia—gunned down when he was trying to negotiate a truce between the two parties.

I was devastated. I couldn't focus on my studies anymore. I dropped all the courses except one course on cultural studies. I thought, "Revenge is sweet," so I convinced two comrades that we should kill off my brother's enemies by night, one by one, stalking them in the dark alleys of Beirut. I got a silencer and guns, and we started to stalk his enemies by night. Those were really dark days, ugly days. I used to go back to the school periodically to make friends with some Christians who belonged to the militia that killed my brother in order to know their movements by night and ambush them more easily.

One of those days I sat down in class, in that course on cultural studies, comparative literature, and religions. The professor was drawing comparisons between Greek mythology, the Bible, the Qur'an, and some Western philosophy. As a Muslim, I considered the Bible something unclean, a book that bishops and rabbis had corrupted, that misled people, but it was part of the curriculum. The professor was quoting short sections. When she got to the New Testament, I, who was stalking my enemies by night to kill them, heard her read the Sermon on the Mount: "Love your enemies." "Wow! That is superhuman," I thought. "Who could love his enemies?" It was like hearing the voice of God in stereo. The figure of Jesus suddenly became an object of intense curiosity for me. How can somebody love his enemies? How can somebody turn the other cheek? My enemy was not someone who cut me off in the traffic or refused to have lunch with me. My enemy had killed my only brother, my only friend.

When the rich young ruler came to Jesus and asked, "What is the greatest commandment?" he replied, "'Love God with all your heart and with all your soul and with all your might,' and the second is 'Love your neighbor as yourself.'" As a Muslim I used to memorize the Qur'an three hours a day, before the dawn, and I thought this was the way to love God. But this man who was supposed to have a corrupted Bible, whose Bible was supposed to mislead people, to guide them toward Satan, was guiding people toward God in the most powerful way I had ever heard. I thought, "Maybe I am missing truth with a capital *T*. Maybe I should read the Bible on my own." And this was what I began to do.

But then I thought, to be fair, to be objective, I should also finish memorizing the Qur'an. But the more I memorized the Qur'an, the more I discovered its language of hatred, its culture of hatred toward the neighbor. So I thought, to be fully objective, I should learn some Eastern philosophy—Hinduism and Buddhism. I got fond of yoga and transcendental meditation, and I was told I could reach God. To have union with God, one must take the first step of physical yoga, and after that six steps. The last step is Samadhi, where you have union with God. But the more I did of meditation and yoga, the more I felt I was sinking in my inner uncleanness. Then it dawned on me: we try with our futile work, our human efforts, to ascend to God, to climb up to God, but we can't make it.

Only Jesus Christ, God, has descended to us: "the Word became flesh and made his dwelling among us." And I felt the door of heaven opened. I felt I was set free from the burdens of praying ritualistic prayers five times, fasting for one month, and so on. I experienced a peace beyond any peace I could have imagined, peace in my heart—my broken heart. I, who was looking for revenge in killing my enemies, started to have peace in my heart, and God gave me a new heart. Instead of stalking my enemy at night with a gun and silencer, I started sneaking into churches on Sunday morning to hear how Christians speak about Jesus.

Having been called to faith, one night I was baptized. After my baptism I lay down to rest. Jesus appeared to me in the most wonderful dream in my life. Jesus grabbed me and we flew together over a wide, abundant, and thunderous river. We flew from a drab riverbank to a lush green one, exploding with green foliage and trees. He left me there and disappeared.

This was the beginning, really, not the end.

> Bless the LORD, O my soul,
>   and all that is within me, bless his holy name! (Psalm 103:1 RSV)

An Appeal

The Christian in the present age needs to be strengthened in his or her faith and awakened to live the Christian life. While Christians are deeply concerned about pervasive secularism, we are called to resist the temptation to become militant: "Love your enemies, do good to those who hate you, bless those who curse you, pray for those who mistreat you" (Luke 6:27–28). Peter, an eyewitness of Jesus's life, death, and resurrection, exhorts Christians to be willing to be "insulted because of the name of Christ" (1 Pet. 4:14). He reminds followers of Christ that if we suffer as Christians, "do not be ashamed, but praise God that you bear that name" (1 Pet. 4:16).

Christians need to be fortified and empowered by the Scriptures and the Holy Spirit to proclaim that "Jesus Christ is Lord, to the glory of God the Father" (Phil. 2:11). More than ever, let us glory in the cross of the Lamb of God, who came to take away the sin of the world (John 1:29). His atonement on the cross is the "plus sign" of God's love and the certainty of eternal life.

The Lord God had a plan. He was reconciling the world to himself, not counting sins against humankind. He was breaking down barriers and uniting hostile people through Christ's strong sacrifice—in a fellowship of love (2 Cor. 5:19; Eph. 2:16). Because of this, Christians value the fellowship of believers and the bond of love. They remember that the Lord commanded, "As I have loved you, so you must love one another" (John 13:34). It was Christ-love that won the hearts of people, changed lives, and transformed the ancient pagan world. Christians today are called to share and to live the love of Christ. We are called to make a difference in a world not unlike the ancient pagan world with the same transforming Christ-love.

Study Guides

Study Guide 1: The Significance of Abraham

In chapter 1, read "A. The Significance of Abraham."

1. How does the Bible view Abraham?
   Why is Abraham so important to Christians? (See Gen. 12:1–3; 22:18; Matt. 1:1; Rom. 4:16; Gal. 3:16.)

2. Why is Abraham so important to Muslims?

3. According to the Qur'an, what is the origin of Islam?

4. Does Islam claim to be a form of Judaism or Christianity?
   Why, or why not?

5. What is the Lord God's gracious and generous promise to Abraham?

6. What does the name "LORD" mean and signify?

7. How are Genesis 22:18 and Galatians 3:16 connected?

8. "Jesus, the Messiah, is by lineage and fulfillment the _____ and _____ of the _____ to Abraham." (See text.)

9. Discuss how the promise given to Abraham is "contained, centered, and culminated in Jesus, the 'offspring' of Abraham." (See the summary.)

10. What does it mean to Christians that they believe in the God of Abraham? (See "H. Who is the God of Abraham?" in chapter 14.)

Read and discuss the summary.

Study Guide 2: Abraham and Righteousness

In chapter 1, read "B. Abraham and Righteousness."

1. What is the basic meaning of the words *Islam* and *Muslim*?

2. In the Qur'an, "What makes Abraham and others righteous and able to enter Paradise is their _____ in _____ and their obedience in fulfilling _____ _____."

3. According to the Bible, how did Abraham become righteous before God? (Note Gen. 15:1, 5–6; see also Rom. 4:5, 13–16.)

4. What is the natural human definition of "righteousness?" What does God say about this? (See Rom. 3:10, 20.) Where is true "righteousness" to be found? (See Rom. 3:21–22.)

5. Abraham's faith was not something willed by him, but "the Lord God's promise was one of grace (undeserved love) and _____ Abraham's response of faith." "Abraham's faith was _____ because the _____ was great." (See text.) "The Lord's gracious promise to Abraham _____ _____ a response of _____." (See the summary.) Discuss how faith is always "created." (Even in human analogy, a child trusts his or her parents because the parents have been loving, caring, and faithful.)

6. What was the Pharisees' false concept regarding their being the children of Abraham? (Note Matt. 3:9.)

7. How does one become a "spiritual child of Abraham?" (Note Gal. 3:29.)

8. What is the profound statement of Jesus in John 8:56–59? What is he saying? What is the reaction of the Pharisees?

9. Jesus by stating, "before Abraham was born, I am" presents himself as the _____ of _____.

Read and discuss the summary.

Study Guide 3: Abraham and Resurrection; Abraham and the Ka'aba

Abraham and Resurrection

In chapter 1, read "C. Abraham and Resurrection."

1. According to the Qur'an (Surah 2:260), how did Abraham supposedly receive proof of the resurrection?

2. The Sadducees did not believe in the resurrection. According to the Bible (Matt. 22:31–32), what proof did Jesus give concerning the resurrection?

3. "The Bible states that Abraham's belief in the resurrection was evidenced in his willingness to _____ _____." (See text.) What was his reasoning according to Hebrews 11:18–19?

4. "No one can have fellowship with him [the great I AM] and not be _____." (See the summary.) What does this mean to you as a believer in Jesus? (See John 3:36; 1 John 5:12.)

Read and discuss the summary.

Abraham and the Ka'aba

In chapter 1, read "D. Abraham and the Ka'aba."

5. According to the Qur'an, why was the Ka'aba supposedly built?

6. Read the section on "Mecca" in "Background Information on the Life of Muhammad." What was the situation of the Ka'aba in Muhammad's day? How did this affect Muhammad?

7. On what day in the Islamic lunar calendar is the hajj to Mecca held? How do the Muslims dress? Why?
What is the ritual of the hajj?
What is the meaning of the throwing of stones at a pillar?
Who is Abraham supposedly willing to sacrifice? Where?
How is the hajj concluded?
Look up the hajj online. What was the attendance at the last hajj?

8. Where, according to the Bible (Gen. 22:2), was Isaac to have been sacrificed? What does this fact do to the whole idea of the hajj?

Read and discuss the summary.

Study Guide 4: Ishmael; Conflict in the Household of Abraham

Ishmael

In chapter 2, read "A. Ishmael."

1. How is it that Ishmael was born (Gen. 16:1–2)?

2. According to Genesis 17:15–16, the plan of the Lord God is that the promise of a son would be through _____. (See text.)

3. What does this "arrangement" with Hagar reveal about Abraham and Sarah?

4. According to the Qur'an, Abraham was given "_____ of a _____ son" (Surah 37:101).
   What status is Ishmael given in the Qur'an?

5. What does the Bible say about Ishmael?
   Why does the Bible not give prominence to Ishmael?

Read the summary.

Conflict in the Household of Abraham

In chapter 2, read "B. Conflict in the Household of Abraham."

6. What is the attitude of Hagar?

7. How does Sarah in turn treat Hagar?

8. What does the angel of the Lord tell Hagar?
   What promise is she given?
   What is she to name her son? Why?

9. Why does Sarah insist on getting rid of Hagar and her son?
   What is her concern (Gen. 21:10)?

10. "Sarah states emphatically what the Lord God had already _____ set forth to Abraham: it is Isaac who is the son of the _____." (See the summary.) Discuss how this is a crucial, crisis situation.

Read and discuss the summary.

Study Guide 5: Abraham's Concern for Ishmael and the Covenant Promise to Isaac; Ishmael or Isaac Offered as a Sacrifice; Isaac

Abraham's Concern for Ishmael and the Covenant Promise to Isaac

In chapter 2, read "C. Abraham's Concern for Ishmael and the Covenant Promise to Isaac."

1. How is Abraham distressed greatly by the conflict in his family? What might have been his conflicting thoughts?

2. What rights could the son of the maidservant have?

3. What comfort does the Lord God offer to Abraham concerning "the boy and your maidservant?" (Note Gen. 21:13 and Gen. 25:16.)

4. What is the clear statement of the Lord God concerning Sarah and Isaac? (Note Gen. 21:11–13 and Gen. 17:19.)

Read the summary. Why did the conflict in Abraham's family arise? Can there be hope for understanding between Jews and Arabs?

Ishmael or Isaac Offered as a Sacrifice

In chapter 2, read "D. Ishmael or Isaac Offered as a Sacrifice."

5. How have the Qur'an and Islamic tradition answered the question whether Ishmael or Isaac are sacrificed?

6. What is the clear teaching of the Bible concerning the sacrifice of Isaac?

Read the summary. Discuss evidence that the son offered was Isaac.

Isaac

In chapter 2, read "E. Isaac."

7. According to Surah 21:72–73, Isaac and Jacob are made righteous without belief in the promise of the "seed" of the Messiah and Savior. (Note and discuss Gal. 3:6–8. See Rom. 4:16.)

8. Who is a recipient of the promise made to Abraham? (Note Rom. 9:6–8.) What is the difference between "natural children" and "children of the promise?"

Read the summary and discuss "righteousness" by faith in the promise of the "seed" of the Messiah and Savior given to Abraham.

Study Guide 6: Jews, Christians, Muslims

In chapter 3, read "A. Jews and Christians in the Qur'an and the Bible."

1. Discuss what the Qur'an states concerning the Jews.

2. Discuss what the Qur'an states concerning Christians.

3. How does the Bible view all people?

4. Finish and discuss: "We did not first have to _____ ourselves by be-lieving in God and doing what is _____, before God loved us in _____." (See text.)

5. How does the love of God in Christ reach out to all people? "God's love was _____, and was _____, _____, and _____ in his Son, Jesus the Messiah. . . . (In contrast, in the Qur'an, 'Allah _____ not the disbelievers')." (See text.)

6. Explain John 3:16 in its original power and emphasis.

7. How would you respond to the view that Christianity is intolerant and narrow?

8. Finish and discuss how the great love of God in Christ provides the "cure for sin," breaks down barriers and unites people. God's "love in Christ is extended to all, breaking down _____ between people by _____ them to God and to _____ _____ through the _____ of _____ _____ on the _____." (See the summary.) What ought this motivate us to do?

Read the summary.

Study Guide 7: The Nature of Allah / Lord God

In chapter 4, read "A. The Nature of Allah / Lord God."

1. How is Allah described in the Qur'an?

2. How does the Qur'an deny Jesus as "the Son of God?"

3. How is the Lord God described in the Bible?

4. Contrast the "love" of the Lord God with the "love" of Allah.

5. Why is Allah not called "Father"? What does it mean to you that the Lord God is "our Father"?

6. Discover and share the names of the Lord God in the Bible. (Use them in your personal meditation.)

7. Finish and discuss: "The Christian faith does not teach the existence of three _____ (tritheism)." (See text.)

8. In what actions did Jesus demonstrate his divinity?

9. What claims did Jesus make of himself?

10. How did the apostles attest to the divinity of Jesus?

11. Finish: "As the _____ of the _____ is inseparable from the _____, 'the _____ is the _____ of God's glory.'" (See text.)

12. Finish: "The Bible uniquely reveals that in his essence *God is* _____." (See the summary.)

13. Give reasons why Allah and the Lord God are not the same. See "H. Who is the God of Abraham?" in chapter 14.

Read and ponder the summary.

Study Guide 8: The Will of Allah / Lord God

In chapter 4, read "B. The Will of Allah / Lord God."

1. Finish and discuss: "Allah determines the present and eternal destiny for good or ill of human beings. This is his _____ will." "The strong message of the Qur'an is that the _____ of Allah _____ and _____ all things." (See text.)

2. What do the often repeated words in the Qur'an, "Allah sendeth whom He will astray, and guideth whom He will," mean for the Muslim in this life and the next?
   (It should be noted that the "majority" of the Shi'a "reject the 'official' Sunnai predestinarianism and believe in the freedom of human choice." See section B.1.e, "Free will and Allah," in chapter 7.)

3. What does it mean that "The Lord God is not the author of evil"? Give examples from happenings today to affirm the truth, "While the Lord God permits evil, he does not cause evil or approve of evil."

4. The believer in Christ "looks back through the _____ and in wonder sees God's love for him or her originating in _____. It is an eternal _____ that chose and _____ him or her to be God's very own by his _____ through _____ in Jesus, the Messiah. This truth is a great _____ to the believer in _____." (See text.) Do we see the "comfort" in this approach?

5. Why do we know that the Lord God predestines no one to damnation?

6. Discuss: "If people are lost it is due to their own sin and persistent unbelief."

7. Read "A. How can I have the certainty of eternal life?" in chapter 14. Note the differences between Allah and the Lord God in dealing with the destiny of humankind.

Read and ponder words of comfort in the summary.

Study Guide 9: Allah / Lord God as Creator; The Person of Jesus

Allah / Lord God as Creator

In chapter 4, read "C. Allah / Lord God as Creator."

1. What does the Qur'an say in Surah 35:11 about the creation of male and female? How does it differ from the biblical creation of female?

2. What does it mean that "man is his [Allah's] vice regent on earth" (Surah 2:30)?

3. What is our responsibility as a "caretaker" of the Lord God's creation?

4. The Bible says that the Lord God has a plan and purpose for each of us. What does this mean to you?

5. What comfort is it to you that the psalmist says, "My times are in your hands" (Ps. 31:15)?

Read and discuss the summary.

The Person of Jesus

In chapter 5, read "A. The Person of Jesus."

6. What misconception is presented concerning Jesus in Surah 6:101?

7. What are some titles the Qur'an gives to Jesus?

8. Consider references from the Bible where Jesus is the Son of God. How often is Jesus referred to as the Son of God in the New Testament?

9. See Daniel 7:13–14 and discover the meaning of the designation "Son of Man." How does this "fit" Jesus?

10. What false view of Mary does the Qur'an attribute to Christians? What is the true description of Mary in the Bible?

11. How does Islam answer the question, "What do you think of Christ— whose son is he?"

Read and ponder the summary.

Study Guide 10: The Nativity; The Mission of Jesus

The Nativity

In chapter 5, read "B. The Nativity."

1. Discuss that in the Qur'an Jesus is "acknowledged as the promised _____." He, however, is "not recognized as the _____ of _____." (See text.)

2. How is the Bible's account of the annunciation unique and different from the Qur'an's?

3. In the Qur'an Jesus is acknowledged as a prophet, "However, Jesus will be 'only a _____' (Surah 4:171), nothing more. He will be a '_____ son' of Mary (Surah 19:19), but _____ more." (See text.)

4. In witnessing to Muslims how might the words of Gabriel be cited to share the true nature of Jesus? (See "2. Quote Gabriel (Arabic: Jibra'il)" under "D. How to Share the Good News with a Muslim" in chapter 15.)

5. Read section 3, "The birth of Jesus," and share the significance of
   * the "decree" of Caesar Augustus as part of God's plan;
   * the universal dimension to the account of the birth of Jesus;
   * the importance of the "town of Bethlehem";
   * the "sign" of the child lying in a manger;
   * the good news being announced first to shepherds;
   * "a Savior" who is "Christ the Lord";
   * the Son of God born humbly in a stable, lying in a manger.

6. When the shepherds saw the baby Jesus, how were their lives changed?

7. Read the summary. In two columns note the differences in the Qur'an and the Bible regarding the annunciation, conception, birth, and name of Jesus.

The Mission of Jesus

In chapter 5, read "C. The Mission of Jesus."

8. What does the Qur'an mean when it says that Jesus was a "slave" to Allah? How is the description of Jesus as a "slave" or "servant" different in the Bible?

9. What does it mean that Jesus "performs the great exchange"?

10. Read and discuss the summary.

Study Guide 11: The Crucifixion

In chapter 5, read "D. The Crucifixion."

1. Concerning the crucifixion of Christ, the Qur'an states that Jesus was not crucified, but only "_____ so unto them; . . . they _____ him _____ for certain" (Surah 4:157). "The generally accepted Muslim view affirms that Jesus did not die, but that Allah _____ him (*rafa'u*) to himself."[1] (See text and discuss.)

2. According to the Qur'an, who was supposedly substituted for Jesus? Why was someone supposedly substituted?

3. According to Islamic tradition, what will Jesus do upon his return?

4. Share facts from the Bible clearly attesting to Jesus's crucifixion.

5. How is Jesus's crucifixion affirmed in his resurrection?

6. Finish: "The crucifixion of Jesus is _____ and _____. If there is no crucifixion, then there is no _____ for sin." (See text.)

7. Jesus rebukes Peter for objecting to his being crucified and states that this prohibition by Peter comes from _____. A denial of the crucifixion of Jesus came not from "the things of _____, but the things of _____" (Matt. 16:21–23).

8. Cite several sources from secular history as evidence to corroborate the fact of the crucifixion of Jesus.

9. Read and share the summary. What does the willingness of Jesus to die as the atoning sacrifice upon the despised cross show? What does Christ's resolve to endure this most humiliating of all deaths demonstrate? Why is the fact of Jesus's crucifixion central to the Christian faith?

Study Guide 12: Ransom and Sacrifice for Sin

In chapter 5, read "E. Ransom and Sacrifice for Sin."

   1. See text and discuss the significance of each statement:
- "In the Qur'an, there is no _____ for sin."
- Yet, Surah 37:107 states, "We [Allah] ransomed him [_____]."
- "There is no _____ for ransom sacrifice."
- "Allah _____ his demands in the words 'We tax not any soul beyond its scope' (Surah 7:42)."

   2. While it is true that one sinful human being cannot ransom another sinful human being (Ps. 49:7–8), Jesus is the _____ Son of God who gave "his life as a ransom for many" (Matt. 20:28).

   3. Why is it true that "without the shedding of blood there is no forgiveness" (Heb. 9:22)?

   4. Note the strong emphasis on sacrifice in the Old Testament.

   5. Note the strong emphasis on sacrifice in the New Testament.

   6. Read and discuss the summary.
- In the Qur'an, "the strict demands of divine justice are _____ to human ability."
- "The denial of ransom and sacrifice is so complete that in the Qur'an there are only _____ plagues by which Allah shows his power to free the Hebrew people."
- "The justice of the Lord God cannot be pushed aside or _____."
- "The demands of the Lord God's holy law are not adjusted down to human _____."
- "Jesus did not say, '_____ your _____ to love your enemies.'"
- "The Lord God, with a _____ that cannot bear to see the sinner condemned, finds a way to deal seriously with sin and meet his own just demands."
- "Sin is not _____. The Lord God's condemnation of sin is not _____. Sin is _____ for. The sacrifice of Jesus was _____ 'once for all' when he willingly offered up himself as the _____ of God for the sins of the whole world (Heb. 7:27)."

Read "A. How can I have the certainty of eternal life?" in chapter 14.

Study Guide 13: Grace and Faith

In chapter 5, read "F. Grace and Faith."

1. The Qur'an states that only Allah is able to forgive sins (Surah 3:135). Discuss how the question is not only, "Does God forgive sins?" but "How and on what basis does God forgive sins?"

2. What does it mean when Paul says that God "presented [Jesus] as a sacrifice of atonement, through faith in his blood. He did this to demonstrate his justice" (Rom. 3:25)?

3. How is the sacrifice of God's Son different from a pagan sacrifice?

4. What problem is there with the idea that "since Allah is able to forgive sins, there is no need for a Mediator or a Savior"?

5. What does it mean that forgiveness is ours by grace "through faith in his [Jesus's] blood" (Rom. 3:25) and that Christ is "our Passover lamb" (1 Cor. 5:7)?

6. Why is righteousness not possible by the law but only "through the righteousness that comes by faith" (Rom. 4:13)? (See Rom. 3:9–20.)

7. What does it mean to you personally that you are saved by grace and through faith in Christ Jesus?

8. What problem is there with the Qur'an stating, "whoso doth good works . . . and he (or she) is a believer such will enter Paradise" (Surah 4:124) and "If ye love Allah . . . Allah will love you and forgive you" (Surah 3:31)?

Share the summary.

9. Comment on: "Jesus not only died for us but suffered *with us*, and so he is able to 'sympathize with our weaknesses.'"

Ponder and share the section "E. How can I face adversity?" in chapter 14.

Study Guide 14: Rebirth

In chapter 5, read "G. Rebirth."

1. In the Qur'an, "Rebirth is not necessary since human beings are basically born _____ _____." (See text.)

2. "Since human beings are born _____ (Ps. 51:5), rebirth is _____ if one is to enter the kingdom of God." (See text.)

3. When is one reborn?

4. Discuss: "To be reborn means to become a _____ of God. Just as we cannot accomplish our own natural _____ or conception, nor our own _____, so we become a child of God not by 'natural descent, nor of human _____ or a husband's will,' but we are 'born [begotten] of God' (John 1:13)."

5. How does Ephesians 5:26 describe baptism?

6. Complete: "Allah does not have an _____ _____ with Muslims, nor does he dwell in them." (See text.) Compare this with the Christian faith.

7. Discuss the "new life in Christ": "filled with a sense of _____, _____, and _____ and the _____ of _____ _____. Christ brings a new _____, a new _____, a new _____, and a new _____ of no longer _____ for _____ 'but for him who died for [us] and was raised again' (2 Cor. 5:15)."

8. Discuss how a Christian has "new life and a new way of living, not by works, not in _____ and _____, but 'by faith in the Son of God.' Now we have a new _____ _____ and _____ by the Holy Spirit. That motivation is not ____ _____ or hope of _____ but the _____ of _____, 'who loved me and gave himself for me' (Gal. 2:20)."

Read and share the summary.
Read and share the section "C. How does God connect with me personally?" in chapter 14.

Study Guide 15: Angels; Jinn and Satan

Angels

In chapter 6, read "A. Angels."

1. What similar things do the Qur'an and the Bible say about angels?

2. What different things do the Qur'an and the Bible say about angels?

3. How have angels served believers in the Lord God?

4. What service did angels render to Jesus?

5. Share times when the Lord's angels ministered to you.

Jinn and Satan

In chapter 6, read "B. Jinn and Satan."

6. From the various views given, what is your answer to the question, "Who are the Jinn?"

7. Compare the views of the Bible and the Qur'an concerning the devil.

8. According to the Qur'an, how do the Jinn tempt the Muslim?

9. How did the Jinn supposedly use their powers on behalf of Solomon?

10. What does the Bible say about evil angels?

11. What is the Christian's weapon against evil angels?

Read and share the summary on angels; also, the summary on Jinn. Say a prayer of thanks to the Lord for his angels who are his servants to protect and defend you and carry your spirit to paradise.

Study Guide 16: The Creation of Humankind; The Nature of Humankind; The Fall of Humankind

The Creation of Humankind

In chapter 7, read "A. The Creation of Humankind."

1. How do the Qur'an and the Bible differ in their descriptions of the creation of man and woman?

2. How does the Lord God express a "personal touch" in his creation of man and woman?

3. What does it mean that in the Bible male and female were created in the image of God? In what respect do human beings no longer have this image of God?

4. How is the image of God restored in the believer in Christ? When will the image be completely restored?

The Nature of Humankind

In chapter 7, read "B. The Nature of Humankind."

5. What does the Qur'an teach about original sin?

6. What do the Shi'a and the Sunni believe with regard to free will?

7. What is Muhammad's answer in the dispute between Abu Bakr and Umar?

8. According to the Bible, what does it mean that humankind is "sinful"?

9. Comment on the following quote from the text: "While a person has the ability to choose in human matters such as whether to go here or there, human beings do not have free will in spiritual matters."

The Fall of Humankind

In chapter 7, read "C. The Fall of Humankind."

10. "The Qur'an offers no promise of a _____."

11. Interpret Genesis 3:15.

12. How does the Lord God show personal tenderness and mercy to Adam and Eve after the fall?

Read and share the summaries.

Read and ponder also the section "B. What is the nature of humankind?" in chapter 14 and "3. What the Bible Teaches about Human Sinfulness," under "C. Be Fortified with Biblical Truth," in chapter 15.

Study Guide 17: Women; Marriage

Women

In chapter 8, read "A. Women."

1. Finish and comment on: "The Qur'an teaches that man and woman are equal in _____ _____. . . . However, 'men are in _____ of women.'"

2. Finish and comment on: "A wife is to be admonished if she is given to 'rebellion.' Then she may be banished to a _____ bed and finally _____ or _____ for her disobedience (Surah 4:34)." (See text.)

3. Using the Internet, share some accounts of recent abuse of women in the Muslim world.

4. Finish and comment on: According to the Bible "women are given _____ and _____ equal to those of men." "In Christ Jesus men and women are given equal _____ as 'sons of God' (Gal. 3:26)."

5. Recall the status and service of women in the ministry of Jesus.

Marriage

In chapter 8, read "B. Marriage."

6. Comment on: "The Qur'an allows a man to marry as many wives as he can afford, up to four wives at a _____. Not so for a woman. . . . The woman may not marry from any '_____ of the _____' [Christians and Jews], as a man may. The husband determines the religion of the _____." (See the summary.)

7. Comment on: "Jesus _____ God's original _____ for marriage." "Christ is the _____ and _____ of marriage relationships." (See text.)

8. Comment on: "All believers are called to 'submit to one another out of _____ for _____' (Eph. 5:21). The believing husband loves his wife 'just as _____ loved the _____ . . .' (Eph. 5:25)." "The believing wife in turn _____ and respects her husband and submits to him 'as to the _____' (Eph. 5:22)." "Christ and his bride, the church, are the model and the _____ for both the believing _____ and the believing _____."

Read and share the summaries.

Study Guide 18: Divorce; Veil and Modesty

Divorce

In chapter 8, read "C. Divorce."

1. What is the Qur'an's teaching with regard to divorce?

2. Finish and comment on: "Divorce is _____ in Islam. The door is wide open for a woman or a man who wants to come out of marriage."[2]

3. How did Muhammad resolve the objection to his marriage with Zainab, the wife of his adopted son Zaid?

4. Finish and comment on: "Jesus elevates marriage by bringing it back to the Lord God's _____ _____."

5. What did Jesus say about divorce?

6. On what basis does the apostle Paul allow divorce?

7. When divorce happens, what is the Christian's attitude and comfort?

Read and reflect on the summary.

Veil and Modesty

In chapter 8, read "D. Veil and Modesty."

8. What are the reasons that a Muslim woman wears a veil?

9. What does the Bible teach concerning purity for Christian men and women? Comment on the need for such purity in our churches, our culture, and in our personal lives today.

10. What is the "inwardly compelling" reason that a Christian is to live a pure and modest life? How can Christians overcome temptation and become a light and leaven of purity in their lives?

Read and reflect on the summary.

Study Guide 19: Homosexuality; Murder, Suicide, Abortion

Homosexuality

In chapter 9, read "A. Homosexuality."

1. What does the Qur'an call homosexual behavior? Do you agree with the statement: "It is unnatural, it is wrong, it is something disgusting"?[3]

2. How do the accounts of Sodom (Gen. 19:5), Gibeah (Judges 19:22), and the Roman world (Rom. 1:18–32) serve as a warning today?

3. Reflect on the summary. Comment on: "While the behavior is abhorrent, the Bible holds out hope to the homosexual to be 'washed . . . sanctified . . . [and] justified in the name of the Lord Jesus Christ and by the Spirit of our God' (1 Cor. 6:11)."

Murder, Suicide, Abortion

In chapter 9, read "B. Murder, Suicide, Abortion."

4. To what does the Qur'an compare the gravity of murder?

5. Comment on this Islamic teaching: "Whatever applies to the crime of murder likewise applies to committing suicide. . . . Soul-life begins with 'four months in the womb.'" Search the Internet to learn about Islam and abortion.

6. What does the Bible say in Psalm 139:13–14 about the sacredness of life?

7. What does the early Christian authority *The Didache* teach about abortion? Search the Internet to learn about your church's teaching on abortion.

8. Search the Internet to learn the total number of children aborted since 1973. How does this affect the regard for human life? How does it affect other social issues such as family life, abuse, Social Security, etc.?

9. How would you comfort someone who is burdened with a past abortion?

10. How does the biblical view of life as being sacred and redeemed by the blood of Christ determine our resolve to nurture, protect, and cherish human life from the womb to the tomb? What can you do to further the biblical view of the sanctity of life?

Share and reflect on the summary.

Study Guide 20: Aggression and Jihad

In chapter 9, read "C. Aggression and Jihad."

1. What is the basic meaning of "jihad" in the Qur'an? What are the various aspects of jihad in the life of a Muslim?

2. Which Surah was quoted by the five Islamic caliphates on February 23, 1998 in the fatwa declaring war against the United States?

3. What attitude are Muslims to have toward "disbelievers"?

4. What was the exhortation of the letter to the 9/11 suicide bombers found in the luggage of Atta and published in the *Washington Post*?

5. Finish: "While the Qur'an teaches that human life is sacred and one is not to take one's own life, in the case of _____ [against infidels] it is not only _____ but _____."

6. Might the Christian agree that "today many Muslims feel their faith and values threatened by the secularism, materialism, and promiscuity of Western influence"? In what respect would a Christian differ with the "Islamic fundamentalists" when threatened by the secular culture?

7. According to the Muslim Pickthall, Muhammad in person led _____ campaigns (nine in hard fighting) and planned and controlled _____. (Suggestion: Read "Background Information on the Life of Muhammad.")

8. Finish and comment on: While the Qur'an states that Muslims are not to be "aggressors," nevertheless, "Extremist Muslims who wish to find reason for aggressive action against _____ . . . will find sufficient _____ in the Qur'an for their actions." What is the mission and vision of Islam?

9. Finish and comment on: "The call of Christ is more than to _____ evil; it is to be active in doing _____ to all people."

10. Finish: "While early Islam was spread by the _____ and the message of Islam, early Christianity was spread by the _____ and the blood of _____."

Read and reflect on the summary.
See "G. How should the faith be propagated?" in chapter 14.

Study Guide 21: Godly Life

In chapter 9, read "D. Godly Life."

1. Describe the godly life of those who worship Allah. How is it outwardly similar to the biblical commandments?

2. What food and drink are forbidden in the Qur'an? What does the Bible say about "unclean" food? (See Acts 10:14–15; Rom. 14:14, 20; 1 Tim. 4:3–5.) (Islam also forbids eating shellfish and lard-based cooking.)

3. What is the law of retribution in the Qur'an? What do Christ and the apostle Paul teach about revenge and retribution? (See Matt. 5:38–45; Rom. 12:17–21.)

4. In the New Testament, what is essential for a godly life?

5. Distinguish between the acts of the sinful nature and the fruit of the Spirit.

6. In contrast to a relative, subjective expression of love, when is love genuine and authentic according to Romans 12:9 and Psalm 97:10?

7. Read and discuss Romans 12:9–21. Do you agree that it would be good to memorize these words along with other portions of Scripture? (Many Muslims memorize the entire Qur'an.)

8. What is the motive and moving force for the godly life of the believer?

9. Read and discuss each paragraph in "D. What meaning does my life have with God?" in chapter 14.

Read and ponder each paragraph of the summary, noting the difference between the Islamic and Christian godly life with regard to source and motivation.

Study Guide 22: Resurrection; Judgment

Resurrection

In chapter 10, read "A. Resurrection."

1. What does Surah 17:13–15 in the Qur'an teach about the resurrection of the body?

2. What do 1 Thessalonians 4:16 and John 11:25 in the Bible teach about the resurrection of the body?

3. Finish and comment on: "The evil works of _____ will _____ them. The _____ works of the believers will be cited as _____ of their saving faith."

4. What is the Father's will according to John 6:40?

5. What does it mean that "the resurrection will usher in the promised new creation for humankind and for all of creation"? (See also the summary.)

Judgment

In chapter 10, read "B. Judgment."

6. What does Surah 39:68–71 in the Qur'an teach about the final judgment?

7. What do Surah 3:106 and Surah 84:7 in the Qur'an teach about belief, scales, and accounting?

8. How is the belief of the Qur'an similar to the belief of the Pharisees?

9. According to the Qur'an, what will Jesus do on the final day?

10. What does the Bible teach concerning the judgment in Matthew 25:31–32?

11. How is a good person like a "good tree" (Matt. 12:35–37)? What does a good tree bear?

12. What is the "book of life"? Whose names are recorded there? (See Rev. 20:12–15; 21:27.)

13. What is a person's only certain hope to escape condemnation on judgment day?

Read and ponder the summary.

Study Guide 23: Paradise

In chapter 10, read "C. Paradise."

1. How does the Qur'an diminish and compromise the justice of God to meet human sinfulness and limitation?

2. How is Paradise described in the Qur'an? What is Paradise for the Muslim man?

3. What does Muhammad twice say about hell and the "majority of its dwellers"?

4. According to the Qur'an, to whom is Paradise promised? What may one have to first pass through before he or she enters Paradise?

5. What comfort does Jesus give to those who believe in him?

6. How is the heavenly Jerusalem described? What does it mean?

7. What will God personally do for the believer?

8. What is the Lord's promise concerning death, mourning, crying, and pain? How does this give hope, strength, and comfort to you?

9. What is "the great blessing of paradise" and the great "emphasis" for the believers in Christ? (This is something not granted to the Muslim, since Allah is transcendent and has no intimate fellowship with his believer.)

10. What did Jesus teach about marriage in paradise?

11. What does the Bible teach about the law of the Lord God and his just demands?

12. How is it possible to be "justified" before the Lord God?

13. Who are those who stand before the throne of God? Do you personally have this certainty?

Read and rejoice in the summary.

Study Guide 24: Sacred Writings

In chapter 11, read "A. Primary Sources: The Qur'an and the Bible" and "B. Conflicting Statements: The Qur'an versus the Bible." Read also "1. The Reliability of the Bible," under "C. Be Fortified with Biblical Truth," in chapter 15.

1. How does the Muslim look at the Qur'an?

2. What does the Qur'an say about the Bible?

3. Why do Christians believe the Bible is the inspired Word of God?

4. How does one answer the conjecture of some that the belief in Jesus as Savior and the Son of God gradually evolved over time?

5. Finish and comment on: "If one rejects Jesus as the _____ and _____ of _____, one must abandon or rewrite the entire New Testament." (See text box.)

6. Share some of the accounts in the Qur'an that conflict with the Bible.

7. Show how the witness of the New Testament is clear and powerful from

   • Jesus
   • St. Peter
   • St. John
   • St. Paul
   • St. Luke the Evangelist

8. How were the discrepancies between the various versions of the Qur'an handled? What questions does this raise?

9. Why did the various books of the Bible become the authentic "canon" of the Word of God?

10. Discuss "F. What about the differences between the Qur'an and the Bible?" in chapter 14.

Read and share the summaries in chapter 11.

Study Guide 25: Practices of Faith

The Creed

In chapter 12, read "A. The Creed."

1. What is the Shahada of the Islam religion? What do the Christian creeds confess about "one God"?

2. Why is Allah not addressed as "Father"? What does the Apostles' Creed confess about the Father?

3. What is the significance of the Creator of the cosmos having a "Father's heart"?

4. Why according to Islam is there no need for a Mediator?

5. What important truths does the Apostles' Creed confess about the person of Jesus?

6. What does the Apostles' Creed confess about the Holy Spirit?

Read and discuss the summary.

Prayer

(Prayer will be discussed separately in study guide 26.)

Almsgiving

In chapter 12, read "C. Almsgiving."

7. Complete: "Besides helping to alleviate fear of _____, giving alms assures the Muslim of eternal reward." Contrast this with the Christian motive for giving.

8. How does Jesus personalize our compassion for the needy? Read and discuss the summary.

Fasting

In chapter 12, read "D. Fasting."

9. What different approach is there to fasting during Ramadan and fasting in the Bible?

Read and discuss the summary.

Pilgrimage

In chapter 12, read "E. Pilgrimage."

Read and discuss the summary.

Study Guide 26: Prayer

In chapter 12, read "B. Prayer."

1. Finish: Prayer is prescribed and obligatory for the Muslim _____ times a day.

2. What are the five times of prayer for the Muslim?

3. What does the Muslim prayer consist of?

4. What does the requirement of ablutions and ritual remind you of?

5. What is the Friday congregation prayer for Muslims?

6. What is prayer for the Christian? How does it differ from the Muslim concept of prayer?

7. What does it mean to pray "in Jesus's name"?

8. What does it mean to "pray continually"?

9. Discuss the various times and occasions for Christian prayer.

10. Identify the times of prayer (Adoration, Confession, Thanksgiving, Supplication) in a Christian worship service.

11. How can you improve your prayer life?

12. How can Christian congregations improve their prayer life?

Read the summary. Note in particular Jesus's prayer life and the prayer life of the early Christians.

To wrap up your study, discuss chapter 13, "Brief Summation." Consider chapter 15, "Sharing the Good News with Muslims."

Notes

Preface

1. Mohammad M. Pickthall, translator's preface to *The Glorious Qur'an: Arabic Text and English Rendering*, 10th rev. ed. (Des Plaines, IL: Library of Islam, 1994), vii–viii.

2. N. J. Dawood, ed., *The Koran Translated with Notes* (London: Penguin, 1999), i.

3. Alan Jones, introduction to *The Koran*, translated by J. M. Rodwell, Everyman's Library (London: J. M. Dent, 1994), xxvii, xxvi (italics added). The "Note on the Editor" (p. vii) states that Alan Jones "has taught Arabic and Islamic Studies there [in Oxford] since 1957. He is a specialist in pre-Islamic and early Islamic Arabic and in Quranic Studies, and, at a much later period, in the literature of Muslim Spain. He is at present writing a book on the pre-Islamic background of the Qur'an."

Chapter 1   Abraham

1. Ergun Mehmet Caner and Fetthi Emir Caner, *Unveiling Islam* (Grand Rapids: Kregel, 2002), 129.

2. John L. Esposito, *Islam: The Straight Path* (New York: Oxford University Press, 1988), 94.

3. Caner and Caner, *Unveiling Islam*, 130.

4. B. K. Wiltker, "Moriah," in *The Zondervan Pictorial Encyclopedia of the Bible*, ed. Merrill C. Tenney (Grand Rapids: Zondervan, 1978), 4:276.

Chapter 2   Ishmael and Isaac

1. David Van Biema et al., "The Legacy of Abraham," *Time*, September 30, 2002.

Chapter 3   Jews, Christians, Muslims

1. Silas, "Errors and Omissions in the PBS Special *Muhammad: Legacy of a Prophet*," January 20, 2003, http://www.answering-islam.org/Silas/pbs-special.htm. See J. Spencer Trimingham, *Christianity among the Arabs in Pre-Islamic Times* (London: Longman, 1979).

Chapter 4   Allah / Lord God

1. The Muslim always says "Amen" after this prayer. As J. M. Rodwell ("Notes," in *The Koran*, Everyman's Library [London: J. M. Dent, 1994], 431) explains, this opening is

> recited several times in each of the five daily prayers, and on many other occasions, as in concluding a bargain. . . . This formula—*Bismillahi 'rrahmani 'rrahim*—is prefixed to each Sura except the ninth.

The former of the two epithets implies that the mercy of God is exercised as occasions arise, towards all his creatures; the latter that the quality of mercy is inherent in God and permanent—so that there is only a shade of difference between the two words. . . . Perhaps, *In the name of Allah, the God of Mercy, the Merciful,* would more fully express the original Arabic.

2. The names of Allah are listed in Maulana Muhammad Ali, *The Religion of Islam* (Chelsea, MI: BookCrafters, 1990), 121–24.

3. The Hadith (a collection of sayings and examples of Muhammad) states that this surah "is held to be worth a third of the whole Qur'an and the seven heavens and the seven earths are founded upon it" (Ergun Mehmet Caner and Fetthi Emir Caner, *Unveiling Islam* [Grand Rapids: Kregel, 2002], 108).

4. Ali, *Religion of Islam*, 108–9.

5. Norman L. Geisler and Abdul Saleeb, *Answering Islam* (Grand Rapids: Baker Books, 2002), 21.

6. Ibid., 22.

7. Chawkat Moucarry, *The Prophet & the Messiah* (Downers Grove, IL: InterVarsity, 2001), 91.

8. Ali, *Religion of Islam*, 242.

9. Geisler and Saleeb, *Answering Islam*, 146.

10. Fazlur Rahman, *Islam*, 2nd ed. (Chicago: University of Chicago Press, 1993), 85–99.

11. Geisler and Saleeb, *Answering Islam*, 30.

12. Walter R. Roehrs and Dean O. Wenthe, "Matthew, 'Pharisees'," in *Concordia Self-Study Bible*, ed. Robert G. Hoerber (St. Louis: Concordia, 1984), 1483.

13. Jen Christiansen, "Predestination and Fatalism." *The World of Islam: Resources for Understanding* (Colorado Springs: Global Mapping International, 2000), CD-ROM.

14. Caner and Caner, *Unveiling Islam*, 167.

15. David Van Biema, Bruce Crumley, "Wahhabism: Toxic Faith?" Islam's Other Hot Spots. *Time.* September 15, 2003, 46.

Chapter 5   Jesus

1. Anis A. Shorrosh, *Islam Revealed: A Christian Arab's View of Islam* (Nashville: Thomas Nelson, 1988), 114.

2. Ergun Mehmet Caner and Fetthi Emir Caner, *Unveiling Islam* (Grand Rapids: Kregel, 2002), 220–21.

3. Helmut Gatje, *The Qur'an and Its Exegesis* (Oxford: Oneworld, 1996), 128.

4. "217: Judas Scourged and Mocked," *The Gospel of Barnabas* 217, http://barnabas.net/barnabasP217.html.

5. Cyril Glassé, "What Do We Know about the 'Gospel of Barnabas'?" *The Concise Encyclopedia of Islam* (San Francisco: Harper & Row, 1989), 64, http://answering-islam.org/Barnabas/.

6. Norman L. Geisler and Abdul Saleeb, *Answering Islam* (Grand Rapids: Baker Books, 2002), 303.

7. A. F. Wells, "Gnosticism," in *Zondervan Pictorial Encyclopedia*, ed. Merrill C. Tenney (Grand Rapids: Zondervan, 1978), 737–38.

8. Caner and Caner, *Unveiling Islam*, 93.

9. Ibid., 221.

10. Geisler and Saleeb, *Answering Islam*, 158.

11. "An Open Letter and Call from Muslim Religious Leaders—A Common Word between Us and You," http://www.islamicity.com/articles/Articles.asp?ref=CM0710-3390 (italics original).

Chapter 6   Angels and Jinn

1. J. M. Rodwell, "Notes," in *The Koran*, Everyman's Library (London: J. M. Dent, 1994), 432.

2. Ibid.

3. Norman L. Geisler and Abdul Saleeb, *Answering Islam* (Grand Rapids: Baker Books, 2002), 38.

4. Syed Abu-Ala' Maududi, *Chapter Introductions to the Quran*, http://www.unn.ac.uk /societies/islamic/quran/intro/io72.htm.

5. Rodwell, "Notes," in *The Koran*, 461n14.

Chapter 7   Humankind

1. Chawkat Moucarry, *The Prophet & the Messiah* (Downers Grove, IL: InterVarsity, 2001), 86.

2. Ibid., 86 (brackets in original).

3. Ibid., 86, quoting Muslim, *Sahih*, trans. Abdul Hamid Siddiqi (1977; repr. New Delhi: Kitab Bhavan, 1982), 1378, no. 6325 (4731).

4. John Bowker, *What Muslims Believe* (Oxford: Oneworld, 1995), 89.

5. Maulana Muhammad Ali, *The Religion of Islam* (Chelsea, MI: BookCrafters, 1990), 248.

6. S. Abul A'la Maududi, "The Islamic Concept of Life," §2, http://www.islam101.com/sociology /conceptLife.htm, reprinted from *The Islamic Way of Life* (Lahore: Islamic Publications, 1948).

7. Ibid., §1.

8. Fazlur Rahman, *Islam*, 2nd ed. (Chicago: University of Chicago Press, 1993), 174.

9. Moucarry, *Prophet & the Messiah*, 213.

10. Norman L. Geisler and Abdul Saleeb, *Answering Islam* (Grand Rapids: Baker Books, 2002), 31.

11. Walter R. Roehrs and Dean O. Wenthe, "Matthew, 'Pharisees'," in *Concordia Self-Study Bible*, ed. Robert G. Hoerber (St. Louis: Concordia, 1984), 1483.

12. Geisler and Saleeb, *Answering Islam*, 148.

Chapter 8   Women and Marriage

1. Ergun Mehmet Caner and Fetthi Emir Caner, *Unveiling Islam* (Grand Rapids: Kregel, 2002), 134.

2. Abraham Sarker, *Understand My Muslim People* (Newberg, OR: Barclay, 2004), 203.

3. John Bowker, *What Muslims Believe* (Oxford: Oneworld, 1995), 126–27.

4. Roland Cap Ehlke, *Speaking the Truth in Love to Muslims* (Milwaukee: Northwestern Publishing House, 2004), 101.

5. Robert F. Worth, "Stoning," *International Herald Tribune*, April 15, 2011.

6. Bowker, *What Muslims Believe*, 127.

7. Ibid., 133.

8. Ibid., 128.

Chapter 9   Ethical Teachings

1. John Bowker, *What Muslims Believe* (Oxford: Oneworld, 1995), 52.

2. Sedki Riad, "Dying and Death: Islamic View," January 21, 2002, http://www.jannah.org /article/death.html.

3. Ahmad Ibn Naqib al-Misri, *Reliance of the Traveller: A Classic Manual of Islamic Sacred Law* (Beltsville, MD: Amana, 1994), 236.

4. Ibrahim B. Syed, "Abortion," Islamic Research Foundation International, http://irfi.org /articles/articles_101_150/abortion.htm.

5. Edgar J. Goodspeed, *The Apostolic Fathers: An American Translation* (New York: Harper and Brothers, 1950), 12.

6. Bowker, *What Muslims Believe*, 79.

7. John L. Esposito, *Islam: The Straight Path* (New York: Oxford University Press, 1988), 95.

8. James A. Beverley, "Is Islam a Religion of Peace?" *Christianity Today*, January 7, 2003, 37.

9. Ergun Mehmet Caner and Fetthi Emir Caner, *Unveiling Islam* (Grand Rapids: Kregel, 2002), 185.

10. Ibid., 181.

11. John L. Esposito, *Islam: The Straight Path*. 3rd ed. (New York: Oxford University Press, 1998), 125.

12. Caner and Caner, *Unveiling Islam*, 197–98.

13. Esposito, *Islam*, 1st ed., 12.

14. Mohammad M. Pickthall, *The Glorious Qur'an: Arabic Text and English Rendering*, 10th rev. ed. (Des Plaines, IL: Library of Islam, 1994), xix.

15. Bowker, *What Muslims Believe*, 73.

16. Ibid, 41.

17. Esposito, *Islam*, 3rd ed., 162–202.

18. Caner and Caner, *Unveiling Islam*, 185.

19. Fazlur Rahman, *Islam*, 2nd ed. (Chicago: University of Chicago Press, 1993), 2.

20. Esposito, *Islam*, 1st ed., 17.

21. Beverley, "Is Islam a Religion of Peace?" 37.

22. Muhammad ibn Ismail Bukhari, *Sahih al-Bukhari*, Vol. 4 Book 53 Number 386, http://www.usc.edu/schools/college/crcc/engagement/resources/texts/muslim/hadith/bukhari/053.sbt.html.

23. "Death: The Hereafter: The Abode of Souls: Barzakh," *The World of Islam: Resources for Understanding* (Colorado Springs: Global Mapping International, 2000), CD-ROM, 1.

24. Pickthall adds in a footnote: "Since the time of Omar II the Omayyad [99–101 A.H./717–720 AD], this verse had been recited at the end of every weekly sermon in all Sunni congregations."

25. Chawkat Moucarry, *The Prophet & the Messiah* (Downers Grove, IL: InterVarsity, 2001), 117.

26. Rahman, *Islam*, 86.

27. W. Montgomery Watt, *What is Islam?* (New York: Fredrick Q. Praeger, 1968), 156.

Chapter 10   The End Times

1. See Revelation 20:12.

2. Ergun Mehmet Caner and Fetthi Emir Caner, *Unveiling Islam* (Grand Rapids: Kregel, 2002), 221.

3. Norman L. Geisler and Abdul Saleeb, *Answering Islam* (Grand Rapids: Baker Books, 2002), 116.

4. Caner and Caner, *Unveiling Islam*, 134.

5. Geisler and Saleeb, *Answering Islam*, 111.

6. Surah 19 v. 71, "Everyone will be brought to Hell, then the righteous will be saved," *Tafsir Ibn Kathir*, http://tafsir.com/default.asp?sid=19&tid=31598.

7. Muhammad ibn Ismail Bukhari, *Sahih al-Bukhari*, Vol. 8 Book 76 Number 577, http://www.usc.edu/schools/college/crcc/engagement/resources/texts/muslim/hadith/bukhari/076.sbt.html.

Chapter 11   Sacred Writings

1. Anis A. Shorrosh, *Islam Revealed: A Christian Arab's View of Islam* (Nashville: Thomas Nelson, 1988), 144.

2. Ibid.

3. H. L. Drumwright Jr., "Crucifixion," *Zondervan Pictorial Encyclopedia of the Bible*, ed. Merrill C. Tenney (Grand Rapids: Zondervan, 1976), 1:1040.

Chapter 12   Practices of Faith

1. Ahmad Ibn Naqib al-Misri, *Reliance of the Traveller: A Classic Manual of Islamic Sacred Law* (Beltsville, MD: Amana, 1994), 110–11.
2. Ergun Mehmet Caner and Fetthi Emir Caner, *Unveiling Islam* (Grand Rapids: Kregel, 2002), 123–24; cf. George Boswell, *Islam* (Nashville: Broadman and Holman, 1996), 62.
3. "How to Perform Salat," March 2, 2002, http://www.submission.org/salat-how.html, 2–10.
4. Caner and Caner, *Unveiling Islam*, 125.
5. Ibid.
6. Ibid., 127.
7. Ibid., 159.

Chapter 15   Sharing the Good News with Muslims

1. Stan Guthrie, "Doors into Islam," *Christianity Today*, September 9, 2002, 44.
2. Ergun Mehmet Caner and Fetthi Emir Caner, *Unveiling Islam* (Grand Rapids: Kregel, 2002), 224–25.
3. Roland Cap Ehlke, *Speaking the Truth in Love to Muslims* (Milwaukee: Northwestern Publishing House, 2004), 172.
4. Caner and Caner, *Unveiling Islam*, 211.
5. Ibid., 230.

Background Information on the Life of Muhammad

1. Wendy Murray Zoba, "Islam, U.S.A.: Are Christians Prepared for Muslims in the Mainstream?" *Christianity Today*, April 3, 2000, 43.
2. Mohammad M. Pickthall, translator's preface to *The Glorious Qur'an: Arabic Text and English Rendering*, 10th rev. ed. (Des Plaines, IL: Library of Islam, 1994), vii.
3. John L. Esposito, *Islam: The Straight Path* (New York: Oxford University Press, 1988), 12.
4. Ibid., 132.
5. Ibid., 13.
6. Fazlur Rahman, *Islam*, 2nd ed. (Chicago: University of Chicago Press, 1993), 24.
7. Pickthall, *Glorious Qur'an*, xv.

Background Information on Shi'ites and Sunnis

1. Paul Marshall, Roberta Green, and Lela Gilbert, *Islam at the Crossroads* (Grand Rapids: Baker Books, 2002), 52.
2. Mary Habeck, *Knowing the Enemy: Jihadist Ideology and the War on Terror* (New Haven: Yale University Press, 2006), 17–18.
3. Ibid., 163, 165.

Testimony of a Former Muslim

1. Rev. Hicham Chehab is available for speaking engagements. Email: hicham.chehab@gmail.com.

Study Guides

1. Ergun Mehmet Caner and Fetthi Emir Caner, *Unveiling Islam* (Grand Rapids: Kregel, 2002), 93
2. John Bowker, *What Muslims Believe* (Oxford: Oneworld, 1995), 128.
3. Ibid., 127.

Bibliography

Ahmad, Hazrat Mirza Tahir. *The Holy Qur'an with English Translation and Commentary*. Vol. 2. Islamabad: Islam International Publications, 1988.

Ali, Muhammad Maulana. *The Religion of Islam*. Chelsea, MI: BookCrafters, 1990.

"Answers to 7 Questions on Islam." http://www.salafipublications.com/sps/sp.cfm?subsecID=NMM01&articleID=NMM010003&articlePages=1.

Associated Press. "Sentenced to Stoning, Woman's Life Spared." *The Herald*, September 23, 2003.

Barry, A. L. *What about Islam?* St. Louis: Office of the President of the Lutheran Church—Missouri Synod, 1999.

Bente, F., and W. H. T. Dau, eds. *Concordia Triglotta*. St. Louis: Concordia, 1921.

Beverley, James A. "Is Islam a Religion of Peace?" *Christianity Today*, January 7, 2003.

Bowker, John. *What Muslims Believe*. Oxford: Oneworld, 2002.

Bukhari, Muhammad ibn Ismail. *Sahih al-Bukhari*. Translated by M. Muhsin Khan. http://www.usc.edu/schools/college/crcc/engagement/resources/texts/muslim/hadith/bukhari/.

Caner, Ergun Mehmet, and Fethi Emir Caner. *Unveiling Islam*. Grand Rapids: Kregel, 2002.

Cleveland, William L. *A History of the Modern Middle East*. 3rd ed. Boulder, CO: Westview Press, 2004.

Cook, David. "The Beginnings of Islam as an Apocalyptic Movement." Pages 79–93 in *War in Heaven/Heaven on Earth*, edited by Steven O'Leary and Glen McGhee. London: Equinox, 2005. Reprint from *Journal of Millennial Studies* 1 (2001): http://www.bu.edu/mille/publications/winter2001/cook.html.

Dawood, N. J, ed. *The Koran Translated with Notes*. London: Penguin, 1999.

DeFiglio, Pam. "A Child Chooses the Veil." *Daily Herald* (Arlington Heights, IL), January 29, 2002.

Dretke, P. James. *A Christian Approach to Muslims*. Pasadena: William Carey Library, 1979.

Ehlke, Roland Cap. *Speaking the Truth in Love to Muslims*. Milwaukee: Northwestern Publishing House, 2004.

Esposito, John L. *Islam: The Straight Path*. New York: Oxford University Press, 1988; 3rd ed., 1998.

————. *What Everyone Needs to Know about Islam*. New York: Oxford University Press, 2002.

The First Gospel of the Infancy of Jesus Christ. http://www.pseudepigrapha.com /LostBooks/infancy1.htm.

Gabriel, Brigitte. *Because They Hate*. New York: St Martin's, 2006.

Gatje, Helmut. *The Qur'an and Its Exegesis*. Oxford: Oneworld, 1996.

Geisler, Norman L., and Abdul Saleeb. *Answering Islam*. Grand Rapids: Baker Books, 2002.

Glassé, Cyril. "The Gospel of Barnabas." Page 64 in *The Concise Encyclopedia of Islam*. San Francisco: Harper & Row, 1989.

Goodspeed, Edgar J. *The Apostolic Fathers: An American Translation*. New York: Harper and Brothers, 1950.

"The Gospel of Infancy of Thomas (the Israelite)." In *The Complete Gospels*, translated by Harold Attridge and Ronald F. Hock. New York: HarperCollins, 1992.

"Gospel of Thomas: Greek Text A." In *The Apocryphal New Testament*, translated with notes by M. R. James. Oxford: Clarendon, 1924.

Gulshan Esther. *The Torn Veil*. Fort Washington, PA: CLC Publications, 1984.

Guthrie, Stan. "Doors Into Islam." *Christianity Today*, September 9, 2002.

Habeck, Mary. *Knowing the Enemy: Jihadist Ideology and the War on Terror*. New Haven: Yale University Press, 2006.

Haneff, Suzanne. *What Everyone Should Know about Islam and Muslims*. Des Plaines, IL: Library of Islam, 1993.

Hoerber, Robert G., ed. *Concordia Self-Study Bible*. St. Louis: Concordia, 1984.

"How to Perform Salat." March 2, 2002. http://www.submission.org/salat-how.html.

Ibn Naqib al-Misri, Ahmad. *Reliance of the Traveller: A Classic Manual of Islamic Sacred Law*. Translated by Nuh Ha Mim Keller. Beltsville, MD: Amana, 1994.

Ibrahim, I. A. *A Brief Illustrated Guide to Understanding Islam*. Houston: Dar-us-Salam, 1997.

Jones, Alan. Introduction to *The Koran*, translated by J. M. Rodwell. Everyman. London: Orion; Rutland, VT: Charles E. Tuttle, 1998.

"Judas Scourged and Mocked." The Gospel of Barnabas, §217. http://barnabas.net /barnabasP217.html.

Khan, Zafrulla Muhammad. *The Quran: Arabic Text English Translation*. Brooklyn: Olive Branch, 1977.

Lacayo, Richard. "About Face: An Inside Look at How Women Fared under Taliban Oppression and What the Future Holds for Them Now." *Time*, December 3, 2001.

Landes, Richard. "Apocalyptic Islam and Bin Laden." November 20, 2001. http://www
.bu.edu/mille/people/rlpages/Bin_Laden.html.

Loochhaas, H. Philip. *How to Respond to Islam*. Rev. ed. St. Louis: Concordia, 1984.

Lueker, Erwin L., ed. *Lutheran Cyclopedia: A Concise In-Home Reference for the Christian Family*. St. Louis: Concordia, 1984.

Maier, Paul L. *In the Fullness of Time*. Grand Rapids: Kregel, 1997.

Malik, Muhammad Farooq-i-Azam. Surah Introduction to "Surah 72: Al-Jinn." http://www.alim.org/library/quran/Surah/Introduction/72/MAL. From *English Translation of the Meanings of al-Qur'an: The Guidance for Mankind*. Houston: Institute for Islamic Knowledge, 1997.

Marshall, Paul, Roberta Green, and Lela Gilbert. *Islam at the Crossroads*. Grand Rapids: Baker Books, 2002.

Maududi, S. Abul A'la. "The Islamic Concept of Life." http://www.islam101.com/sociology/conceptLife.htm. From *The Islamic Way of Life*. Lahore: Islamic Publications, 1948.

———. "Chapter Introductions to the Qu'ran." http://www.usc.edu/schools/college/crcc/engagement/resources/texts/muslim/maududi/. From *The Meaning of the Qur'an*. Lahore: Islamic Publications, 1993.

Mayer, F. E. *The Religious Bodies of America*. St. Louis: Concordia, 1956.

McDowell, Josh. *More Than a Carpenter*. Wheaton: Living Books, 1977.

McGirk, Tim, et al. "Roots of Terror: Islam's Other Hot Spots." *Time*, September 15, 2003. http://www.time.com/time/magazine/article/0,9171,1005667,00.html.

Momen, Moojan. *An Introduction to Shi'i Islam: The History and Doctrine of Twelver Shi'ism*. New Haven: Yale University Press, 1985.

Montrecroce, Riccoldo da, and Martin Luther. *Islam in the Crucible: Can It Pass the Test?* Translated by Thomas C. Pfotenhauer. Kearney, NE: Morris, 2002.

Moucarry, Chawkat. *The Prophet & the Messiah: An Arab Christian's Perspective on Islam & Christianity*. Downers Grove, IL: InterVarsity, 2001.

Naeir, Samuel Masgood. "Bridges and Barriers between Christianity and Islam." Lecture at Immanuel Lutheran Church, Glenview, IL, January 2004.

"The Nature of Muhammad's Prophetic Experience." http://www.answering-islam.org/Gilchrist/Vol1/3d.html, accessed September 7, 2002.

"9/11 One Year Later." *Time*, September 11, 2002.

"An Open Letter and Call from Muslim Religious Leaders—A Common Word between Us and You." http://www.islamicity.com/articles/Articles.asp?ref=CM0710-3390.

Parrinder, Geoffrey. *Jesus in the Qur'an*. New York: Oxford University Press, 1977.

Parshall, Phil. *Muslim Evangelism*. Waynesboro, GA: Gabriel, 2003.

Pickthall, Mohammad Marmaduke, *The Glorious Qur'an: Arabic Text and English Rendering*, 10th rev. ed. Des Plaines, IL: Library of Islam, 1994.

———. *The Meaning of the Glorious Koran: An Explanatory Translation*. New York: Meridian / Penguin, 1997.

Plass, Ewald M. *What Luther Says*. 3 vols. St. Louis: Concordia, 1959.

Qutb, Syyid. *Basic Principles of the Islamic Worldview*. Translated by Rami David. North Haldedon, NJ: Islamic Publications International, 2006.

Rahman, Fazlur. *Islam*. 2nd ed. Chicago: University of Chicago Press, 1993.

Reagan, R. David. "The Truth about Islam." Lamb and Lion Ministries, November 20, 2001. http://www.lamblion.com/ articles/articles_islam1.php.

Riad, Sedki. "Dying and Death: Islamic View." January 21, 2002. http://www.jannah .org/articles/death.html.

Rodwell, J. M., trans. *The Koran*. Everyman's Library. London: J. M. Dent, 1994.

Saritoprak, Zeki. "The Eschatological Descent of Jesus: Muslim Views." *The Fountain*, January–March 2000. http://www.fountainmagazine.com/article .php?ARTICLEID=641.

Sarker, Abraham. *Understand My Muslim People*. Newberg, OR: Barclay, 2004.

Schmidt, Alvin J. *The Great Divide*. Boston: Regina Orthodox, 2004.

Shorrosh, Anis A. *Islam Revealed: A Christian Arab's View of Islam*. Nashville: Thomas Nelson, 1988.

"Should Christians Convert Muslims?" *Time*, June 30, 2003.

Silas. "Errors and Omissions in the PBS Special *Muhammad: Legacy of a Prophet*." January 20, 2003. http://www.answering-islam.org/Silas/pbs-special.htm.

Spencer, Robert. *Islam Unveiled: Disturbing Questions about the World's Fastest-Growing Faith*. San Francisco: Encounter Books, 2002.

"Stampede Mars Annual Hajj Ritual." *Daily Herald* (Arlington Heights, IL), February 2, 2004.

Strobel, Lee. *The Case for Christ*. Grand Rapids: Zondervan, 1998.

"Surah 19, v 71, 'Everyone will be brought to Hell, then the righteous will be saved.'" *Tafsir Ibn Kathir*. http://tafsir.com/default.asp?sid=19&tid=31598.

Syed, Ibrahim B. "Abortion." Islamic Research Foundation International. http://irfi .org/articles/articles_101_150/abortion.htm.

Taymiyyah, Shaikh ul-Islaam Ibn. "Creed of Hamawiyyah—Chapter 11: Concerning Allaah Being with His Creation (Al-Ma'eeyah)." http://www.salafipublications.com /sps/sp.cfm?subsecID=AQD07&articleID=AQD070011&articlePages=1.

Tenney, Merrill C., ed. *The Zondervan Pictorial Encyclopedia of the Bible*. 5 vols. Grand Rapids: Zondervan, 1978.

Trimingham, J. Spencer. *Christianity among the Arabs in Pre-Islamic Times*. London: Longman, 1979.

Van Biema, David, and Bruce Crumley. "Wahhabism: Toxic Faith?" *Time*, September 15, 2003. http://www.time.com/time/magazine/article/0,9171,1005664,00.html.

Van Biema, David, Azadeh Moavevi, Nadia Mustafa, Matt Rees, and Jamil Hamad. "The Legacy of Abraham." *Time*, September 30, 2002.

Watt, W. Montgomery. *What Is Islam?* New York: Frederich Q. Praeger, 1968.

"What Do We Know about the 'Gospel of Barnabas'?" http://www.answering-islam .org/Barnabas/.

"Whoever is killed amongst us as a martyr shall go to Paradise." Online comment. http://nzanswers/yaho.com/question/index?quid=20071121113445AA5hPlW.

The World of Islam: Resources for Understanding. Colorado Springs: Global Mapping International, 2000. CD-ROM.

Worth, Robert F. "Stoning." *International Herald Tribune.* April 15, 2011.

Zepp, Ira G., Jr. *A Muslim Primer.* 2nd ed. Fayetteville: University of Arkansas Press, 2000.

Zoba, Wendy Murray. "Islam, U.S.A.: Are Christians Prepared for Muslims in the Mainstream?" *Christianity Today*, April 3, 2000.

Topical Index

in the Qur'an
  divorce is easy 106
  Muhammad marries
    Zaid's wife 107

fasting
  blessing for Christians, not as
    Pharisees 156
  for Muslims (Ramadan)
    from sunrise to sunset 155

God of Abraham 169–71. *See
  also* Allah; Lord God
  in the Bible
    belief in 16–17
    "connects" to us 166
    and God of love 44
    Jesus is 171
    and Jesus is "I AM" 17, 19,
      46, 171, 185
    loved Abraham before
      circumcision 170
    and personalized
      compassion 77, 149
  in the Qur'an
    belief in Allah to gain
      Paradise 163
    why Allah and Lord God are
      not the same 17, 19, 43, 44,
      52, 159–60

hajj (pilgrimage)
  in the Bible
    not required 157
  in the Qur'an
    example of what is
      necessary for Paradise 23
    and Ka'aba, "cube", place
      of worship 22–23
    pillar of Islam 156–57
    return as newborn, reborn
      at hajj 23
    and time, dress, observance
      23
humankind. *See* man
homosexual, hope for 112–13

Isaac
  in the Bible
    at heavenly feast 135
    bury Abraham 30
    conflict 27–28
    and Ishmael 25–26
    offered as sacrifice 30–31

promise of 28
prophet/patriarch,
  "laughter" 32
  "raised" from dead 21
  righteous 32–33
Ishmael
  in the Bible
    Abraham's concern for 28
    father of twelve tribes 29
    mocks Isaac 28
  in the Qur'an
    and Abraham build Ka'aba
      22
    Allah of Abraham revealed
      to 16
    Allah offers ram 23
    messenger and prophet
      25–26
    place of sacrifice Mina 23

Jesus
  and amazing grace through
    faith 76, 77, 191–93
  annunciation/birth of 59
  cast out demons 187
  certainty in 163–64, 191
  and comfort in
    predestination 52
  conceived by Holy Spirit 60
  crucifixion of 66–68
  deity of 44–47, 181–82
  and faith frees from
    condemnation 132
  as good shepherd 166
  and great exchange 164, 189
  as great "I AM" 17, 19, 46,
    171, 185
  and godly life 123, 125–27
  God's love in 34–35, 37–38,
    113
  and good tree and good fruit
    123, 132
  and heart of love 167
  and Isaiah 53, 188
  as judge 132
  justice dealt with 74
  Jews/non-Jews in 37
  love as a magnet 81
  and love enemies 120
  and loving Father 148–49
  and man slave to sin 91,
    94–95
  not just a prophet 60
  and peacemakers 115, 120–22

and poor care for 154
promise contained, centered,
  culminated in 17
in the Qur'an
  created like Adam 57
  crucifixion "only appeared
    so," Gospel of Barnabas
    67
  not Son of God 56
  "only a messenger" 45,
    60, 68
  and Muslim belief of
    Jesus, similarity and
    difference 176–77
  ransom of Ishmael 70,
    72, 189
  as "slave of Allah" 64
  speaks from cradle 62
  as ransom, Passover lamb
    72–73, 77
  and rebirth necessary 79
  and resurrection and life
    128–30
  righteousness in 33
  returns with angels 83, 85
  as Savior 35, 37, 62, 64–66,
    70–78, 182, 187–89
  secular corroboration of 69
  as sinless ransom 72–74,
    189
  as son of Abraham,
    fulfillment of promise 17
  as Son of God 45–46, 57–58,
    60
  God of God 181
  and sympathy/empathy
    77, 78
  and two Kingdoms 120–21
  as the vine 126
  as Word 58, 185
  and works evidence of
    saving faith 132–33
  and "Yahweh saves" 66
jihad. *See* aggression
Jinn
  in the Bible
    Jesus came to destroy the
      devil 187
  in the Qur'an
    Allah filled hell with Jinn
      85
    created of essential fire 85
    halfway between men and
      angels 86

Reference Index

Bible

Old Testament

Genesis